THE TENACITY OF PREJUDICE

The Tenacity of Prejudice

ANTI-SEMITISM IN CONTEMPORARY AMERICA

Gertrude J. Selznick and Stephen Steinberg

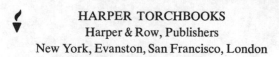

HARPER TORCHBOOKS
Harper & Row, Publishers
New York, Evanston, San Francisco, London

Volume Four in a series based on
the University of California Five-Year Study of Anti-Semitism
in the United States
being conducted by the Survey Research Center,
Charles Y. Glock, Program Coordinator,
under a grant from the Anti-Defamation League of B'nai B'rith

First HARPER TORCHBOOK edition published 1971
STANDARD BOOK NUMBER: 06-131611-3

Contents

APPENDIX

Tables

Acknowledgments

This book is part of the Five-Year Study of Anti-Semitism sponsored by the Anti-Defamation League and conducted by the Survey Research Center of the University of California, Berkeley. We owe special thanks to Oscar Cohen, the program director of the Anti-Defamation League, who first conceived of the research program and has been its most indefatigable supporter. We are also grateful for the support of the Charles Weinfeld Memorial Foundation.

The field work for this study was done by the National Opinion Research Center at the University of Chicago and we are indebted to the staff, especially Eve Weinberg, for the skill and efficiency with which they managed this operation. We also thank the staff of the Survey Research Center: Wendy Shuken, Toni Brown, and Sheila Babbie who aided us in data processing; Charles Yarbrough, who developed computer programs that spared us much drudgery; Beverly Fellows, who typed the manuscript with skill and patience; Eleanor Stevenson, who kept track of the money; and Eva Sinacore, who helped the authors keep track of each other.

Philip Selznick, Marjorie and Leo Lowenthal, and Judith Steinberg read the entire manuscript and we are grateful to them for their many helpful comments. Numerous other friends and colleagues offered advice and criticism: Earl Babbie, Charles Y. Glock, Ruth Kornhauser, Gary Marx, David Nasatir, William Nichols II, Philippe Nonet, Melvin Polner, and Rodney Stark. We are particularly indebted to Charles Y. Glock for the perspective on survey analysis that guided this study.

G.J.S.
S.S.

Introduction

This study asks three questions: *How much* anti-Semitism is there? *Where*—among what kinds of people—is it most prevalent? And, finally, *Why* are some kinds of people more likely than others to be anti-Semitic? The book is divided into three parts corresponding to these three central questions.

Part I (Chapters 1 to 4) examines anti-Semitism along three dimensions: beliefs about Jews, support of discriminatory practices, and susceptibility to political anti-Semitism. In these chapters we ask:

How prevalent are anti-Semitic beliefs and stereotypes?

How many Americans are anti-Semitic in the sense that they hold a large number of derogatory beliefs about Jews?

Of those not anti-Semitic, how many have merely failed to take on this particular prejudice and how many oppose anti-Semitism in principle?

To what extent does contemporary anti-Semitic prejudice express itself in a willingness to support discrimination? Are there some forms of discrimination even non-anti-Semites are willing to engage in?

Are Americans prepared to combat political anti-Semitism or would they respond with apathy?

The major preoccupation of Part I is with measuring the extent of contemporary anti-Semitism, and this portion of the book is largely descriptive. Part II (Chapters 5 to 7) turns to a more analytic problem, that of identifying the social and demographic strata in which anti-Semitism is most prevalent. It examines education, occupation, income, age, sex, nativity, religion, region, and race, and through multivariate analysis establishes the relative importance of each in contemporary anti-Semitism.

Part III seeks to understand why anti-Semitism is more likely to be found among some kinds of individuals than among others. This theoretical analysis is an extension of the factual analysis of Part II and not a separate undertaking. Knowing what kinds of people tend to be anti-Semitic is the first step toward explaining what makes them so.

Our theoretical concerns are limited in several ways. First, this study deals with the differential presence of anti-Semitism in contemporary individuals, not the historic genesis of anti-Semitic beliefs in Western society or the United States.[1] We mention this at the outset because some of the empirical findings and interpretations of this study are in conflict with a number of widely held theories. The conflict is partly resolved, however, once it is recognized that quite different factors may account for contemporary and for historic anti-Semitism; indeed, they may be of an almost opposite nature. For example, the role of the Catholic Church in medieval anti-Semitism is well documented, and helps to explain why anti-Semitism is characteristic of Western rather than Eastern societies. But from the historic role of the Catholic Church it cannot be inferred, as is often done, that Catholics are more anti-Semitic than Protestants. Whatever its origin, once anti-Semitic ideology was embedded in Western culture, it became available to Protestants and Catholics alike. In point of fact, as *Christian Beliefs and Anti-Semitism* has already shown, in the United States Catholics are, as a group, somewhat less anti-Semitic than Protestants.[2] Unless the difference between historical and contemporary sources is understood, there is apt to be fruitless debate as to whether some factor is or is not a "cause" of anti-Semitism. Some theories are oriented toward explaining the presence of anti-Semitism in the society as a whole; others, like the present study, are designed to explain why, among members of the same society, some accept and others reject its historic ethos.

That explaining the presence of anti-Semitism in a group can be different from explaining the anti-Semitism of its members is further illustrated by the following hypothetical example: Suppose one were to find that physicians tend to be higher on anti-Semitism than members of other professions. This might suggest that the greater anti-Semitism of physicians stems from their being in economic competition with Jewish doctors. However, even if this conjecture were correct, one might still find that being in competition with Jews has absolutely no relation to the anti-Semitism of individual doctors. Indeed, physicians in remote rural areas, with no Jewish competitor within 100 miles, may be far more anti-Semitic than urban physicians in frequent competition with Jews. The reason for

---

[1] For a recent study of the historic origins of anti-Semitism, see *Léon Poliakov, The History of Anti-Semitism* (New York: Vanguard Press, 1965).

[2] Charles Y. Glock and Rodney Stark, *Christian Beliefs and Anti-Semitism* (New York: Harper & Row, 1966), pp. 129 and 202.

this is simple. Competition with Jews may create an anti-Semitic ethos within a social group; yet individuals may respond to this ethos, not in terms of their personal competition with Jews, but in light of other factors, such as their general intellectual sophistication. Similarly, an anti-Semitic ethos has long characterized Western society. But the task of this book is to explain, not the origins of this ethos, but its acceptance and rejection at the present time.[3]

Second, the main theoretical conclusions of this study are based on factors that make a major rather than a minor contribution to contemporary anti-Semitism. One reason for the great diversity of theories in the literature is that many single out "causes" of anti-Semitism that could not possibly be operative except in small segments of the population. A theory may be valid, but only for numerically insignificant subgroups; it may account for very little of the total pool of anti-Semitism to be found in the general population. One example is the emphasis sometimes placed on the social snobbery of the rich as a source of anti-Semitism.[4] Since only 1 per cent of the population have annual incomes of $25,000 or more, a theory of this kind—however significant in other respects—can account for only a minute proportion of present-day anti-Semitism.

Finally, it is with the routine anti-Semitism of contemporary American society that this study is primarily concerned. There is a tendency in the literature to see anti-Semitism as a sign of personal psychopathology, and psychoanalysts have offered evidence of this from their clinical practice.[5] While personal psychopathology may explain excesses of anti-Semitism in some individuals, it can throw little light on the ordinary sources and manifestations of anti-Semitism in everyday life.

The Sample

Interviews were conducted with a representative cross section of the national population during the three week period preceding the 1964 presi-

[3] The rate of anti-Semitism in any society or social group is determined by two variables: the extent to which individuals are exposed to an anti-Semitic ethos and the extent to which they are able to resist it. As will be seen, most respondents were familiar enough with anti-Semitic beliefs to have opinions about them. However, it is also true that Americans are differentially exposed to anti-Semitism, a fact about which we shall have much to say in later chapters. The main point to be emphasized now is that anti-Semites do not have to invent anti-Semitism; it is part of the cultural heritage and available to them in the same way as many other beliefs and attitudes.

[4] For example, E. Digby Baltzell, *Philadelphia Gentlemen* (New York: Free Press of Glencoe, 1958) and *The Protestant Establishment* (New York: Random House, 1964).

[5] For example, in Nathan W. Ackerman and Marie Jahoda, *Anti-Semitism and Emotional Disorder* (New York: Harper & Row, 1950).

dential election.[6] The original sample design called for 2,000 interviews. As inevitably happens, a small number of interviews were lost. In this case, a hurricane, a local flood, and interviewer illness conspired to reduce the sample to 1,976 cases. This figure was further reduced to 1,915 by the 61 Jewish respondents who were omitted from the analysis and to 1,913 by two cases that mysteriously disappeared in the bowels of the computer.[7]

No sample can pretend to be an exact replica of the total adult population of the United States. But the representativeness of samples can be gauged by comparing their results with Census Bureau materials. For example, as shown below, the educational distribution of our sample is virtually identical to that reported by the 1964 Population Survey and based on a sample many thousand times larger.[8] The main difference is

	National Sample	1964 Population Survey
Grade school	30%	34%
Some high school	19	18
High school graduate	30	30
Some college	11	9
College graduate	10	9

at the grade school level. The Population Survey reports 34 per cent of the adult population with only a grade school education; the figure in our sample is 30 per cent. This difference may reflect the fact that most opinion surveys do not include the "group quarters population," those living in penitentiaries, old age homes, and the like. Because these people tend to be uneducated, their omission may explain some of the discrepancy between our sample and the 1964 Population Survey. In any event, the discrepancy is small.[9] While a small margin of error is always involved,

[6] Sampling and interviewing were carried out by the National Opinion Research Center at the University of Chicago. The sample is a modified probability (block quota) sample. Such a sample uses probability methods down to the block level. Interviewers are then given a random starting point and directed to call at every house, following a prescribed route, seeking to fill age-sex quotas and an additional quota on employed women. A full probability sample uses probability methods down to the particular individual who is to be interviewed, and requires numerous callbacks, intensive efforts to convert refusals, and a great deal of time and money. While a modified probability sample falls somewhat short of the ideal, it is adequate for the purposes of this study.

[7] The number of cases in most tables do not add up to 1,913 since, on most questions, information on a few respondents is missing.

[8] *Statistical Abstract of the United States, 1965*, U.S. Dept. of Commerce, Bureau of the Census, p. 112.

[9] Other comparisons were made on sex and age (for which there were quota controls) and on race and income. No large discrepancies were found. It can also be noted that the religious breakdown of our sample closely parallels that of the national population. For example, Jews, who form about 3 per cent of the national population, constitute about 3 per cent of the sample.

for most purposes a sample of 2,000 cases can adequately represent the national population.

Most past research in anti-Semitism has been based on unrepresentative samples, frequently of college students. This has led to many contradictory findings about the kinds of people most apt to be anti-Semitic, and thus to many contradictory theories. Generalizations from special samples, besides often being descriptively inaccurate, easily lead theory astray. Except for limited studies based on occasional questions in national polls,[10] this is the first extensive analysis of anti-Semitism based on nationally representative data.

Do Respondents Tell the Truth?

Can it be assumed that respondents are willing to divulge their prejudices to a stranger with pencil in hand? Perhaps the best reason for not doubting the veracity of respondents is that so many reveal themselves as prejudiced. The data clearly indicate that both anti-Jewish and anti-Negro prejudice are at high levels. In view of this, it is hard to imagine that many respondents were purposefully distorting their responses in an attempt to appear unprejudiced.

Why this is so touches on the very nature of prejudice. Many anti-Semites would agree that prejudice is wrong. But since they are convinced that their beliefs describe reality, they do not see themselves as prejudiced. A sizable majority of respondents believe that Jews are wealthier than other Americans. Why shouldn't they? The middle-class status of Jews is firmly established fact.[11] But the anti-Semite tends to hold all his beliefs about Jews with the same conviction: Jews *are* shrewd and tricky. Jews *do* have too much power in the business world. Jews *are* more loyal to

---

[10] The most recent being Charles Herbert Stember, "The Recent History of Public Attitudes," in Stember *et al.*, *Jews in the Mind of America* (New York: Basic Books, 1966).

[11] Like every other major group in American society, Jews are found at all social and economic levels. Comparisons with other religious groups, however, yield substantial differences. The following results are based on data collected in 1957:

	Jews	Protestants	Catholics	Nation
Attended college	33%	19%	14%	19%
Working in professions or as owners, managers, or officials	51	21	19	21
Annual family income of $7500 or more	52	18	18	19

Large differences were also reported among the various Protestant denominations. Episcopalians and Presbyterians exhibit roughly the same distribution as Jews with respect to education, occupational prestige, and family income. [Bernard Lazerwitz, "Religion and Social Structure in the United States," in Louis Schneider (ed.), *Religion, Culture and Society* (New York: John Wiley and Sons, 1964), pp. 428–429].

Israel than to America. These beliefs can and often do provoke feelings of hostility in the person who holds them. But the point is that people who hold such beliefs regard them as objective fact, and thus feel little restraint in opening their minds to interviewers.

An example of this appears in *Christian Beliefs and Anti-Semitism,* an earlier volume in this series. Data were gathered by means of a mail questionnaire that offered respondents a space at the end for comments. Remarks such as these by a San Francisco housewife were not uncommon:

This questionnaire is apparently for the use of finding out if I am prejudiced against Negroes or Jews *which I can say I am not* [respondent's emphasis]. I feel they should have a place in the community if they earn the right. So far the Negroes are uneducated and unclean and haven't earned their place in the average community. The Jews are neither, and they fit in most any place, *but they are underhanded and sneaky* [respondent's emphasis].[12]

The social scientist might cite these remarks as a classic example of prejudice. But the average bigot does not entirely share the social scientist's conception of prejudice. He understands well enough that prejudice has something to do with being irrational and unfair. But he defines irrationality as disliking or hating people for no reason at all. Since he has reasons, he sees himself as unprejudiced. But what the bigot cites as reasons the social scientist defines as prejudice.

Undoubtedly, some respondents hide their prejudices. It is frequently contended that high-status respondents are aware that prejudice is frowned upon and conceal their real attitudes from interviewers, who themselves are predominantly middle class. There is some merit in this observation, but a good deal less than is commonly supposed. The *kind* of respondent who has scruples about appearing to be prejudiced is unlikely to be prejudiced in the first place. A reluctance to accept vulgar stereotypes and to go against what is recognized as ethically proper is one thing that leads people to repudiate prejudice. Moreover, it is in the very nature of authoritative norms that they should produce some measure of dissimulation and hypocrisy. However, in segments of society governed by the desire not to *appear* prejudiced, there is apt to arise the desire not to *be* prejudiced.

The claim that large numbers of high-status respondents hide their anti-Semitic beliefs overlooks what has been shown by much past research, namely, that prejudice always correlates highly with a host of other attitudes having nothing to do with prejudice. High-status respondents consistently reject unsophisticated and erroneous beliefs more frequently than do lower-status respondents even when these beliefs are respectable

---

[12] Glock and Stark, *op. cit.,* p. 105.

and do not violate any social standard. One may doubt the depth of their conviction in all these matters, but that is another question.

The widespread belief in middle-class dissimulation has an understandable basis in reality. The anti-Semitism of the middle class is apt to be visible, especially to Jews, who are themselves largely middle class. Since the uneducated poor are relatively inarticulate and powerless, the educated are the leaders and spokesmen in most areas of public life, and anti-Semitism is no exception. This fosters the impression that the uneducated poor are less anti-Semitic than the middle class, who are then assumed to be systematically dissembling in face-to-face encounters with interviewers.

This is not to say that no evasiveness is present, but it may be of an opposite kind to that commonly supposed. There is evidence, in Chapters 1 and 2, that some respondents refuse to accept even quasi-factual statements about Jews that might be exploited by anti-Semites or suggest anti-Semitism on their own part. In other words, they consistently go out of their way to deny that Jews and non-Jews are in any way different. That the 61 Jews in the sample behave in the same way suggests that dissimulation frequently came from the genuinely unprejudiced rather than the "respectable" anti-Semite.

There was one other possible source of evasiveness in the present study. Twelve per cent of the sample had Jewish interviewers. To gauge whether evasiveness occurred, we used the Index of Anti-Semitic Belief described in Chapter 2. By this standard, respondents interviewed by Jews scored as slightly (8 percentage points) less anti-Semitic than others. At first glance it appeared that using Jewish interviewers did slightly bias the results, but further analysis showed otherwise. A disproportionate number of respondents with Jewish interviewers live in urban areas; they are also slightly more educated than respondents interviewed by non-Jews. When these two factors are held constant, religion of interviewer no longer has an effect.[13]

It is also sometimes argued that lower-status respondents tend to acquiesce in an interview, that is, agree to questions and statements without regard to their content. When statements are pejoratively worded (as customarily happens in a study of prejudice), lower-status respondents may appear to be high on prejudice only because of their tendency to acquiesce. However, like evasiveness, acquiescence is not irrelevant to prejudice. One of the themes of this book is that prejudice itself is a kind of acquiescence to common stereotypes and modes of behavior. When people acquiesce in an interview situation, they reveal that they

---

[13] It can also be noted that 87 of the 244 Negro respondents were interviewed by whites because in some areas Negro interviewers were not available. However, Negroes interviewed by whites exhibit the same rate of anti-Semitism as those interviewed by Negroes.

lack principled reasons for rejecting prejudice. If they do not actually hold the beliefs they assent to, it is likely they would adopt them if they were under pressure to do so. Indeed, discriminatory practices and political anti-Semitism typically depend on the acquiescence of the many to the actions of a few.[14]

We have argued, largely on logical grounds, that acquiescence and evasiveness pose no great problem in studies of prejudice. At the worst, there may be a slight tendency to underestimate anti-Semitism among the upper classes and to overestimate it among the lower classes. However, the basic conclusions of this study are based on such large percentage differences that a small margin of error is not a serious matter.[15] Besides, there is empirical evidence, presented in Chapters 1, 2, and 5, that neither acquiescence nor evasiveness was more than an incidental factor.

Do Attitudes Matter?

The objection is sometimes raised that attitudes are inconsequential. What difference does it make if people dislike Jews, so long as they are unable or unwilling to behave in a discriminatory way? Or, on the national level, what difference does it make if there is prejudice in the population, so long as our institutions succeed in putting a brake on discrimination?

It would be false to assume that there is no correspondence between belief and behavior, even though, as our data show, the correlation is far from perfect. To deny this is tantamount to telling Jews they should feel easy in the company of bigots until they have suffered some actual abuse. To be sure, it is far from certain that a person who is prejudiced will act out his prejudices in behavior. Whether or not he does depends on many factors, including the situational pressures and restraints to which he is subject. Many prejudiced people cooperate with Jews in public life just as many unprejudiced people participate in discrimination; for example, when they join clubs and organizations that tacitly or explicitly exclude Jews. But it can hardly be doubted that, all other things being equal, people who are prejudiced in their attitudes are more likely than the

---

[14] "Response sets to agree or disagree first appeared as sources of error in personality inventories but we have come to realize that they are also personality characteristics in their own right; they may be characteristics of greater interest than most of those that the inventories were designed to measure" [Roger Brown, *Social Psychology* (New York: Free Press of Glencoe, 1965), p. 512].

[15] This study does not use tests of significance. Since the sample is a block quota sample, standard errors are not calculable, and therefore tests of significance would be only approximate at best. However, if the sample had been drawn by strict probability methods, the major relations would obviously be significant at the .05 level or better, given the large percentage differences and the substantial number of cases on which they are based.

unprejudiced to practice discrimination and, what is equally important, less likely to oppose the discriminatory practices of others.

It was partly a disregard for attitudes that led the world, including some German Jews, to minimize the significance of Hitler's access to power. Even today many people are puzzled by the fact that pre-Nazi Germany was not characterized by an unusual amount of discrimination. Had a survey been conducted during that period, there would probably be less grounds for bafflement. Undoubtedly such a survey would have uncovered abundant anti-Semitism in the form of attitudes and beliefs prevalent in the population, and perhaps even widespread support for or indifference to political anti-Semitism.[16] The lesson of the Nazi holocaust is that attitudes are not to be ignored, even during periods when public forms of discrimination are not a serious problem.

A Note to the Reader

As few sociologists will wish to dispute, there are problems in reporting and talking about survey data. To be perfectly accurate in all our formulations would be a bar to reading and understanding. One finding in this book is that, when people are classified into age categories, with every increase in age there is a corresponding increase in the proportion scoring as anti-Semitic. While precise, such language is cumbersome. Hence we often substitute such language as: The old are more likely than the young to be anti-Semitic or, even more simply, the old are more anti-Semitic than the young. Or, instead of asking, Why are the old more anti-Semitic than the young? we may ask, Why are the old anti-Semitic? What such formulations lose in accuracy, they gain in brevity.

The distinction in this study between anti-Semitic beliefs and support of discriminatory practices raises awkward problems of terminology. We use the term "anti-Semitism" to refer to either or to both, relying on the context to make the meaning clear. However, we have reserved the term "anti-Semitic prejudice" to refer to anti-Semitic beliefs only. If it is remembered that a person can be prejudiced without "acting out" his prejudice in behavior, this usage may appear less arbitrary.

---

[16] One survey was conducted in 1931 by a group of German social scientists, some of whom later participated in the research program that produced *The Authoritarian Personality* [*Studien über Authorität und Familie*, Forschungsberichte aus dem Institut für Sozialforschung (Paris: Libraire Felix Alcan, 1936)]. According to one member of the research team, Leo Lowenthal, "The conclusion of the Institut staff when it went over these data in late 1931 was that the advent of Hitler would not find a reservoir of strong resistence among the masses because of the prevalence of the authoritarian and ambivalent character types" (personal communication).

PART I   EXTENT

Most research on anti-Semitism was carried on during and immediately after the Nazi holocaust when there was an urgent need to understand the causes of anti-Semitism. The result is a heavy theoretical emphasis in the literature and the neglect of purely descriptive issues. The first purpose of this study, therefore, is to assess the extent and nature of contemporary anti-Semitism, two decades after the end of World War II.

1 : The Prevalence of Anti-Semitic Beliefs

The amount of anti-Semitism found in a population depends in part on how anti-Semitism is defined. Problems of measurement beset all social research, and it is impossible to give an absolute and unequivocal answer to the question: How much anti-Semitism is there in the United States? Some degree of arbitrariness is inescapable. However, it *is* possible to avoid radical overestimation or radical underestimation and to arrive at a balanced and informed assessment. At the present time, acceptance of negative stereotypes of Jews far outruns support of discrimination. To focus solely on anti-Semitic beliefs would exaggerate contemporary anti-Semitism; to focus solely on discrimination would minimize it. A first step, then, is to distinguish between beliefs and behavioral orientations, and to examine the two dimensions separately.

Even when attention is restricted to belief, difficulties remain. Just as anti-Semitic beliefs exceed willingness to discriminate, so some derogatory beliefs are more widespread than others. To classify people as anti-Semitic because they accept the belief that Jews are clannish would give the impression that a majority of Americans are anti-Semitic. To count as anti-Semitic only those who believe that Jews have too much power in the United States would give the impression that relatively few Americans are anti-Semitic. This was one reason for including a large number of beliefs in the interview schedule. That these beliefs cover a wide range—from mild stereotypes to hard-core tenets of anti-Semitic ideology—is reflected in the fact that some were accepted by a majority, others by only 10 or 15 per cent of the population.

How Beliefs Were Chosen

In choosing beliefs about Jews for the interview schedule, various principles of selection came into play. With some exceptions, only beliefs peculiarly

3

relevant to Jews were considered. Anti-Semitism, while not entirely distinct from other kinds of prejudice, is nonetheless a relatively unique ideological entity. A few people might conceivably think of Jews as childlike, primitive, and improvident, but this complex of traits is traditionally applied to Negroes, not to Jews. A few people might imagine Jews to be submissive, priest-ridden, and ignorant, but this syndrome of traits is typically an expression of anti-Catholic prejudice. Had such beliefs been included in the study they would no doubt have been massively rejected, not because Americans are free of anti-Semitism but because these are not among the unfavorable traits traditionally assigned to Jews. It is quite different for images of the Jew as clannish, as engaging in sharp or unethical practices, or as excessively powerful in business and finance. At least in the United States, these beliefs are as distinctive of anti-Semitism as they are irrelevant to other kinds of prejudice. The first task, therefore, was to formulate or borrow statements from past studies that seemed to represent traditional tenets of anti-Semitic ideology. For example: "Jews stick together too much"; "The trouble with Jewish businessmen is that they are so shrewd and tricky that other people don't have a fair chance in competition"; "International banking is pretty much controlled by Jews."

Although anti-Semitism has retained a common core over the centuries, it has also been subject to the vagaries of time and place. A second guiding principle was the possible emergence of new or distinctively American stereotypes and their fusion with traditional anti-Semitic ideology. With the establishment of a Jewish state the charge has arisen that Jews place loyalty to Israel above their loyalty to the United States, and a statement to this effect was offered to respondents. The present civil rights struggle suggested the following item: "Jews have stirred up a lot of the trouble between whites and Negroes."

A few beliefs were included precisely because they seemed free of the distinctive rhetoric of anti-Semitic ideology. The sophisticated person may reject vulgar and intemperate statements and yet be willing to confess to a mild dislike of Jews. One of the negative statements included in the interview was that "Jews have a lot of irritating faults." This can hardly be called a tenet of anti-Semitic ideology; besides, as some respondents pointed out, everyone has a lot of irritating faults. Nevertheless, it was hoped that, especially among the well-educated and sophisticated, agreement with statements of this type would serve to distinguish between the determinedly unprejudiced, unwilling to single out Jews even for slight criticism, and those willing to do so.

The desire to test certain theories about anti-Semitism suggested the inclusion of a number of beliefs that might otherwise have been safely omitted. Some theories link the prevalence of anti-Semitism to certain "objective" characteristics of Jews. These theories frequently center around the theme of *ressentiment*, claiming that non-Jews resent Jewish wealth, the Old Testament status of Jews as God's Chosen People, or Jewish intellectuality and facility with ideas.[1] Each of these factors has been advanced at one time or another as central to anti-Jewish hostility, and questions were included to assess the place of each in contemporary American attitudes.

There is another kind of theory to which we wished to give attention. Some traditional anti-Semitic beliefs have been interpreted as mutually contradictory. It is often remarked that one of the more peculiar claims of anti-Semites is that Jews are both too seclusive and too intrusive, and that this illogicality is a distinctive trait of anti-Semitism.[2] Thus in addition to questions on Jewish clannishness, we borrowed the following question from past studies: "Do you think that Jews today are trying to push in where they are not wanted?"

The above considerations, and the desire to present respondents with a broad spectrum of beliefs, led to the inclusion in the interview of more than twenty potentially negative or hostile belief items. Questions were posed in different ways. Some gave respondents several alternatives to choose from, for example: "Do you think that on the average Jews have more money than most people, less money, or about the same?" A second group of frankly judgmental questions called for a yes or no answer, for example: "Do you think the Jews have too much power in the United States?" Finally, a long battery of statements about Jews was presented to respondents who were asked to say for each whether they thought it was "probably true" or "probably false."

Table 1 reports responses to eighteen of the interview items, ranking the various beliefs about Jews from least prevalent to most prevalent.[3] In the following discussion, responses are considered under six headings or traditional images of the Jew: as monied; as clannish; as prideful; as unethical; as power-hungry; and as pushy and intrusive.[4]

---

[1] "The anti-Semite readily admits that the Jew is intelligent and hard-working; he will even confess himself inferior in these respects. This confession costs him nothing . . . the more virtues the Jew has the more dangerous he will be" [Jean-Paul Sartre, *Anti-Semite and Jew* (New York: Grove Press, 1962), p. 22].

[2] For example, T. W. Adorno *et al., The Authoritarian Personality* (New York: John Wiley and Sons, 1964), pp. 75–76.

[3] Responses of the 61 Jewish respondents to this series of questions are reported in Appendix B.

[4] This classification is largely for convenience of presentation. It cannot be assumed that beliefs subsumed under the same heading form a "cluster" or are more highly correlated with each other than with beliefs in some other category. The correlations among some of the key beliefs appear in Appendix C.

Table 1. POTENTIALLY NEGATIVE BELIEFS ABOUT JEWS

(in order of their acceptance)

	True	False	Don't Know
Jews are always stirring up trouble with their ideas.	10%	70%	20%
Jews have too much power in the United States.[a]	11	77	12
Jews have stirred up a lot of the trouble between whites and Negroes.	13	60	27
Jews today are trying to push in where they are not wanted.	18	68	14
Jews don't care what happens to anyone but their own kind.	26	62	12
Jews are [not] just as honest as other businessmen.	28	64	8
Jews have too much power in the business world.[a]	29	59	12
Jews are more loyal to Israel than to America.	30	47	23
International banking is pretty much controlled by Jews.	30	24	46
The trouble with Jewish businessmen is that they are so shrewd and tricky that other people don't have a fair chance in competition.	35	53	12
Jews have a lot of irritating faults.	40	43	17
Jews are more willing than others to use shady practices to get what they want.	42	46	12
You can usually tell whether or not a person is Jewish just by the way he looks.	44	53	3
The movie and television industries are pretty much controlled by Jews.	47	21	32
Jewish employers go out of their way to hire other Jews.	49	32	19
Jews stick together too much.	52	38	10
Jews always like to be at the head of things.	54	32	14
Jews still think of themselves as God's Chosen People.	59	17	24

[a]These were posed in the form of questions to which respondents answered "yes," "no," or "don't know."

The Jew as Monied

American Jews are now predominantly middle class and exhibit at least their fair share of concern for achievement and success.[5] At the same time, the connection of Jews with money is one of the oldest elements in anti-Semitic ideology. Respondents were asked whether they thought that on the average Jews have more money than most people, less money, or about the same. Sixty per cent said "more money." That so many did so suggests

[5] For evidence of the relatively middle-class position of American Jews see Introduction, footnote 11.

that in present-day America this belief does not necessarily entail or stem from anti-Semitic hostility. Respondents who said that Jews have more money were asked whether this bothered them; fully 97 per cent answered "no." Typical comments were: "They work for it and earn it, they're entitled to it." "If they're smart enough to get it, they deserve it." "It's their money. It doesn't bother me, wish I had some of it." How people would feel about "Jewish money" in a period of economic crisis is another matter, but at the present time almost no one, whether prejudiced or not, admits to resenting the relatively privileged position of Jews.

While almost universally held by confirmed anti-Semites, some beliefs are also frequently accepted by the unprejudiced, and the belief in Jewish economic success is one of them. Of all the beliefs in the interview, this is the second most popular among the unprejudiced. Put another way, that Jews have more money tends more than almost any other belief to be held in isolation, unaccompanied by other beliefs whose anti-Semitic content is beyond question. Undoubtedly, for some Americans the belief that Jews have more money is merely an affirmation of assumed fact, without anti-Semitic implications or anti-Semitic roots.

This does not mean that belief in Jewish money represents nothing but simple recognition of fact. Even unprejudiced Americans probably have exaggerated notions of Jewish wealth, and the confirmed anti-Semite would insist that Jews have more money regardless of the actual economic status of the majority of Jews. Furthermore, as will be seen in the next chapter, despite the quasi-factual nature of the belief and the overwhelming denial of resentment, saying that Jews have more money is correlated with holding other beliefs of an undeniably anti-Semitic character. For some, the image of the monied Jew is an integral part of a larger syndrome of anti-Semitic ideas. In its own distorted way, anti-Semitic ideology is a "theory" that either explains why Jews have so much more money than other people or treats alleged Jewish wealth as evidence that Jews are money-mad, unethical, and power-hungry. It is largely because of the ideological nature of anti-Semitism that even quasi-factual beliefs about Jews have a certain anti-Semitic potential and can be exploited in periods of economic crisis. Perhaps for this reason, many of the unprejudiced go out of their way to deny differences, at least in the interview situation. Among the unprejudiced, as among Jewish respondents, the most characteristic response was to say that Jews have the same amount of money as others.[6]

By itself, the question on Jewish money tells us little about the extent

---

[6] Precise figures can be found in Chapter 2, Table 5. It might be suspected that disproportionately more low-income respondents would see Jews as having more money than others, but analysis showed no consistent relation between income and response to the money question.

of anti-Semitism in the United States, but it says a good deal about the continued salience of Jews as a group to Americans. Only 3 per cent answered "don't know" to the question on Jewish money. Without the historic presence of anti-Semitism in Western culture, the middle-class status of Jews would go as unremarked as the middle-class status of Episcopalians.[7] Despite the fact that Jews constitute only 3 per cent of the population, and are nonexistent in many parts of the United States, people apparently single them out and remark upon the fact of Jewish economic success. There is little doubt that Jews remain a salient social category to most Americans.

To further assess American attitudes toward Jewish economic success, respondents were asked: "Do you think of Jews as being more ambitious than other people, less ambitious, or about the same?" Virtually the identical proportion (57 per cent) said "more ambitious" as said Jews have more money (60 per cent). Forty-one per cent accepted the composite image that Jews possess both more money and more ambition. It is tempting to interpret this image as a favorable one—as representing the belief that Jews have more money *because* they have more ambition. The evidence suggests otherwise. Again it is precisely the unprejudiced who reject this characterization of Jews. Not only does this image single out Jews as a group, it is congruent with the typical charge that Jews have too much money and are, if anything, overambitious. The tendency among the unprejudiced, as among Jewish respondents, was to say that Jews have the same amount of money and ambition as others. (About 4 out of 10 in both groups did so.)[8]

Earlier we suggested the role that fact plays in anti-Semitism: not only does the bigot use facts about Jews to support his prejudice, he has a ready-made ideology with which he can interpret the facts to others. However, some facts lend themselves to distortion more easily than others, and anti-Semitic ideology selects certain kinds of facts while ignoring others. This consideration led us to include the following question: Do you think that Jewish children do better in school, worse, or about the same as other children? This question elicited a far different response from the

---

[7] In 1957, 46 per cent of Episcopalians and 42 per cent of Jews had annual incomes of $7,500 or more. The figure for the nation as a whole was 19 per cent [Bernard Lazerwitz, "Religion and Social Structure in the United States," in Louis Schneider (ed.), *Religion, Culture and Society* (New York: John Wiley and Sons, 1964), pp. 428–429].

[8] That the unprejudiced tend to deny differences could mean either that they are hiding their prejudice or that they are going out of their way to reject even the hint of prejudice. That Jewish respondents also tend to deny differences supports the latter interpretation. Denial of differences could also stem from lack of acquaintance with Jews or with stereotypic images of Jews. But again the Jewish responses belie this interpretation.

questions on money and ambition: whereas 57 per cent said "more ambitious" and 60 per cent said "more money," only 19 per cent said Jewish children do better in school. "About the same" is now the modal response, with 64 per cent choosing this answer. It might be argued that few adults are in a position to observe the school performance of Jewish and non-Jewish children. Nevertheless, most people had an opinion on the school question, and one different from their opinion on Jewish money and ambition. This again suggests that the money and ambition replies represent more than innocent recognition of fact. The image of Jewish money and ambition is a historic component of anti-Semitic ideology whereas the performance of Jewish school children is not.

Responses to the questions on Jewish money, ambition, and scholastic performance underscore the observation, frequently made in the literature, that once anti-Semitic prejudice exists in a society, even facts about Jews take on an ambiguous quality. It is characteristic of ideological anti-Semites to believe firmly in various untruths and fantasies about Jews. But it is also characteristic of ideological anti-Semites to interpret certain "facts" about Jews in perverse and malicious ways.

Common sense tells us that there are two roads to tolerance. One is to acknowledge that Jews are different—comparatively more privileged, more ambitious, more self-segregating—and yet remain nonblaming and non-discriminatory. The other is to deny that Jews are in any way different in order to remove all possible vestiges of an attitudinal basis for anti-Semitism. Of the two, the first is the more complex, mature, and sophisticated attitude. But the decline of anti-Semitic prejudice will probably be marked as much by a denial of differences as by an increasing tolerance of differences.

The Jew as Clannish

For centuries in Europe Jews were segregated from the life of the general community and were strict in enforcing their own patterns of self-segregation. This situation began to change only with the Emancipation, beginning around the middle of the eighteenth century. Jews were gradually freed from centuries of oppression and persecution, and Jewish self-segregation became problematic. Officially accepted as equal members of society, Jews became vulnerable to the charge that they were clannish and self-segregating. At the time of the survey, large numbers of Americans— 52 per cent of the sample—agreed with the statement that "Jews stick together too much." Almost the same proportion (49 per cent) agreed that "Jewish employers go out of their way to hire other Jews." Two other beliefs imply that Jews are not only clannish but disloyal to others. These were accepted less frequently: 26 per cent said that "Jews don't care about anyone but their own kind"; 30 per cent, that "Jews are more loyal to Israel than to America." Many people who see Jews as clannish do not go on to affirm the two harsher beliefs. However, almost everyone who said that Jews don't care about others also said that Jews stick together too much. While this latter belief can be said to have some basis in reality, it is an essential element in the image of Jews as disloyal to others and cannot be dismissed as entirely innocuous.

The Jew as Prideful

Anti-Semitic propaganda often refers to Jews euphemistically and with mixed overtones of scorn and resentment as the Chosen People. For this reason, respondents were presented with the statement "Jews still think of themselves as God's Chosen People." The proportion agreeing is as high as that found for the questions on money and ambition: 59 per cent agree. Another quarter of the sample (24 per cent) said "don't know." Only a relative handful of 17 per cent denied that "Jews still think of themselves as God's Chosen People." Since this is a traditional religious belief among Jews, one would hardly wish to treat it as an indicator of anti-Semitism. Nevertheless, this item conforms to the pattern already observed for other quasi-factual beliefs about Jews. It is accepted by a majority of anti-Semites, but the unprejudiced tend to reject this "fact" as they do others. A majority of Jewish respondents (64 per cent) also denied that "Jews still think of themselves as God's Chosen People." Once again we see the ambiguity of fact where prejudice is concerned.

The Jew as Unethical

Economic stereotypes of Jews as mercenary, unscrupulous, and guileful date back at least to the Middle Ages. For centuries in Europe, Jewish economic activities, such as money lending—forbidden to Christians—and international trade, were carried on in an environment of intense religious hostility. For this and other reasons, economic stereotypes of the unethical Jew became deeply embedded in the European mind and underwent little change in their subsequent journey to the New World.

One statement in the interview referred specifically to Jewish business-men: "Jewish businessmen are so shrewd and tricky that other people don't have a fair chance in competition." A third of the sample (35 per cent) agreed. Another statement referred to Jews in general: "Jews are more willing than others to use shady practices to get what they want." In this case 42 per cent agreed. It is safe to assume that when Americans think of Jews as shady, they usually have business practices in mind. The two statements are highly correlated and about a quarter of the sample (26 per cent) agreed to both.

Partly as a methodological control one statement about Jewish businessmen was worded positively: "Jewish businessmen are just as honest as other businessmen." This is a severe test of anti-Semitism: To go out of one's way to deny a positively worded statement is a more direct expression of hostility than to accept a negatively worded statement. Still, over a quarter of the sample (28 per cent) denied that Jews are as honest as other businessmen. From this and the other two statements, it is apparent that at least a quarter of the population see Jews as unethical in business.

In the introduction we raised the issue of respondent acquiescence and its relevance for studies of prejudice. The criticism is sometimes made that respondents indiscriminately answer "yes" to questions regardless of their content, and thereby invalidate survey findings. The inclusion of the positively worded statement that "Jews are just as honest as other businessmen" permits us to assess the extent to which respondents were in fact acquiescent.

One early indication that acquiescence was minimal is that the proportion giving anti-Semitic responses varies greatly from one belief to the next, from 10 per cent at one extreme to over 50 per cent at the other. This shows that respondents discriminated among the items, and that on at least one item no more than 10 per cent can be accused of acquiescing. Moreover, if the proportions are examined in the order in which stereotypes were presented to respondents (see Appendix A), no pattern can be discerned: percentages rise and fall with the content of the stereotype, and no build-up of an acquiescent response set emerges.[9]

In including the positively worded statement it was reasoned that if acquiescence were a powerful factor, then a large proportion of respondents would "contradict" themselves by saying "yes, Jews are shady"; "yes, Jews are shrewd and tricky"; and "yes, Jews are just as honest as other businessmen." In fact this response pattern was exhibited by only 8 per cent of the sample.[10] Even this figure of 8 per cent represents a maximum estimate

[9] In the pilot interviews, we found that one series of questions did produce a response set. When queried about their preferences for shopping in Jewish or non-Jewish stores, joining clubs with or without Jewish members, and so on, once respondents answered, "It makes no difference to me," they tended to adhere to this response on subsequent questions. The result was a build-up of no-difference responses at the bottom of the list, and the decision to exclude this type of question from the final interview schedule.

[10] Inconsistency was higher among the less educated. But even among grade schoolers only 12 per cent said "yes" to all three questions. The figure for high schoolers is 7 per cent; for college graduates, 2 per cent.

of acquiescence since some who believe that Jewish businessmen are shady, even shrewd and tricky, may not believe that Jews are more dishonest than other businessmen. It is also noteworthy that only a handful—2 per cent of the sample—answered "no" to all three questions. We are confident that neither acquiescence nor a negative response set is a serious problem in this study.

The Jew as Power-Hungry

Respondents were asked five questions touching on the theme of Jewish power and control. Three were presented as statements:

"Jews always like to be at the head of things."

"The movie and television industries are pretty much run by Jews."

"International banking is pretty much controlled by Jews."

Of these three, the belief that Jews always like to be at the head of things is the most common, accepted by 54 per cent of the sample. Less frequent but nevertheless widely held is the belief that Jews pretty much control movies and television; 47 per cent indicated they thought this was true. Fewer, but still a substantial minority (30 per cent), believe that international banking is pretty much controlled by Jews. Like the movie and television item, to which 32 per cent answered "don't know," this belief drew an extremely high proportion of "don't know" responses—46 per cent, greater than for any other question in the entire interview. While only a minority accept the belief that Jews control international banking, only a minority of 24 per cent definitely reject it.[11]

In 1936, when cries of "Jewish power" were common in this country, the editors of *Fortune* magazine did an exhaustive survey of American business and came to the following conclusions:

. . . there is no basis whatever for the suggestion that Jews monopolize U.S. business and industry. . . . First of all and very definitely, they do not run banking. . . . Something of the same situation exists in automobiles. There are only three Jews of any prominence in the executive end of manufacturing. . . . The coal industry is almost entirely non-Jewish. It is doubtful whether the roster of the leading twenty-five companies would show a single Jew from miner to manager or on up to the board of directors. . . . Rubber is another non-Jewish industry. . . . Shipping and transportation are equally non-Jewish.

A vast continent of heavy industry and finance may therefore be staked out in which Jewish participation is incidental or non-existent. To this may be annexed other important areas into which Jews rarely penetrated such as light and power and telephone and telegraph and engineering in general and heavy machinery and lumber and dairy products. In brief, Jews are so far from con-

---

[11] Subsequent chapters analyze the sources and significance of don't-know responses.

trolling the most characteristic of present-day American activities that they are hardly represented in them at all.[12]

The facts showed that Jews played a significant role only in certain light industries, such as textiles, clothing, retailing, and scrap metal, and could also be found in large numbers in the professions and the literary field. That Jews tend to be in highly visible occupations may help to explain why people find credible the claim that Jews are taking over the business world. The *Fortune* study showed how little basis there was for this belief in the 1930s; ironically, the anti-Semitism that fosters the myth of Jewish power is also the rationale for economic discrimination.

Two questions in the interview asked about Jewish power: "Do you think Jews have too much power in the United States?" "How about the business world—do you think the Jews have too much power in the business world?" Only 11 per cent said Jews have too much power in the United States, but over a quarter of the sample (29 per cent) said they have too much power in the business world. Respondents who accepted either of these beliefs were then asked: "Do you think something should be done to take power away from the Jews?" Twenty-eight per cent of this group, or 8 per cent of the sample, answered in the affirmative. Ordinarily, such a small percentage would not be noteworthy. However, those who feel that something should be done about "Jewish power" are taking an extreme position, and for this reason were asked what they thought should be done.

Almost no one expressed a willingness to use violence. One person suggested "we might shoot a bunch of them," another said we ought to "bring Hitler back to life," and two proposed that we "send them back to where they came from." Some merely repeated the ancient cry, "There oughta be a law."

They already got most of the money and power so let somebody else have some say so. I don't know what ought to be done. I do know something. They ought to pass some kind of law.

There should be some kind of law that would limit what they could and couldn't do especially when they try to undersell other merchants. Pretty soon they're going to own all business.

A few mentioned voting and "the power of the ballot." Others appealed to government.

The only thing is the government just take it over and not let them do it. I think they got rights just the same as everyone else. I don't think anybody but the government got the right to do that.

[12] "Jews in America," *Fortune*, February 1936, pp. 130 and 133.

Well, that's the $64,000 question. I don't know unless they limit their business to a certain volume per year. (*Who should limit it?*) The government, I guess.

Congress ought to do something because the way Jews are acting, they'll have as much power as Congress.

These comments reveal primitive conceptions of democracy and legality. Some respondents equate democracy with majority rule and believe that repression is legitimate so long as it is initiated by government or sanctioned by law. As one respondent phrased it in answering a question about Hitler: "Killing people is wrong and to take the lives of those people was terrible. He should have used his power by laws and not the terrible and cruel thing as this was."

Some people, because they believe that Jews control big business, suggest enforcement of antimonopoly laws.

We have laws that restrict monopolies that are not enforced. Big business is run by Jews. We should enforce the laws we have. If we don't restrict them they'll be running the country.

Some of their monopolies should be controlled. (*Which ones?*) The paint business. (*Any others?*) The steel scrap business. One Jew I know saved steel scraps for twenty years before the last war and he got to be a millionaire from selling it during the last war.

Monopoly on property should be taken away. Remove monopoly on grocery stores. No competition allowed for the little man. Big Jews' chain stores force out little businessmen.

A few respondents did not advocate taking action against Jews but suggested hard work and more aggressiveness on the part of others.

Let's face it, Jews are called money-changers by the majority of people. I can't think of any way to solve this problem. Christian people will have to have more push and forge ahead of the Jewish race.

Have the rest become as aggressive and interested in taking on more responsibilities in business organizations, in law and government. If they don't want the Jews to get ahead and be more powerful, we have to become more aggressive.

All in all, about a third of those who said power should be taken away from the Jews proposed restrictive laws or government action. But half could not offer any specific proposals. Some merely reiterated their belief that *something* ought to be done; others frankly admitted they had no ideas to offer. That so many had no opinion is one indication that the question of "Jewish power" has lost much of its salience, even to anti-Semites. However, it is clear that, should an anti-Semitic movement arise in the future, these people would be vulnerable to its appeals. Though they do not personally advocate violence, they might condone the violence of others.

The Jew as Pushy and Intrusive

One of the paradoxes of prejudice is that a minority seeking to overcome the barriers of discrimination is often perceived as overly aggressive and intrusive. In this way, the repertory of prejudice is expanded, and the image of the "pushy" Jew has become an element in anti-Semitic ideology. Respondents were asked: "Do you think Jews today are trying to push in where they are not wanted?" A small minority of 18 per cent answered in the affirmative.[13]

Many writers have suggested that the belief in Jewish clannishness and the belief that Jews are pushy are in logical contradiction, and that this contradictory image of the Jew is a distinctive trait of anti-Semitism. For example, the authors of *The Authoritarian Personality* found a high correlation between intrusive and seclusive images of Jews, and concluded that this "reveals a deep contradiction in anti-Semitic ideology. . . . As a matter of simple logic, it is impossible for most Jews to be both extremely seclusive and aloof and at the same time too intrusive and prying."[14] They interpret this alleged self-contradition as a symptomatic expression of the irrationality of the anti-Semite.

It is overly academic, however, to see the two beliefs as contradictory. When the anti-Semite accuses Jews of being both seclusive and intrusive, he has in mind a process whereby a few Jews "push in" and then exhibit their clannishness by "bringing their own kind in." This is a familiar defense of social club discrimination as well as the rationale for fears of "Jewish power." As one respondent put it: "They monopolize so much. . . . The Jews class up together and crowd others out." Far from being incompatible, the notion of Jewish clannishness is combined with the notion of Jewish pushiness to create the image of the Jew as conspiring to dominate others.

Two other beliefs that see the Jew as intrusive and a trouble-maker in society are also rarely accepted. Only 10 per cent agreed that Jews stir up trouble with their ideas, only 13 per cent blamed Jews for causing trouble between whites and Negroes. This latter item was included in the interview partly to test whether the civil rights conflict has resulted in a tendency

---

[13] By a yes answer an unprejudiced person might be expressing approval of Jewish efforts to overcome discriminatory barriers such as exist in many social clubs. However, this belief is accepted principally by extreme anti-Semites (Chapter 2, Table 3).

[14] Adorno *et al., op. cit.*, p. 75.

to single out Jews for blame. This evidently has not occurred on a wide scale, even in the South.

The Trend of Anti-Semitic Beliefs

One way to gauge present levels of acceptance of anti-Jewish beliefs is to compare them with past levels. Political anti-Semitism—defined as a pre-occupation with alleged Jewish power—has declined radically in recent decades and is now almost at the vanishing point. In 1938 as many as 41 per cent agreed that Jews have too much power in the United States. This figure increased during the war years, reaching a peak of 58 per cent in 1945, but by 1962 it had declined to 17 per cent.[15] In 1964 the figure was even lower—11 per cent.

It is necessary, however, to distinguish between political anti-Semitism and conventional anti-Semitism. By "conventional" anti-Semitism we mean beliefs in Jewish clannishness and unethical business practices.[16] Such beliefs, while they have undoubtedly declined since the 1930s and 1940s, have not declined radically and are still far from vanishing. In 1952 and again in 1966 national samples were asked: "Do you think the Jews stick together too much, or not?" In 1952, 47 per cent, in 1966, 39 per cent said Jews stick together too much, a decline of only 8 percentage points over the 14-year period.[17] The same conclusion applies to other questions whose anti-Semitic content is less open to doubt. In 1952 a national sample of Christians was asked: "Compared with most people of your religion would you say most Jews are the same, better or not as good in generosity toward public charities?" At that time, about 2 out of 10 answered "not as good."[18] In 1964 at least as many (26 per cent) agreed that "Jews don't care what happens to anyone but their own kind." Though the two items differ in wording, their implications are similar,

[15] Charles Herbert Stember *et al.*, "The Recent History of Public Attitudes," in *Jews in the Mind of America* (New York: Basic Books, 1966), p. 121.

[16] When the data were factor analyzed, clannish and unethical beliefs consistently appeared on the same factor, power beliefs on a different factor. See Appendix D.

[17] *Catholic Digest*, April 1967, p. 116. Responses were reported for Catholics and Protestants separately; we have combined them, adjusting for the religious composition of the population. In our 1964 sample respondents were asked whether the statement "Jews stick together too much" was probably true or probably false, and 52 per cent said "probably true." The discrepancy between this figure and the 1966 *Catholic Digest* poll may reflect the different ways in which the item was presented. In the *Catholic Digest* survey it was posed as a question and, in addition, respondents were asked first whether Protestants and then whether Catholics stick together too much, thereby putting respondents into the position of having explicitly to single out Jews.

[18] Charles Herbert Stember, *Education and Attitude Change* (New York: Institute of Human Relations Press, 1961), p. 22.

and it appears that the image of Jews as indifferent to others did not decline between 1952 and 1964.

A similar picture emerges with respect to economic images. In 1952 and in 1966 the question was asked: "Compared with most people of your religious beliefs, would you say most Jews are about the same, better or not as good in being fair in business?" The proportion replying "not as good" declined 11 percentage points, from 37 to 26 per cent, in the 14-year period.[19] Another comparison shows no decline in recent years. In 1956 and 1959 national samples were presented with the statement, "Jewish businessmen are so shrewd and tricky that other people don't have a fair chance in competition." Each time about a third agreed (35 and 30 per cent).[20] In our 1964 sample, the figure was 35 per cent. Thus it appears that certain clannish and unethical stereotypes have undergone at best a moderate decline since the 1950s and are still widespread.[21]

These conclusions are at variance with those of Stember's recent trend analysis.[22] According to Stember, "notions of 'Jewish clannishness' are no longer widespread" and have "very nearly disappeared." He goes on to add that perhaps the most significant of all changes has been "the waning of the 'Shylock' image—the notion that Jews as a group are 'greedy,' 'dishonest' or 'unscrupulous.' "[23] His data indicate that in 1962 less than 10 per cent of the population believed in each case that Jews are "too clannish," are "unscrupulous," and "have too much power in business."[24] The large discrepancies between Stember's conclusions and our own are easily explained. Let us use the belief that Jews are "too clannish" as an example. In the present study respondents were presented with the statement, "Jews stick together too much," and were asked whether it was probably true or probably false. Half the sample agreed that it was probably true. In contrast, Stember bases his conclusions on an open-ended question asked in 1940 and again in 1962: "Are there

[19] *Catholic Digest*, August 1967, p. 118.

[20] Stember, "Recent History of Public Attitudes," *op. cit.*, p. 70.

[21] The trend comparisons with respect to conventional anti-Semitism cover only a fourteen-year span, and it might be argued that this is too short a period to measure trends in beliefs. However, during this same period the belief in excessive Jewish power seems to have declined sharply. In 1952 a national sample was asked: "Do you think the Jews are trying to get too much power in the United States, or not?" Thirty-four per cent said "yes" (*Catholic Digest*, April 1967, p. 115). In contrast, in 1964 only 11 per cent agreed with the statement that "Jews have too much power in the United States." While the two questions differ somewhat, the decline is unquestionably real. As we saw, in 1964 only small minorities accepted any of the beliefs concerning Jews as intrusive or as troublemakers in society.

[22] Stember, "Recent History of Public Attitudes," *op. cit.*

[23] *Ibid.*, p. 211.

[24] *Ibid.*, Fig. 123, p. 209.

any objectionable qualities which you think Jews generally have to a greater extent than other people?" In 1940, 63 per cent answered "yes"; in 1962, 22 per cent did so.[25] Among this 22 per cent, 18 per cent mentioned "clannishness; discrimination against non-Jews" as an objectionable quality. This 18 per cent is equal to 5 per cent of the total sample, and from this last figure Stember concludes that the belief in Jewish clannishness has "very nearly disappeared." But this conclusion is clearly unwarranted. The data merely show that, in 1962, 5 per cent of Americans felt strongly enough about Jewish clannishness to volunteer this as an objectionable trait. We do not know from Stember's data how many of the remaining 95 per cent held the belief in Jewish clannishness.[26] Moreover, Stember's own data indicate that in 1962 anti-Semitism was far from disappearing: there were still 22 per cent who were sufficiently negative toward Jews to say that they have objectionable traits. But the tendency of this 22 per cent to mention a particular trait as objectionable does not accurately reflect the prevalence of particular beliefs in the general population.

Stember's method of calculation also leads him to conclude that beliefs in Jewish "unscrupulousness" and excessive business power are now confined to minuscule minorities of less than 10 per cent. But as our data show, when respondents are directly confronted with these beliefs, about a third accept each. The conclusion seems justified that conventional anti-Semitism not only continues at fairly high levels, but has hardly declined since 1952.

Evaluation of the Findings

The prevalence of the various beliefs about Jews tells us something about both the extent and the nature of contemporary anti-Semitism. As we have seen, most beliefs concerning Jewish power are at low levels and are not typical of present-day anti-Semitism. However, a large number of traditional tenets of anti-Semitic ideology are accepted by sizable proportions:

[25] *Ibid.*, Table 12, p. 65.

[26] That this belief is one of the most accepted of all stereotypes suggests, as we said, that many people do not feel especially negative about Jewish clannishness and that this belief is often held by the unprejudiced. Precisely because clannishness is generally not regarded as a serious indictment, those who wished to comment about "objectionable qualities" of Jews would not be apt to mention it; they have more serious complaints and accusations to make. Thus while in 1962 18 per cent mentioned clannishness, about a quarter mentioned *each* of the following: unscrupulousness, aggressiveness, and too much emphasis on money (*loc. cit.*). Ironically, one can virtually infer from Stember's data that the belief in Jewish clannishness is not the least but one of the most accepted of all beliefs, as is in fact the case.

Jews don't care what happens to anyone but their own kind.	26%
Jews are [not] just as honest as other businessmen.	28
Jews have too much power in the business world.	29
International banking is pretty much controlled by Jews.	30
Jews are more loyal to Israel than to America.	30
The trouble with Jewish businessmen is that they are so shrewd and tricky that other people don't have a fair chance in competition.	
Jews are more willing than others to use shady practices to get	35
what they want.	42

Based on these figures, a good guess would put the level of anti-Semitic prejudice midway between 26 and 42 per cent or at about a third of the population. More substantial evidence for this estimate is presented in the next chapter.

Certain other beliefs are more widespread. For example, the following are held by roughly half the population:

The movie and television industries are pretty much controlled by Jews.	47%
Jewish employers go out of their way to hire other Jews.	49
Jews stick together too much.	52
Jews always like to be at the head of things.	54

It is frequently contended, often by Jews themselves, that beliefs such as these should not be regarded as anti-Semitic since they have at least some basis in reality. This argument assumes a basic distinction between "true" beliefs and "false" beliefs about Jews. Undoubtedly some generalizations about Jews are more warranted than others. But the distinction between "true" and "false" beliefs is misleading if it implies that people typically acquire their "true" beliefs about Jews in one way and their "false" beliefs in another. One might suppose that people frequently in contact with Jews would be the most apt to accept "true" beliefs and the least likely to accept "false" beliefs. But this is not the case. The data show that contact with Jews has much the same relation to "true" beliefs that it has to "false" beliefs: nearly every belief about Jews is most often accepted by people with the *least* contact with Jews.[27] Even the belief that "you can usually tell whether or not a person is Jewish just by the way he looks" is most frequently held by persons who report absolutely no contact with Jews.[28]

[27] Persons without contact more often answered "don't know" but, when they had an opinion, tended to accept anti-Semitic beliefs more often than those with contact.

[28] Respondents were asked about eight possible contacts with Jews (Appendix A, question 42). Among those who had 0, 1, or 2 contacts, 49 per cent said, "You can usually tell whether or not a person is Jewish just by the way he looks." Among

As has been frequently remarked, people become prejudiced not by becoming acquainted with Jews, but by becoming acquainted with the prejudiced beliefs current in their environment. From the perspective of linguistics, prejudice is a social grammar. Every language has rules, most of them implicit, for the use of adjectives. A man is handsome, a woman, beautiful; rooms are long and narrow, people tall and thin. Any prejudice, including anti-Semitism, can similarly be viewed as a set of implicit rules specifying which adjectives are relevant or appropriately applied to which groups: Negroes are lazy, Irish are drunkards, Scots are stingy, Mexicans fall asleep at the drop of a hat, and Jews are rich and clannish. It would be a mistaken view of prejudice, and its viability, to define only a false ascription as prejudice. Above all else, a prejudiced ascription is a differential ascription: the same trait may be as applicable to one group as to another, yet it is applied only to one. In the absence of countervailing forces prejudice is as easily acquired as language itself.

But anti-Semitism is more than a social grammar: It is also an ideology. Not only does it connect the idea of Jews with the idea of money and clannishness, it connects the belief that Jews have money or are clannish with other beliefs of a far more noxious character, for example, that Jews are avaricious and actively seek to control and dominate. To hold that Jews have money or are clannish is, by itself, no evidence of anti-Semitism or hostility toward Jews, and many people who hold such beliefs do not draw invidious conclusions. That Jews are well off economically does not necessarily imply that Jews have an inordinate love of money or are bent on controlling the economy. Yet because of the existence of anti-Semitic ideology, the link is always there as a potentiality. For many of those not now prejudiced, it may be a short step from accepting a quasi-factual belief in normal times to embracing an anti-Semitic belief system in times of crisis.

The purpose of this chapter has been to examine the prevalence of various beliefs about Jews. Present levels of acceptance provide a benchmark against which past and future levels can be measured. At the present time, American anti-Semitism appears to be far less political in content

---

those with 3 to 6 contacts, the figure declines to 38 per cent; among those with 7 or 8 contacts, to 21 per cent. Additional findings on the relation between contact and anti-Semitism are reported in Chapter 7.

Lack of knowledge of Judaism produces much the same result. Respondents were asked two questions: (1) "Protestants and Catholics go to church on Sundays. Do you happen to know what day of the week Jews have their weekly religious service?" (Sixty-three per cent gave the correct answer.) (2) "The Ten Commandments are part of the Christian religion. As far as you know, are the Ten Commandments also part of the Jewish religion?" (Fifty-five per cent answered "yes.") Those lower on knowledge are more likely to accept anti-Semitic beliefs.

than it was in past eras. On the other hand, beliefs in Jewish clannishness and unethical business practices persist and give us a broad suggestion of the nature of contemporary anti-Semitism and the number of individuals who can be characterized as anti-Semites. But it is only a suggestion. We turn now to a more central problem for this study—that of measuring anti-Semitism in the individual.

2 : How Many Anti-Semites?

It may be possible in everyday life to distinguish between the prejudiced and the unprejudiced in an unequivocal way. In social research, no such hope can be held out. The best that can be done is to rank individuals according to their numerical score on some measure of anti-Semitic prejudice. From the large number of beliefs about Jews included in the interview, the following eleven were chosen for this measure:

Do you think Jews have too much power in the United States?

How about the business world—do you think Jews have too much power in the business world?

Jews are more willing than others to use shady practices to get what they want.

Jews are more loyal to Israel than to America.

Jews are [not] just as honest as other businessmen.

Jews have a lot of irritating faults.

International banking is pretty much controlled by Jews.

Jews don't care what happens to anyone but their own kind.

Jews always like to be at the head of things.

Jews stick together too much.

The trouble with Jewish businessmen is that they are so shrewd and tricky that other people don't have a fair chance in competition.

These eleven items constitute the Index of Anti-Semitic Belief.[1] One point was assigned for each belief accepted; respondents could thus score from 0 to 11. Groups with higher scores are assumed to be more anti-Semitic

---

[1] Each of these eleven beliefs is correlated with all of the others (Appendix C). When all beliefs about Jews included in the interview were subjected to factor analysis, the result confirmed the choice of items for the index: Ten of the eleven items chosen had the highest loadings on the first principal component factor (Appendix D). The eleventh was the belief that Jews control international banking, which was included because it is a traditional anti-Semitic tenet. The reason for its low loading will become apparent in Chapter 6.

than groups with lower scores. In view of the evident anti-Semitic content of most of the beliefs in the Index, this is a reasonable assumption. Nevertheless, the Index must be validated and tested. Its validity is shown by its capacity systematically to predict three things: (1) acceptance of each of the eleven beliefs included in the Index, (2) acceptance of other derogatory beliefs not included in the Index, and (3) discriminatory attitudes and support for political anti-Semitism.

Validating the Index of Anti-Semitic Belief

A good index ought to manifest a high degree of internal consistency or internal predictive power. Persons with a score of 2 ought to be more likely than persons with a score of 1 to accept each of the eleven beliefs in the index, persons with a score of 3 ought to be more likely to do so than those with a score of 2, and so on. With negligible exceptions, the Index of Anti-Semitic Belief meets this test: the higher the score, the more frequent the anti-Semitic response to each of its constituent items. For example, on the belief that Jews don't care about anyone but their own kind, the proportions agreeing rise steadily from 2, 6, and 10 per cent at points 1, 2, and 3 on the Index up to 71, 85, and 95 per cent at points 8, 9, and 10 on the Index (Table 2).

Not all beliefs included in the Index are equally anti-Semitic. Two stand out as relatively weak indicators of anti-Semitism: "Jews always like to be at the head of things" and "Jews stick together too much." More often than others, these beliefs are typical of low scorers; in other words they are frequently held in isolation. Nevertheless, they were included in the Index for two reasons. First, these beliefs are held by progressively higher proportions as scores on the Index increase. Secondly, a sensitive index should distinguish not only between degrees of anti-Semitism but also between those who accept some mild beliefs about Jews and those who will not accept any negative ascription, however mild. The inclusion of two "soft" beliefs gives the Index this added sensitivity.

Internal consistency is a weak test of validity, and Table 3 subjects the Index to a more challenging test: Does it systematically predict responses to negative beliefs about Jews that are not included in the Index? With few deviations, the higher the score on the Index, the greater the likelihood of accepting other negative beliefs about Jews. For example, acceptance of the belief that Jews today are trying to push in where they are not wanted rises steadily with greater anti-Semitism from 1 and 3 per cent among those with scores of 0 and 1 on the Index to 50 and 76 per cent among those with scores of 10 and 11. This pattern holds for each of the validating beliefs in Table 3. Chapters 3 and 4, which explore the link between prejudice and

Table 2. INTERNAL VALIDATION OF THE INDEX OF ANTI-SEMITIC BELIEF

					Score on Index of Anti-Semitic Belief								Total
	0	1	2	3	4	5	6	7	8	9	10	11	
Number of Respondents	(316)	(289)	(227)	(183)	(192)	(156)	(125)	(130)	(108)	(95)	(58)	(34)	(1,913)
Beliefs in Index													
Too much power in U.S.	0%	0%	1%	1%	4%	6%	10%	25%	29%	40%	66%	100%	11%
Care only about own kind	0	2	6	10	15	34	52	54	71	85	95	100	26
Not as honest as other businessmen	0	2	7	16	28	39	51	55	76	74	79	100	28
Too much power in business world	0	3	10	21	30	40	37	56	64	82	98	100	29
More loyal to Israel than to America	0	5	18	24	30	33	43	65	65	83	90	100	30
Control international banking	0	11	21	24	33	34	42	48	54	73	87	100	30
Shrewd and tricky in business	0	4	11	18	34	51	69	76	90	94	100	100	35
Have a lot of irritating faults	0	13	22	39	50	56	60	73	80	83	91	100	40
Use shady practices to get ahead	0	6	20	41	53	61	77	80	92	95	96	100	42
Stick together too much	0	29	39	50	64	72	81	86	88	97	100	100	52
Always like to head things	0	24	48	58	64	78	85	86	94	97	98	100	54

Note: In this and all subsequent tables the number in parentheses represents the number of respondents on which the percentages are based.

Table 3. EXTERNAL VALIDATION OF THE INDEX OF ANTI-SEMITIC BELIEF

	Score on Index of Anti-Semitic Belief												Total
	0	1	2	3	4	5	6	7	8	9	10	11	
Number of respondents	(316)	(289)	(227)	(183)	(192)	(156)	(125)	(130)	(108)	(95)	(58)	(34)	(1,913)
Validating Items													
Jews are always stirring up trouble with their ideas	0%	1%	1%	2%	5%	10%	16%	22%	22%	40%	55%	70%	10%
Jews have stirred up a lot of the trouble between whites and Negroes	1	3	2	5	13	11	18	28	29	37	50	62	13
Jews today are trying to push in where they are not wanted	1	5	5	14	19	22	26	32	39	50	50	76	18
You can usually tell whether or not a person is Jewish just by the way he looks	18	37	33	40	48	51	59	63	58	72	72	74	44
The movie and television industries are pretty much run by Jews	22	35	44	49	51	52	58	61	62	67	86	88	47
Jewish employers go out of their way to hire other Jews	17	31	44	47	54	66	68	70	75	81	78	91	50

discriminatory attitudes, constitute further validations of the Index of Anti-Semitic Belief.

Describing the Population

Having partially validated the Index of Anti-Semitic Belief, we can now use it to describe the population. Table 4 reports the proportions of the sample with each of the scores from 0 to 11; the figures in parentheses

Table 4.   DISTRIBUTION OF THE SAMPLE ON THE INDEX OF
ANTI-SEMITIC BELIEF

Index Score	Per Cent	Number	
0	16	(316)	Least anti-Semitic third
1	15	(289)	(31 per cent)
2	12	(227)	
3	10	(183)	Middle anti-Semitic third
4	10	(192)	(32 per cent)
5	8	(156)	
6	6	(125)	
7	7	(130)	
8	6	(108)	Most anti-Semitic third
9	5	(95)	(37 per cent)
10	3	(58)	
11	2	(34)	
100% (N) =		(1,913)	

Average score = 3.75

show the absolute number of cases. As can be seen, 16 per cent did not accept any of the eleven beliefs in the Index; somewhat fewer, or 15 per cent, accepted one belief, and still fewer, or 12 per cent, accepted two beliefs. At the other end of the Index, 5 per cent accepted nine of the beliefs, 3 per cent accepted ten, only 2 per cent accepted all eleven.

The exact point on the Index where one distinguishes between anti-Semites and non-anti-Semites is necessarily somewhat arbitrary. One criterion is average score on the Index, in this case 3.75. By this standard 47 per cent of the sample can be said to be high on anti-Semitism in the sense that they exceeded the average. However, we decided on a slightly more stringent standard. Only at score 5 do acceptance rates begin to exceed acceptance rates for the sample as a whole (Table 2). For instance, 26 per cent of the sample say Jews care only about their own kind, but at score 5, 34 per cent do so. Respondents are therefore classified as anti-Semitic only if they gave anti-Semitic responses to at least five of the eleven items that make up the Index.[2] By this standard roughly a third of the sample (37 per cent) are high on anti-Semitism.

This finding can be stated another way: The most anti-Semitic third of the sample accept at least five of the eleven beliefs in the Index. It is significant that to locate the most anti-Semitic third one has to dip as low as five on the Index. Had a survey been conducted twenty years ago using the same Index, the most anti-Semitic third might well have accepted as many as eight beliefs. This does not mean that the most anti-Semitic third in our sample is not really anti-Semitic. With but one exception, every belief in the Index was accepted by a majority of the most anti-Semitic third. If the beliefs in the Index were put to a vote among this group all but one would pass (Table 5, last column). If the population as a whole were as anti-Semitic as the most anti-Semitic third, Americans would be very anti-Semitic indeed.

What about the least anti-Semitic third of the population? How anti-Semitic are they? We find from the distribution on the Index that the least anti-Semitic third (31 per cent of the sample) accept no more than one belief (Table 4). This group we designate as the "unprejudiced." Again, it is not inevitable that the least anti-Semitic third should be as free of prejudice as our data show. Twenty years ago the least anti-Semitic third might have accepted as many as four or five of the eleven beliefs. As matters now stand, the general level of anti-Semitism is sufficiently low that a third accept no more than one belief on the Index.[3]

In short, both the unprejudiced and the anti-Semitic seem to be properly defined, from a descriptive as well as an analytic point of view. Those classified as unprejudiced are not only relatively less likely to hold anti-Semitic beliefs, they are unprejudiced in an almost absolute sense. On the other hand, those classified as anti-Semitic are as a group definitely and unequivocally so, in the sense that majorities accept most of the negative beliefs about Jews included in the interview.

The Structure of Anti-Semitic Belief

As Table 5 shows, the anti-Semitic thirds differ not only in the number but also in the kinds of anti-Semitic beliefs each tends to accept. The un-

---

[2] As we said earlier, in order to distinguish subtle degrees of anti-Semitism at the lower end of the scale, we included in the Index three mild beliefs: that Jews have a lot of irritating faults, stick together too much, and always like to head things. These are the three beliefs most often accepted by those who had a score of 1 on the Index (Table 2). However, in order to achieve a score of 5 and be classified as anti-Semitic, respondents had to accept at least two of the more hard-core anti-Semitic tenets. On the average, those classified as anti-Semitic accepted seven of the eleven beliefs in the Index.

[3] The extent to which the least prejudiced third accept beliefs not included in the Index is shown in Table 3.

Table 5. ACCEPTANCE OF ANTI-SEMITIC BELIEFS AMONG LEAST, MIDDLE, AND MOST ANTI-SEMITIC THIRDS OF THE POPULATION

Beliefs in Index	Least Anti-Semitic Third	Middle Anti-Semitic Third	Most Anti-Semitic Third	Total
Too much power in U.S.	0%	2%	27%	11%
Care only about own kind	1	10	62	26
Not as honest as other businessmen	1	16	60	28
Too much power in business world	2	20	60	29
More loyal to Israel than to America	2	23	60	30
Control international banking	5	26	54	30
Shrewd and tricky in business	2	20	77	35
Have a lot of irritating faults	6	36	72	40
Use shady practices to get ahead	3	37	81	42
Stick together too much	14	50	86	52
Always like to head things	12	56	88	54
Money-ambition images:				
More money, more ambition	26%	44%	52%	41%
More money, same ambition	13	15	19	16
Same money, more ambition	18	16	9	14
Same money, same ambition	34	18	11	20
Other	9	7	9	9
100% (N) =	(605)	(602)	(706)	(1,913)

prejudiced third tend to reject all anti-Semitic beliefs; among the middle third half accept the clannish belief that Jews stick together too much; only among the most anti-Semitic third do sizable proportions accept unethical as well as clannish beliefs. Finally, the belief that Jews have too much power in the United States tends to be restricted to the small group of extremely high scorers.

That the anti-Semitic thirds are characterized by different kinds of beliefs indicates that anti-Semitism is not a haphazard conglomeration of beliefs but has a definite structure. As suggested in Chapter 1, certain beliefs seem to form a foundation for the acceptance of others, or to put it more accurately, the acceptance of "harsher" beliefs often appears to entail or to be contingent on the acceptance of "milder" ones. To illustrate this, we analyze three items representing three different levels of anti-Semitism: "Jews stick together too much," "The trouble with Jewish businessmen is that they are so shrewd and tricky that other people don't have a fair chance in competition," "Jews have too much power in the United States." Since respondents could say "yes," "no," or "don't know" to each question, twenty-seven different response patterns are possible.

As Table 6 shows, most of the sample (83 per cent) gave "scalar" responses to the three questions. That is to say, they did not deny a "mild" belief and say "yes" or "don't know" to a "stronger" belief. Very few people accepted the power belief without also accepting the unethical and clannish beliefs (only four respondents in the entire sample did so). Similarly, few people hold the image of Jews as unethical without also agreeing that Jews are clannish. Finally, when people denied that Jews stick together too much, the overwhelming majority rejected both the unethical and the power beliefs. When respondents who had one or more "don't knows" are omitted, 91 per cent gave logically consistent responses.[4]

It is not at all certain that data from other countries or from another period in history would yield the same result. During the Hitler era many Germans may have accepted the belief in excessive Jewish power without also accepting beliefs in Jewish dishonesty and clannishness. Indeed, this probably occurred in the United States during the same period. As mentioned earlier, polls during the 1940s found that almost 60 per cent of Americans believed that Jews had too much power in the United States. While no evidence is available, it is possible that many held this belief

---

[4] No attempt was made to see whether more than three beliefs in the Index scaled. We chose a clannish, an unethical, and a power belief because these are three central themes that run through anti-Semitic ideology. The ideological nature of anti-Semitism virtually insures that certain pairs of beliefs "scale," for example, that Jews stick together too much and that Jews don't care about anyone but their own kind, since the latter tends to be logically contingent on holding the former.

Table 6. PATTERNS OF RESPONSE TO THREE QUESTIONS ABOUT JEWS

Stick Together Too Much	Shrewd and Tricky	Too Much Power in U.S.	Number	
Consistent response patterns (scale types)				
Yes	Yes	Yes	137	
Yes	Yes	No	311	
Yes	No	No	313	
No	No	No	538	
				1,299
Yes	Yes	Don't know	80	
Yes	Don't know	Don't know	29	
Yes	Don't know	No	53	
Don't know	Don't know	Don't know	35	
Don't know	Don't know	No	25	
Don't know	No	No	66	
				288
	Subtotal		1,587	
Inconsistent response patterns (nonscale types)			314	
Total			1,901	

$$\frac{\text{number with consistent response patterns}}{\text{total number of cases}} = \frac{1,587}{1,901} = 83\%$$

$$\text{(among those with no don't-know responses)} \quad \frac{1,299}{1,429} = 91\%$$

without holding other, less extreme beliefs. This is not an unimportant observation. If people who would ordinarily score low on anti-Semitism can suddenly take on extreme beliefs when they become current, it is not surprising that anti-Semitism has often flared up after periods of decline.

One final observation should be made. When the three beliefs—"stick together," "shrewd and tricky," and "power in the United States"—are combined into an index, the following result is obtained: 40 per cent of the sample do not accept any of the three beliefs, 29 per cent accept one, and 31 per cent accept two or three. These figures correspond closely to those based on the more elaborate Index of Anti-Semitic Belief.[5] The short index would therefore appear to be adequate as a parsimonious measure for charting future trends in anti-Semitism.

[5] The short index strongly predicts score on the long Index of Anti-Semitic Belief. As scores on the short Index increase from 0 to 3, the proportion scoring as anti-Semitic on the long Index increases from 7 per cent to 24, 81, and 100 per cent. Thus a score of 2 or 3 on the short Index isolates the anti-Semitic, a score of 0 or 1 the non-anti-Semitic.

The Don't-Know Response

Each question in the interview produced a certain number of respondents who either said "don't know" or avoided a direct reply. The majority gave few don't-know answers to the eleven items in the Index of Anti-Semitic Belief; 62 per cent had no more than one don't know, 83 per cent no more than three don't knows. The remaining 17 per cent had four or more don't knows. In opinion research, don't-know responses are often given a score of one-half. This could have been done in the present study; insofar as respondents answer "don't know," they reveal a failure to reject anti-Semitism in principle, and therefore manifest a certain susceptibility to anti-Semitism. Nevertheless, in order to make the category of anti-Semites as unambiguous as possible, it was decided to give a score only to definite acceptance of a belief.[6] In this way the reader can be sure that when a person scores between 5 and 11 he has definitely accepted between 5 and 11 beliefs. Any other procedure would jeopardize our descriptive estimates of the extent of anti-Semitism.

The meaning of don't knows is far from self-evident, and is explored in subsequent chapters. However a first step can be taken by observing the kinds of beliefs that evoked few, and the kinds that evoked many don't knows. The following beliefs received a small don't-know response:

Jews are just as honest as other businessmen.	8%
Jews stick together too much.	10
Jews are more willing than others to use shady practices to get what they want.	12
The trouble with Jewish businessmen is that they are so shrewd and tricky that other people don't have a fair chance in competition.	12
Jews don't care about anyone but their own kind.	12
Jews have too much power in the business world.	12
Jews have too much power in the United States.	12

The following items elicited relatively large don't-know responses:

Jewish employers go out of their way to hire other Jews.	19%
Jews are more loyal to Israel than to America.	23
Jews still think of themselves as God's Chosen People.	24
Jews have stirred up a lot of the trouble between whites and Negroes.	27

[6] Missing information—due either to the failure of interviewers to ask a question or the unwillingness of respondents to answer—was scored zero in constructing the Index of Anti-Semitic Belief. This decision applied to only 28 respondents, and with few exceptions information was missing on only one of the eleven items in the Index.

The movie and television industries are pretty much controlled
   by Jews.   32

International banking is pretty much controlled by Jews.   46

One possible interpretation of the don't knows is that they represent evasion and are therefore equivalent to an anti-Semitic response. If this were the case, then don't knows should be most frequent on items that are most conspicuously anti-Semitic. But both mild and harsh beliefs appear in each of the two groups listed above. Since there is no correspondence between the proportion of don't knows and the virulence of a belief, it is doubtful that respondents were saying "don't know" in order to conceal anti-Semitism.[7]

A closer examination of the items in the two groups suggests why the second group drew so many don't knows. The first group contains the standard clannish, unethical, and power stereotypes that characterize traditional anti-Semitism. In contrast, the second group contains several items that were invented for this study and with which respondents were presumably unfamiliar. A second clue comes from the finding, reported in Chapter 1, that the same kind of people who answer "don't know" to beliefs about Jews tend to accept anti-Semitic beliefs when they do have opinions.[8] In many cases, therefore, saying "don't know" is equivalent to saying that the belief in question may well be true but the respondent does not know it for a fact. Presumably if someone in an "authoritative" position were to inform him of the "fact," he would readily accept it. When all the evidence is considered together, it would appear that those who are inclined to accept anti-Semitic beliefs tend to answer "don't know" when presented with beliefs with which they are not familiar.

At the least, don't-knowism indicates a susceptibility to anti-Semitism. However, susceptibility cannot be equated with anti-Semitism, as will be evident in Chapter 4. For this reason, we chose not to contaminate the category of anti-Semites by including chronic don't-knowers. But by the

[7] Stated more accurately, the beliefs least accepted in the over-all sample should have elicited the most don't knows, those most accepted the fewest don't knows. However, this did not occur. Table 1 in Chapter 1 ranks the beliefs in the order of their acceptance. Among the first nine of the eighteen beliefs, four had high don't-know responses, five had low don't-know responses. Of the nine most accepted beliefs, again four had high don't-know responses, five had low. In other words, there was no correlation between the frequency of a belief (and presumably its harshness) and the number of don't knows it evoked.

[8] Chapter 1 reported that people with little or no contact with Jews tended either to accept anti-Semitic beliefs or to answer "don't know." Among those with no contacts, 35 per cent had four or more don't knows on the Index of Anti-Semitic Belief; among those with 1 or 2 contacts, the figure is 19 per cent; among those with 3 or more contacts, 5 per cent. Further evidence that the same kinds of people who tend to accept anti-Semitic beliefs also tend to answer "don't know" appears in Chapters 5–7.

same token, we did not want to contaminate the category of non-anti-Semites. We therefore distinguish between two kinds of non-anti-Semites: the convinced, who consistently reject anti-Semitic beliefs, and the unconvinced, who score as non-anti-Semitic largely because they say "don't know" when presented with anti-Semitic statements.[9]

Bringing the don't knows into the picture requires a reassessment of the proportion of the population who are unprejudiced. Earlier we said that a third accepted no more than one belief on the Index. However, some of this group were chronic don't-knowers. When they are removed only 20 per cent of the population can be characterized as unprejudiced. This is a stringent standard, but one that attempts to estimate the extent of self-conscious and principled opposition to anti-Semitism.

Some of My Best Friends

It is in the nature of prejudice that positive beliefs coexist with negative ones. Negroes are seen as good athletes and musicians, Orientals as well-disciplined, Italians as spirited. Positive elements also enter into the stereotypic picture of Jews. In the interview, we included the statement that "Jews are warm and friendly people," and 75 per cent agreed. Large proportions also agreed that "the more contact a person has with Jewish people, the more he gets to like them" (67 per cent) and that "Jews are becoming more and more like other Americans" (73 per cent). No negative belief was as widely accepted as each of these positive statements.

While most characteristic of the unprejudiced, each of the positive beliefs was accepted by a majority of the most anti-Semitic third of the population. Undoubtedly, anti-Semites who deny Jews any possible virtue are even more prejudiced than those who agree to positive statements. This does not mean, however, that those who hold both negative and positive images are not genuinely prejudiced. As one respondent said: "To me the Jewish religion makes them become selfish. Some law should be passed . . . so that Jews should help everybody rather than just Jews. They only help each other. Apart from that, they're very nice and friendly people."

Accepting both pejorative and favorable beliefs about Jews is in part a reflection of the familiar assertion of anti-Semites that some of their best friends are Jews. This is frequently conceived to be another example of the

[9] Both convinced and unconvinced non-anti-Semites accepted no more than four beliefs on the Index. But unconvinced non-anti-Semites had four or more don't knows, convinced non-anti-Semites three or fewer. Analysis showed that four don't knows seriously reduced the chances of scoring as anti-Semitic (seven don't knows made it impossible). However, those with three don't knows were as likely as those with none to score as anti-Semitic. Thus four don't knows is used as the cutting point for distinguishing between the convinced and the unconvinced.

irrationality, if not outright duplicity, of the confirmed anti-Semite, similar to his tendency to regard Jews as both too seclusive and too intrusive. In Chapter 1 it was argued that the seclusive-intrusive image is not self-contradictory but constitutes an interpretation of the insidious process by which Jews group together to gain power over others. In the same way, it may be profitable to regard the claim of the anti-Semite that "some of my best friends are Jews" not as a cover-up for prejudice but as a clue to its nature. When Americans speak about Jews as clannish, dishonest in business, and inordinately powerful, it is not their Jewish friends or acquaintances whom they have in mind. In explaining why something should be done to take power away from the Jews, only one respondent mentioned a personal experience; people generally described Jews as cheating *others* or as being powerful in remote places.[10] It is in the nature of prejudice that fear and hatred are typically aroused far more by fantasy images than by individual members of the group against whom prejudice is directed and with whom the respondent comes into contact. The anti-Semite is always ready to make an exception, to speak of his friend as a "white Jew" and as different from the mythical or symbolic Jew who is the object of his fear and hatred. Indeed, the plea of the anti-Semite that "some of my best friends are Jews" is implicit recognition on his part of how he came to his anti-Semitism: by becoming acquainted not with individual Jews but with anti-Semitic ideology.

Changing Images of the American Jew

In remarks volunteered to interviewers, a few respondents distinguished between Jews and "kikes." In response to a question concerning intermarriage, one highly anti-Semitic respondent said: "Now I make a difference between a Jew and a kike. I wouldn't mind a Jew but I would mind a kike." Words like "kike," "Wop," "Polack" once reflected the realities of an ethnically divided country. Newcomers were in fact strange to each other and to native-born Americans. Since immigrants were invariably of low social status, their cultural peculiarities easily evoked suspicion and contempt. With rising social status, minority groups have in fact become "more and more like other Americans." With this, much of the original common-sense rationale for prejudice has disappeared, and there is now an even wider gap than in the past between stereotypic images of minorities and social reality.

When asked, "Do you think that Jews have changed in some ways in

---

[10] To some extent Negroes are an exception to this pattern. The protocols of Negro respondents sometimes mentioned unpleasant personal experiences with Jewish shopkeepers and employers.

recent years?" about a third of the sample said "yes." When asked how Jews had changed, almost everyone implied they had changed for the better by becoming more like other Americans. As one respondent said: "They have become more like ordinary American citizens. You might say they *have* become Americans. You take when I was a kid, Jews walked funny. They had a funny accent. They were penny pinchers and when they could grab a nickel they would do so."

Hardly anyone implied that Jews should assimilate totally. One woman said: "There are so many Jews converting to the Protestant religion. I think that's wonderful." But she was the rare exception. For the most part when people mentioned religion they had in mind that Jews, especially the younger generation, are abandoning certain "un-American" customs and practices.

Their religion is not nearly as strict as they used to be. The younger generation are getting away from such strict observances like not eating pork or things like that.

Yes, they're loosening up a little. You don't find as many Orthodox. They ride to church; they don't walk.

He's gotten more like everybody else. He used to wear a long beard and not eat ham and now things are changed.

Most frequently mentioned was that Jews have become less clannish. Many connected Jewish clannishness with unfriendliness, and saw Jews as unfriendly to Christians rather than the other way round.

They want to fraternize more with Christians. Before they were inclined to be by themselves.

They seem to be more friendly and they don't seem to be as distant with other groups as they used to be. They are mixing with other groups of people more.

They are more outgoing, more friendly. They don't keep to their own group as much.

Many respondents see both clannishness and religious orthodoxy as evidence of parochialism, narrow-mindedness, and intolerance on the part of Jews for others.

The rabbis are trying to work with the Christian leaders and that would have an effect on the congregations. They will change along with the rabbis.

I don't think they have as much hate in them as they used to have.

They are permitting intermarriage with Gentiles more so than they used to, letting Gentiles into the synagogue. On the whole they are more friendly and tolerant.

Some respondents emphasized increasing civic responsibility on the part of Jews.

They have become less segregated. They share more in community activities and tend to mix with others.

I think they have come to assume more responsibility. The ones I've been associated with have not set themselves off as a minority group. They fit in with the community now in the business and social groups more than they have in the past.

With the gradual reduction of the immigrant population, there has undoubtedly been an increase in the belief that, like other ethnic groups, Jews are becoming "more and more like other Americans." However, there is no correlation between anti-Semitic prejudice and thinking Jews have changed for the better. One reason for this is the inherent ambiguity of the question. To the unprejudiced, saying that Jews have changed for the better might represent a desire to express favorable attitudes toward Jews; to the prejudiced, it might mean that Jews were in need of change. Conversely, saying that Jews have not changed for the better might mean that they are just as bad as they always were or it might reflect the tendency of the unprejudiced to deny differences between Jews and "other Americans." In any event there is nothing in the data to suggest that believing Jews have changed reduces anti-Semitism in the individual; as we said, such a belief is compatible with prejudice. However, the changing image of Jews may be important for the climate of tolerance and for the long-run erosion of traditional stereotypes.

Evaluation of the Findings

This chapter had two objectives: (1) to construct and validate the Index of Anti-Semitic Belief and (2) to use this Index to estimate the extent of anti-Semitic prejudice in the population. The Index divides the population into thirds: an unprejudiced third virtually free of anti-Semitic beliefs; another third that holds some of the less noxious stereotypes of Jews; and an anti-Semitic third, in which majorities accept all but one of the beliefs on the Index. In subsequent chapters the anti-Semitic third is sometimes divided into high scorers (5 to 7) and extremely high scorers (8 to 11). High scorers constitute 21 per cent of the population; extreme anti-Semites, 16 per cent. It must be emphasized that those classified as High or Extreme on anti-Semitism are designated as such only on the basis of their consistent acceptance of anti-Semitic beliefs. Even those called Extreme often reject discrimination and fall far short of the classical image of the rabid anti-Semite.

3 : Discrimination and the Limits of Tolerance

As we cautioned earlier, to focus solely on beliefs about Jews would be to overestimate the extent of contemporary anti-Semitism. In recent decades discrimination against Jews—in college admissions, in resorts, hotels, and housing, and in public life generally—has sharply declined. Perhaps for this reason few Americans now express support for the more flagrant forms of discrimination.

In order better to understand the decline in popular support for discrimination, this chapter examines the extent to which acceptance of anti-Semitic beliefs predicts support for discrimination. A decline in discriminatory attitudes in a population may have two sources. It may stem either from a decline in prejudice or from a decline in the eagerness of the prejudiced to support discriminatory practices. People can harbor negative beliefs about Jews and still be unwilling to act on them. Especially in an era when the Jewish question is not salient, even the most extreme anti-Semite may place limits on his intolerance.

Questions about discrimination are relevant for the unprejudiced as well. People who reject negative stereotypes about Jews may not always be willing to act in a nondiscriminatory way. Even the most unprejudiced may sometimes draw back from accepting Jews on an equal footing with non-Jews. This chapter therefore looks at discrimination from two perspectives: How tolerant is the anti-Semite? How intolerant are the unprejudiced?

How Tolerant Are Anti-Semites?

Discrimination in Hiring

In the pilot interviews conducted for this study, even frankly prejudiced respondents showed little desire to avoid Jews or to uphold most restrictive practices. For this reason relatively few questions on discrimination were included in the final interview. One question that was asked illustrates present-day unwillingness to support discrimination against Jews. This question concerned hiring practices, and offered four alternative policies that "big companies" should follow. Virtually everyone (90 per cent) chose the statement "Hire the best people whether they are Jewish or not"; a bare 2 per cent chose "Hire no Jews at all." In 1948, when a similar question was asked, the corresponding figures were 65 and 10 per

Table 7. ATTITUDES TOWARD EMPLOYMENT DISCRIMINATION BY LEVEL
OF ANTI-SEMITIC BELIEF

Reply to: "Which of the things on this card do you think big companies should do when they are hiring people?"

| | Level of Anti-Semitic Belief | | | | |
	Unprejudiced	Low	High	Extreme	Total
"Hire the best people whether they are Jewish or not."	96%	94%	88%	73%	90%
"Hire Jews in proportion to the number that there are in the community."	1	2	4	5	3
"Hire Jews only when they are so good that no one else could do the job as well."	1	2	5	11	4
"Hire no Jews at all."	0	1	2	10	2
"Don't know."	2	1	1	1	1
100% (N) =	(603)	(602)	(411)	(295)	(1,911)

cent.[1] It is evident that there has been a sharp decline in support for discrimination in hiring.

The unprejudiced almost unanimously favor equality in hiring: 96 per cent said big companies should hire the best people whether they are Jewish or not. This figure declines to 94, 88, and 73 per cent among those Low, High, and Extreme on the Index of Anti-Semitic Belief (Table 7). Even among extreme anti-Semites support for employment discrimination is limited to a minority.

[1] Charles Herbert Stember, "Recent History of Public Attitudes," *Jews in the Mind of America* (New York: Basic Books, 1966), p. 93. The wording of the 1948 question was as follows: "Which of the things on this card do you think people who employ large numbers of workers should do?" Our question read: "Which of the things on this card do you think big companies should do when they are hiring people?"

Residential Discrimination

Respondents were also asked, "How do you feel about having Jews in your neighborhood? Would you like to have some Jewish neighbors, wouldn't it make any difference to you, or would you prefer *not* to have any Jewish neighbors?" A similar question was asked in six past national polls. In every instance, from 1953 on, at least 80 per cent said that having Jewish neighbors would make no difference to them.[2] In the present study, 86 per cent gave the no-difference response (Table 8). Only 7 per cent said they would prefer not having any Jewish neighbors, and 6 per cent said they would like to have some Jewish neighbors.

Table 8.   ATTITUDES TOWARD JEWISH NEIGHBORS BY LEVEL OF
ANTI-SEMITIC BELIEF

Reply to: "How do you feel about having Jews in your neighborhood? Would you like to have some Jewish neighbors, would it make any difference to you, or would you prefer *not* to have any Jewish neighbors?"

| | Level of Anti-Semitic Belief | | | | |
	Unprejudiced	Low	High	Extreme	Total
"Like to have some Jewish neighbors"	7%	6%	7%	5%	6%
"Wouldn't make any difference"	90	90	80	75	86
"Prefer not to have any Jewish neighbors"	2	3	12	19	7
"Don't know"	1	1	1	1	1
100% (N) =	(604)	(602)	(411)	(295)	(1,912)

The no-difference response is usually assumed to be a tolerant response. But it has other possible meanings. Sometimes it may be an expression of hostility. As one respondent who scored as extreme on the Index explained: "It would make no difference to me if I had some Jewish neighbors; I wouldn't have anything to do with them anyway." The no-difference response may also be an expression of anomie or apathy. Suppose the question had read: "How do you feel about having Jews deprived of

[2] *Ibid.*, p. 96. In past polls, the question was worded: "Suppose a Jewish family were going to move in next door to you. Would you say you wouldn't like that at all, or that you wouldn't like it but it wouldn't matter too much, or that it wouldn't make any difference to you?"

their citizenship?" In such a case, a no-difference response could not possibly be given a benign interpretation. Direct evidence for the ambiguous nature of the no-difference response is found in the next chapter.

Although the large no-difference response undoubtedly gives a misleading impression of the extent to which Jews would be welcomed as neighbors, it does show that few people are so adamantly anti-Semitic as to choose the frankly discriminatory response of preferring not to have any Jewish neighbors. Even among extreme anti-Semites this figure is only 19 per cent. Responses to the neighborhood question are meaningful in another way. When a comparable question is asked concerning Negroes, the no-difference response is much lower.[3] Poll materials confirm what is apparent in everyday experience, that more Americans oppose Negroes as neighbors than oppose Jews. Unlike Negroes, Jews are not generally threatened with ghettoization.

Anti-Semitic prejudice tends to be directed against a "mythical" Jew and does not necessarily extend to individual Jews. Anti-Negro prejudice, on the other hand, while it certainly contains mythical elements, is more directly focused on the individual and includes a desire to avoid intimate contact. Even in the case of Negroes, however, close contact is not universally avoided; certainly it is not avoided when Negroes are employed as domestics. But close personal contact *is* avoided when it implies that Negroes have equal status with whites.[4] In other words, the dynamic

---

[3] A 1963 national survey asked: "If a Negro with the same income and education as you moved into your block, would it make any difference to you?" Sixty-four per cent answered "it would make no difference" (Herbert H. Hyman and Paul B. Sheatsley, "Attitudes Toward Desegregation," *Scientific American*, July 1964, pp. 16–23). Whenever a question gives the respondent the option, no-difference responses are always high. While the percentage who say they would be indifferent to Negro neighbors is unrealistically high (64 per cent), it is lower than the 86 per cent who say they would be indifferent to Jewish neighbors.

Acceptance of Jews as neighbors is also evident from a 1959 national sample which was asked to agree or disagree with the statement: "The trouble with letting Jews into a nice neighborhood is that sooner or later they spoil it for other people." Agreement was limited to a small minority of about 10 per cent (only 2 per cent strongly agreed). Over a quarter of the sample were uncertain, however. [Charles Herbert Stember, *Education and Attitude Change* (New York: Institute of Human Relations Press, 1961), p. 21.]

[4] "It is not the sitting next to a Negro at a table or washing at the next basin that is repulsive to a white, *but the fact that this implies equal status* [Clark's emphasis]. Historically, the most intimate relationships have been approved between Negro and white so long as status of white superiority versus Negro inferiority has been clear. Trouble comes only when Negroes decide not to be servants or mistresses and seek a status equal to that of whites. When Negroes start to assume symbols of upward mobility, then a pattern of residential segregation develops in the South, too" [Kenneth B. Clark, *Dark Ghetto* (New York: Harper & Row, 1965), p. 22]. See also Gordon W. Allport, *The Nature of Prejudice* (New York: Anchor, 1958), pp. 263–264; Thomas F. Pettigrew, *A Profile of the Negro American* (Princeton: D. Van Nostrand Company, 1964), p. 168.

behind avoidance of personal contact with Negroes—as neighbors, friends, co-workers—is fear of white status degradation. If fear of status degradation operates in all discrimination, then the point at which it is evoked is considerably higher in the case of Jews than in the case of Negroes. Having some Jewish neighbors does not appear to be threatening to most Americans. This does not mean that living in a "Jewish neighborhood" would not be. As one respondent put it, "It wouldn't make any difference if some Jews moved into this neighborhood, but I wouldn't like it if this became a Jewish neighborhood."[5]

Political Discrimination

The Gallup Poll periodically asks nationally representative samples what they would do if their party "nominated a generally well-qualified man for President and he happened to be a Jew." The proportion willing to vote for a Jewish candidate has steadily increased over the years. A 1937 poll reported that only 46 per cent were willing to vote for a Jew for President. By 1958 the figure was 62 per cent, and since then has increased to 68 per cent in 1961, 77 per cent in 1963, and 80 per cent in 1965. Opposition to a Catholic or Negro President has also declined.[6]

In the present study respondents were not asked whether they would or would not vote for a Jew for President. Instead they were asked how disturbed they would be if their political party nominated a Jew for President. It was necessary further to modify the Gallup question because interviews were conducted in the midst of a presidential campaign in which one of the candidates, while a member of a Protestant denomination, was partly Jewish in ancestry. We rephrased Gallup's question to read: "Suppose your political party wanted to nominate a Jew for President of the United States—that is, a religious Jew who would go to synagogue every week the way a Christian goes to church every Sunday. Would this disturb you very much, somewhat, very little, or not at all?" Only 2 per cent had no opinion. Twelve per cent said they would be very much disturbed, a figure close to the 15 per cent who in the 1965 Gallup sample said they would *not* vote for a Jewish candidate of their own party. However, an additional 17 per cent said they would be somewhat disturbed. A substantial majority—69 per cent—said they would be disturbed very little or not at all.

[5] Also involved in such attitudes is the assumption, however ungrounded, that the values and life style of a minority group are different from one's own. [Milton Rokeach, *The Open and Closed Mind* (New York: Basic Books, 1960).]

[6] Reported in Gallup news releases for August 22, 1965, and June 3, 1967.

Table 9 examines the presidential issue by level of anti-Semitism. As one would expect, as anti-Semitism increases, reservations concerning a Jewish President also increase. Among extreme anti-Semites, 53 per cent said they would be disturbed (very much or somewhat) by the prospect of a Jewish President; the comparable figure for the unprejudiced is 13 per cent. Despite this large difference, it should not be overlooked that almost half (46 per cent) of the extreme anti-Semites say they would be disturbed very little or not at all. As remarked earlier, rabid anti-Semitism

Table 9. ATTITUDES TOWARD A JEWISH PRESIDENT BY LEVEL OF ANTI-SEMITIC BELIEF

Reply to: "Suppose your political party wanted to nominate a Jew for President of the United States—that is, a religious Jew who would go to synagogue every week the way a Christian goes to church every Sunday. Would this disturb you very much, somewhat, very little, or not at all?"

| | Level of Anti-Semitic Belief | | | | |
	Unprejudiced	Low	High	Extreme	Total
"Very much"	3%	8%	16%	32%	12%
"Somewhat"	10	16	23	21	17
Total disturbed	13%	24%	39%	53%	29%
"Very little"	16	17	17	14	16
"Not at all"	68	57	42	32	53
Total undisturbed	84	74	59	46	69
"Don't know"	3	2	2	1	2
100% (N) =	(600)	(602)	(411)	(294)	(1,907)

is rare. At the present time even extreme prejudice, as measured by beliefs about Jews, has limits when it comes to refusing to vote for a Jewish candidate for President.

Increasing acceptance of a Jewish candidate testifies to a growing commitment on the part of Americans to norms of tolerance. In a period when civil rights are being emphasized, and there is little overt anti-Semitism, one would expect even the prejudiced to show less of a tendency to act out their prejudice in behavior. But their commitment to equality in public life is inherently unstable. Not only do they hold numerous anti-Semitic beliefs, including some hard-core tenets of anti-Semitic ideology, but as later chapters show, they exhibit other signs of a weak commitment to democratic principles.

How Intolerant Are the Unprejudiced?

In pilot interviews, several other areas of possible discrimination were explored, for example, hotels and resorts, patronizing Jewish stores, joining clubs with Jewish members. Discriminatory responses were so rare that these questions were excluded from the final interview. The two questions on hiring and neighborhoods were included to document what the pilot interviews strongly suggested: At the present time few Americans support clearly illegitimate forms of discrimination against Jews. The situation is far different for Negroes, and in this respect anti-Semitism differs sharply from racial prejudice.

We turn now to three areas of discrimination that are more ambiguous: religious intermarriage, social club discrimination, and Christmas carols in the public schools. These are areas in which even the unprejudiced often give discriminatory responses, not because they are anti-Semitic, but because other values come into play, for example, the desire to maintain the distinctive values and unique character of the Christian majority. Few defenders of political democracy would regard this as a legitimate aspiration when it entails rejection of a Jewish candidate for President. But the issues to be examined in this section lie in a different realm. While disapproval of intermarriage can have roots in hostility toward Jews, it can also follow from a legitimate desire on the part of non-Jews to maintain their religious and cultural identity.

Intermarriage

The following question was asked: "Suppose you had a child who wanted to marry a Jew who had a good education and came from a good family. How would you feel about this—would you object strongly, somewhat, a little, or not at all?" A majority (55 per cent) answered "a little" or "not at all." On the other hand, 42 per cent said they would object strongly or somewhat. Table 10 shows that disapproval of intermarriage increases with greater anti-Semitism, from 31 per cent among the unprejudiced to 55 per cent among extreme anti-Semites.

Why should as many as 44 per cent of extreme anti-Semites say they would *not* seriously object to intermarriage? At first glance this seems to be a contradiction on their part, but the interview protocols suggest otherwise. Apparently even when they are anti-Semitic, Americans place a high value on a person's right to marry whom he pleases.

A retired truck driver from South Carolina, besides giving an anti-Semitic response to every one of the questions on the Index of Anti-

Table 10. ATTITUDES TOWARD INTERMARRIAGE BY LEVEL OF
ANTI-SEMITIC BELIEF

Reply to: "Suppose you had a child who wanted to marry a Jew who had a good education and came from a good family. How would you feel about this—would you object strongly, somewhat, a little, or not at all?"

| | Level of Anti-Semitic Belief | | | | |
	Unprejudiced	Low	High	Extreme	Total
"Strongly"	12%	19%	26%	38%	21%
"Somewhat"	19	23	22	17	21
Total objecting	31%	42%	48%	55%	42%
"A little"	15	14	18	16	16
"Not at all"	48	41	33	28	39
Total not objecting	63	55	51	44	55
"Don't know"	6	3	1	1	3
100% (N) =	(599)	(602)	(411)	(295)	(1,907)

Semitic Belief, favored action to take power away from Jews because they "take advantage of the unlearned people—they get in second-class goods and sell them to people who don't know better than to buy them." Nevertheless, his response to the marriage question was: "I'd leave this up to the child. If he or she wanted it, I would not object."

A ranch hand from California said: "I wouldn't object about a kid of mine marrying anyone, if that's what he wanted." In other respects his anti-Semitism was explicit. He scored 9 on the Index, indicated he would consider voting for an anti-Semitic candidate ("I'd make up my mind on other issues"), and would not vote for a Jew for President ("I just wouldn't want a Jew to be head of our country").

A worker on a newspaper in Houston, Texas, also scored 9 on the Index and would be indifferent to the anti-Semitism of a candidate for public office ("If he's a Democrat I'd vote for him; if he's a Republican I'd vote against him"). Yet on the question of intermarriage, he took a benign view: "If they loved each other I wouldn't object at all."

A stenographer from California had a score of 7 on the Index, thought something should be done to take power away from the Jews (". . . there should be a limit as to what any person can have"), and indicated she would vote for a candidate who declared himself against the Jews. Yet she says she would not mind at all if her child wanted to marry a Jew, offering the following explanation: "My daughter's sister-in-law is Jewish and we all like her very much. Her family are very wealthy but she is one Jew who doesn't seem to care about making a big show."

This last comment once again reveals the underlying logic of the characteristic claim of anti-Semites, "Some of my best friends are Jews." The Jewish friend or relative is always the exception, and may be all the more admired precisely because he is an exception. In addition to the taboo against interfering in the marital choices of one's children, this is another reason why some anti-Semites can without contradiction accept intermarriage.

Opposition to intermarriage is less frequent but not uncommon among the unprejudiced; 31 per cent are strongly or somewhat opposed. When the results on the intermarriage question are placed next to those on the question concerning a Jewish President, an important finding emerges. The unprejudiced make a sharp distinction between opposition to intermarriage and opposition to a Jewish President whereas extreme anti-Semites do not. Among the unprejudiced, disapproval of intermarriage exceeds rejection of a Jewish President (31 per cent versus 13 per cent). In contrast, among extreme anti-Semites as many disapprove of a Jewish President (53 per cent) as disapprove of intermarriage (55 per cent). The unprejudiced tend to limit their intolerance to the *private* area of intermarriage. The extreme anti-Semite, on the other hand, is as willing to discriminate against Jews in the *public* as in the private realm.[7]

Social Club Discrimination

It is not surprising that the social club is one of the last bastions of discrimination against Jews. One important reason is that conflicting values are involved, and social club discrimination can be defended on principled grounds. As our data show, a majority of Americans feel that it is wrong for a social club to discriminate against Jews. However, a majority also believe that Christians have a right to their own clubs. These are not necessarily contradictory tenets. Few would deny that Christians have a right to exclude Jews from organizations whose functions are primarily religious. But religious and social activities are often intermeshed, and when this is the case, the issue becomes ambiguous. Are exclusionary policies justifiable in the case of an Indian peyote cult? a church bowling league? a Catholic fraternal lodge? a sectarian university? In a pluralist society, the point at which the individual's freedom of association begins to impinge on the rights of others is often difficult to define.

To explore attitudes toward social club discrimination, respondents were presented with the following situation: "Mr. Smith is a member of a

[7] Among extreme anti-Semites who disapproved of religious intermarriage 66 per cent also disapproved of a Jewish President. This figure declines as anti-Semitism declines—to 49 per cent among those with high scores, 34 per cent among those low on anti-Semitism, and 22 per cent among the unprejudiced.

social club where there are no Jewish members. Although he knows many of the members would prefer not to have Jews in the club, he decides to try to get his Jewish friend Mr. Cohen into the club. First of all, do you think that the other members have a right to be angry at Mr. Smith for trying to get Mr. Cohen in the club?" As shown in Table 11, 6 out of 10 deny that the other members have a right to be angry with Mr. Smith. To the next question, "Do you think that the other members have a right to keep Mr. Cohen out just because he is Jewish?" 68 per cent

Table 11.   ATTITUDES TOWARD SOCIAL CLUB DISCRIMINATION

Reply to: "Mr. Smith is a member of a social club where there are no Jewish members. Although he knows many of the members would prefer not to have Jews in the club, he decided to try to get his Jewish friend, Mr. Cohen, into the club."

"First of all, do you think that the other members have a right to be angry at Mr. Smith for trying to get Mr. Cohen in the club?"

"Yes"	33%
"No"	61
"Don't know"	6
100% (N) =	(1,900)

"Do you think that the other members have a right to keep Mr. Cohen out just because he's Jewish?"

"Yes"	28%
"No"	68
"Don't know"	4
100% (N) =	(1,907)

"Now suppose the members did vote to keep Mr. Cohen out of the club. What do you think Mr. Smith should do—quit the club, stay in the club and keep trying to get Mr. Cohen in, or stay in the club and forget the whole thing?"

"Quit the club"	10%
"Stay in and keep trying"	32
"Stay in and forget the whole thing"	51
"Don't know"	7
100% (N) =	(1,906)

"Do you think that *Mr. Cohen* should feel angry or do you think that he should realize that Christians have a right to their own clubs?"

"Should feel angry"	17%
"Should realize that Christians have a right to their own clubs"	74
"Don't know"	9
100% (N) =	(1,906)

responded "no." So far the impression is that a solid majority of Americans are opposed to social club discrimination.

Respondents were then asked what they thought Smith should do if the members voted to keep Cohen out of the club. Three alternatives were offered: Smith should quit the club, stay in the club and keep trying to get Mr. Cohen in, or stay in the club and forget the whole thing. We now find half the sample advising Smith to stay in the club and forget the whole thing. A minority—one-third—said Smith should stay in and keep trying. Few (10 per cent) said Smith should quit the club, and some of these were defenders of social club discrimination who presumably felt that Smith should resign because he had violated a gentlemen's agreement.

The final question is a stringent test of opposition to social club discrimination: "Do you think Mr. Cohen should feel angry or do you think he should realize that Christians have a right to their own clubs?" We realized that these alternatives are not mutually exclusive, but the intent of the question was to see how many respondents were so adamantly and self-consciously opposed to social club discrimination that, forced to make a choice, they would give more weight to the injustice done to Cohen than to the principle that Christians have a right to their own clubs. As it turns out, only 17 per cent thought Cohen should feel angry. Three out of four (74 per cent) said he should realize that Christians have a right to their own clubs.

Responses to this series of questions show that many Americans are in conflict concerning social club discrimination. On the one hand, 68 per cent denied that the members had a right to exclude Jews. On the other hand, at least as many said that Christians have a right to their own clubs. Furthermore, of those who denied that the club had a right to exclude Jews, 4 out of 10 said that Smith should forget the whole thing rather than persist in trying to get Cohen admitted. In other words, many opponents of social club discriminations show no readiness to combat it.

For purposes of analysis respondents were classified into four types: (1) defenders of social club discrimination—those who said that a social club has a right to exclude Jews; (2) token opponents—those who denied this right but said that Smith should stay in and forget the whole thing; (3) militant opponents—those who in addition to denying the right to exclude Jews said that Smith should either quit the club or stay in and keep trying; and (4) the opinionless.[8]

This classification produced the following result (Total column, Table

[8] The opinionless are those who said "don't know" to either of the two questions. However, the 38 respondents who defended the right of the club to exclude Jews but did not know what Smith should do are classified as defenders.

12). Slightly over a quarter of the population were defenders of social club discrimination: they said social clubs have a right to exclude Jews. Another 29 per cent were token opponents: they opposed social club discrimination in principle, but were not willing to do anything to combat it. About a third (36 per cent) qualified as militant opponents by opposing social club discrimination in practice as well as in principle.[9] The remaining 7 per cent were opinionless.

Table 12.   ATTITUDES TOWARD SOCIAL CLUB DISCRIMINATION BY LEVEL OF ANTI-SEMITIC BELIEF

| Attitudes Toward Social Club Discrimination[a] | Level of Anti-Semitic Belief | | | | |
	Unprejudiced	Low	High	Extreme	Total
Defenders	22%	26%	28%	42%	28%
Token opponents	20	32	36	33	29
Militant opponents	48	35	29	22	36
Opinionless	10	7	7	3	7
100% (N) =	(598)	(601)	(410)	(295)	(1,904)

[a]The categories are defined in the text.

While social club discrimination is related to anti-Semitic belief, the relation is not strong (Table 12). Extreme anti-Semites are most likely to defend social club discrimination (42 per cent); the unprejudiced are most likely to be militant opponents (48 per cent). But among the unprejudiced 22 per cent are defenders and 20 per cent are token opponents. As noted earlier, there are sources of discrimination other than prejudice, and support of the restricted social club is one example of this. The following comments, all by respondents scoring as unprejudiced, make it evident that at least some of the unprejudiced see exclusion by a social club as entirely legitimate and even a matter of democratic right:

If it's a private club they have a right to do as they please.

A private club is a private club; you can keep anybody out if you want to.

If it's their club they have a right to decide what they want.

The majority should rule; if they made a rule they should live by it.

That other less exalted motives are also involved becomes evident in Chapter 5.

[9] Obviously, we are talking about attitudes expressed in an interview, not about how people would actually behave. These figures probably overestimate the amount of active opposition that could be expected in actual practice.

Christmas Carols

The issue of Christmas carols in public schools is, in its own way, no less ambiguous than the issue of social club discrimination. The arguments pro and con typically run as follows:

Because schools are public institutions, they have no right to give preferential status to any religion, even in so innocent a form as Christmas carols. Carols are sung to celebrate a Christian holiday and are not simply one aspect of a teaching program that treats all religions impartially. The constitutional separation of church and state forbids giving preference to Christian holidays. The issue is not only constitutional but moral and religious: No child should be required to sing songs from a religion not his own.

In defense of Christmas carols it is argued that, while religious minorities have a legal right, they have no moral right to ask the majority to divorce their religion from their public life, especially since most schools have few or no Jewish children. When the singing of Christmas carols is not accompanied by efforts at conversion, they represent no more than an expression of the religious culture of the vast majority of Americans. The religious loyalties of Jewish children are not threatened by singing carols any more than they are threatened by exposure to the exclusively Christian art of medieval society.

As in the case of the social club issue, the question of Christmas carols was explored in depth. Respondents were first asked, "Do you feel that a public school teacher should teach Christmas carols to her class even if some of the children are Jewish?" A second question was then posed: "Suppose the parents of some Jewish children go to the principal and ask that the Christmas carols not be sung in the classroom. How much would you sympathize with the Jewish parents—very much, somewhat, a little, or not at all?" This question served to remind respondents that the singing of Christmas carols might offend Jews and arouse protest. Respondents were then given the opportunity to modify their original position: "What do you think should be done—continue singing the Christmas carols, or stop singing them?"

In response to the first question, "Should a public school teacher teach Christmas carols even if some of the children are Jewish?" 83 per cent answered with an unqualified "yes"; only 5 per cent said "no." When asked whether they would sympathize with the Jewish parents, 56 per cent said "not at all" and 21 per cent said "a little," making a total of 77 per cent with little or no sympathy. Even after being confronted with the hypothetical objections of Jewish parents, very few respondents changed their minds; 83 per cent began and 74 per cent ended by feeling that

Christmas carols should be sung.[10] There is no doubt that most Americans favor the singing of carols in public schools, and would be unsympathetic to dissenting opinion on this issue.[11]

This holds for the unprejudiced as well as for anti-Semites (Table 13). Before being reminded of possible Jewish objections, even the least prejudiced third of the population gave overwhelming approval to Christmas carols: 80 per cent versus 88 per cent for extreme anti-Semites. The unprejudiced were more likely to say they would sympathize with the Jewish parents somewhat or a little, but only 5 per cent said "very much." Almost half—48 per cent—said they would not sympathize at all. The major difference between the unprejudiced and extreme anti-Semites is that almost no extreme anti-Semites modified their original position: 88 per cent began and 85 per cent ended by approving of Christmas carols. More of the unprejudiced changed their minds; 80 per cent began, 67 per cent ended by defending Christmas carols. Nevertheless, this represents a solid majority who continued to defend Christmas carols after being reminded of possible Jewish objections.

That support for Christmas carols is not always motivated by anti-Semitic prejudice is also suggested by the responses of the 61 Jewish respondents: 54 per cent began, 44 per cent ended by saying Christmas carols should be sung. Furthermore, while 38 per cent said they would be very sympathetic to the Jewish parents, 48 per cent said they would not be sympathetic at all. It is clear that Jewish opinion on the issue of Christmas carols is sharply divided.

The implication of the data is that challenges to prevailing religious practices in the schools would meet with stiff opposition. And in fact in some communities where such challenges have been made the result has been open conflict. A few years ago, in Boulder, Colorado, a group of Jews and Christians protested to the school board that Christmas observances had become excessive. As moderate as their objections were, they precipitated a month-long crisis that included a cross-burning and threatening telephone calls.[12] More recently, in Wayne, New Jersey, a member of the school board issued a public statement warning against the election of Jewish candidates to the school board. One of his charges was

---

[10] Eleven per cent suggested that Jewish children be excused, 3 per cent that Jewish songs also be sung. These responses were not offered to respondents but were available as coding categories for the interviewer.

[11] Support for prayers in the schools is almost as great as that for carols. When asked, "How do you feel about prayers being said in the public schools?" 58 per cent of the sample were strongly in favor and 26 per cent somewhat in favor, a total of 84 per cent. It is evident that the Christian majority are reluctant to give up their traditional practices nor their special claim to religious preference in the public schools.

[12] Leonard Gross, "Christmas, To Observe or Not? From a New Generation, a New Answer," *Look*, December 28, 1965, pp. 22–24.

Table 13.   ATTITUDES TOWARD CHRISTMAS CAROLS IN THE PUBLIC SCHOOLS
BY LEVEL OF ANTI-SEMITIC BELIEF

| | Level of Anti-Semitic Belief | | | | |
	Unprejudiced	Low	High	Extreme	Total
"Do you feel that a public school teacher should teach Christmas carols to her class even if some of the children are Jewish?"					
"Yes" (unqualified)	80%	83%	83%	88%	83%
"Yes" (qualified)	10	9	8	8	9
"No"	5	4	6	2	5
"Don't know"	5	4	3	2	3
100% (N) =	(604)	(601)	(410)	(295)	(1,910)
"Suppose the parents of some Jewish children go to the principal and ask that the Christmas carols not be sung in the classroom. How much would you sympathize with the Jewish parents—very much, somewhat, a little, or not at all?"					
"Not at all"	48%	52%	62%	73%	56%
"A little"	24	25	18	14	21
"Somewhat"	18	16	12	8	15
"Very much"	5	4	6	2	5
"Don't know"	5	3	2	3	3
100% (N) =	(604)	(601)	(410)	(294)	(1,909)
"What do you think should be done—continue singing the Christmas carols, or stop singing them?"					
"Continue singing them" (unqualified)	67%	70%	79%	85%	74%
"Continue singing them if Jewish children are excused"[a]	12	13	9	8	11
"Continue singing them if Jewish songs are also sung"[a]	5	4	2	1	3
Other	7	5	5	2	5
"Stop singing them"	3	4	2	1	3
"Don't know"	6	4	3	3	4
100% (N) =	(604)	(602)	(411)	(295)	(1,912)

[a]These response categories appeared on the interview schedule but interviewers were instructed not to read them to respondents.

that Jews must be prevented from "taking what's left of Christ out of our Christmas celebrations." The extent to which voters responded to this particular charge is open to question, but the two Jewish candidates were overwhelmingly defeated.[13] Such events bear out the finding that sentiment on the Christmas carol issue is united and adamant.

[13] Rodney Stark and Stephen Steinberg, "Jews and Christians in Suburbia," *Harper's*, August 1967, pp. 73–78.

Evaluation of the Findings

The separation of beliefs from behavioral orientations is crucial to an understanding of the ambiguous nature of present-day anti-Semitism. Chapter 2 showed that at least a third of the population are anti-Semitic in terms of their beliefs about Jews. However, as this chapter has shown, support of the more illegitimate forms of discrimination is generally low even among the most prejudiced third of the population. The anti-Semitism typical of the present is not the rabid anti-Semitism of past eras that has too often served as the model for all anti-Semitism.

How are we to interpret the gap between continuing acceptance of anti-Semitic beliefs and declining support for discrimination? It is frequently argued that prejudiced beliefs typically decline only after actual discriminatory practices decline. According to this interpretation, the first step in this process is official opposition to discrimination by government and other elites, resulting in a decline in discriminatory practices. Both have occurred in the United States since World War II. These are then followed by a corresponding decrease in attitudinal support for discrimination in the general population, even among anti-Semites. This also appears to have happened. As a final step, possibly a generation later, beliefs are brought into line with behavioral orientations, just as behavioral orientations were earlier brought into line with actual practice. On this view anti-Semitic beliefs, though widespread, are a residue that will decline and atrophy in the future.

It might be argued, however, that so long as a substantial reservoir of anti-Semitic beliefs exists, the decline in discriminatory attitudes is precarious. The reluctance of the prejudiced to support discrimination may represent little more than conventional conformity to the present climate of opinion. To the extent that this is the case, opposition to discrimination could dissolve under less favorable political conditions.

Both interpretations may be correct. We may be witnessing a decline in anti-Semitism but a precarious decline. If the prejudiced have other beliefs and attitudes consistent with their opposition to discrimination, the decline in discriminatory attitudes toward Jews might be judged to be firm. If in subsequent chapters we find otherwise, this would suggest the precariousness of present-day opposition to discrimination against Jews.

4 : Political Anti-Semitism and Apathy

The previous chapter explored the extent to which Americans are tolerant of Jews. This chapter explores the extent to which Americans are tolerant of anti-Semitism. Responses to two questions are analyzed:

1. If a candidate for Congress should declare himself as being against the Jews, would this influence you to vote for him or to vote against him?
2. If the United States government wanted to pass a law to stop more Jews from immigrating to this country, would you be in favor of this or against this?

Both questions center around the introduction of anti-Semitism into the political process, and in this sense deal with the issue of political anti-Semitism.[1] Needless to say, responses have little bearing on the realistic chance that an anti-Semitic candidate will appear or that discriminatory legislation will be proposed. In this country there are many institutional defenses which, so long as they remain intact, are effective barriers to political anti-Semitism. An occasional candidate might inject anti-Semitism into a political campaign, but at the present time a program of political action against Jews is virtually inconceivable. This does not mean that American attitudes toward political anti-Semitism are irrelevant. They are the only clue we have as to how Americans might behave if actually confronted with a situation of political anti-Semitism.

It is frequently assumed that so long as few Americans openly advocate political anti-Semitism, this settles the question: Could it happen here? But the German experience tells us otherwise. How many Germans actively supported the anti-Semitic program of the Nazis is impossible to say. But

[1] In Chapter 1 we used the term "political anti-Semitism" to refer to beliefs concerning Jewish power. In the present chapter, political anti-Semitism has a related but different meaning: it refers to the willingness to introduce anti-Semitism into the political process. Political anti-Semitism in this sense is also different from political discrimination, or the refusal of individuals to vote for a Jewish political candidate.

that most Germans were indifferent to the fate of the Jews is hardly open to doubt. The crucial question, therefore, is not the extent to which Americans advocate or would support political anti-Semitism but the extent to which they would be indifferent and apathetic should it arise. We are thus concerned with the question: Can Americans be counted on to oppose political anti-Semitism or would many respond with indifference and apathy?

The Anti-Semitic Candidate

Between 1945 and 1964 the proportion saying they would vote for an anti-Semitic candidate declined from 23 per cent to 5 per cent (Table 14). Conversely, opposition to the candidate increased from 31 per cent in 1945

Table 14.   ATTITUDES TOWARD AN ANTI-SEMITIC CANDIDATE FOR CONGRESS,

1945 AND 1964

(whites only)

Reply to: "If a candidate for Congress should declare himself as being against the Jews, would this influence you to vote for him or to vote against him?"[a]

	1945	1964[b]
"Vote for him"	23%	5%
"Vote against him"	31	58
"Would make no difference"	35	33
"Don't know"	10	4
No answer	1	0
100% (N) =	(2,444)	(1,651)

[a]The exact wording in the 1945 survey was as follows: "If a candidate for Congress in this state should declare himself as being against the Jews, would this influence you to vote for him or against him?"

[b]Figures are for whites only, in order to make them comparable to the 1945 data. The responses of Negroes were virtually identical to those of whites, and these are combined in subsequent tables.

to 58 per cent in 1964. The latter figure still constitutes only a bare majority, however. In 1964, as in 1945, a third of the respondents volunteered the response that the candidate's anti-Semitism would make no difference to them.[2]

[2] The question reads: "If a candidate for Congress should declare himself as being against the Jews, would this influence you to vote for him or to vote against him?"

Some insight into the meaning of the no-difference response can be gleaned from explanations offered by respondents. Only 38 explanations were recorded (interviewers were not instructed to probe), but they provide valuable clues. One possibility is that the no-difference response is simply another expression of anti-Semitism. One recorded explanation was frankly hostile: "It wouldn't make any difference to me if a candidate came out against the Jews; I don't like Jews anyway." Perhaps other anti-Semitic respondents would have given similar explanations had they been pressed to do so. However, on the evidence of the explanations recorded, the no-difference response usually had a less cynical, more politically naïve meaning.

Most respondents said they would decide their vote on the basis of other issues or the quality of the man himself. Especially striking is that this group includes persons who scored as unprejudiced as well as people who scored as anti-Semitic. Moreover, comments by unprejudiced respondents were indistinguishable from those of anti-Semites. The four quoted below are from respondents who scored as extreme anti-Semites on the Index of Anti-Semitic Belief:

Neither way, I would make up my mind on other issues. (A retired ranch foreman from Bakersfield, California.)

If he is a good candidate, I'd vote for him. (A housewife from Dorchester, Massachusetts.)

Would depend on the man. (A cabinetmaker from Ft. Worth, Texas.)

According to the man. (A retired truck driver from Seattle, Washington.)

It is impossible to tell these comments apart from the following made by unprejudiced respondents:

Well, I don't think it would influence me to vote for him one way or the other. (A housewife from Long Beach, California.)

If I liked the man, I'd vote for him anyway. (A machinist from Portage, Indiana.)

If he was a good man for the job. (A keypunch operator from Utica, New York.)

However, interviewers were provided with both a no-difference and a don't-know coding category.

The 1945 data appear in Charles Herbert Stember, *Education and Attitude Change* (New York: Institute of Human Relations Press, 1961), p. 62, by categories of education. The number of cases on which percentages were based is not reported, and the figures for the total 1945 sample in Table 14 were graciously supplied by the American Jewish Committee.

I'd vote for the best man even if he was against Jews. (A housewife from Utica, New York.)

A few respondents, unprejudiced against Jews, were equally unprejudiced against the candidate:

He is entitled to his own opinion. (A machine operator from Philadelphia, Pennsylvania.)

It is good for anyone in politics to give their honest opinions. (A drill operator from Los Angeles, California.)

That's his own opinion. I don't think it would be smart of him to say so. (A housewife from Pitcairn, Pennsylvania.)

The explanations suggest that a sizable minority of the sample went out of their way to reject the underlying assumption of the question, namely, that anti-Semitism in a political candidate is sufficient grounds for deciding

Table 15. ATTITUDES TOWARD AN ANTI-SEMITIC CANDIDATE BY LEVEL OF ANTI-SEMITIC BELIEF

Attitudes Toward Anti-Semitic Candidate	Level of Anti-Semitic Belief				
	Unprejudiced	Low	High	Extreme	Total
In favor	1%	2%	7%	16%	5%
Indifferent	28	31	38	43	33
Opposed	66	63	51	38	58
Don't know	5	4	4	3	4
100% (N) =	(601)	(601)	(411)	(295)	(1,908)

whether to vote for or against him. As will be seen, few anti-Semites now feel that a candidate's anti-Semitism is, by itself, an adequate reason for supporting him. However, at least some non-anti-Semites respond in an analogous way: They do not feel that anti-Semitism in a political candidate is sufficient reason to vote *against* him. In effect, both are saying they might buy political anti-Semitism as part of a package deal, provided the package as a whole was attractive to them.[3]

Table 15 analyzes attitudes toward the anti-Semitic candidate by level of

[3] This might be considered an overly strong interpretation, since the question did not say the candidate would urge action against Jews. One respondent said she would vote for him so long as he was "within reason, so long as he wasn't like Hitler." Nevertheless, respondents' comments corroborate the apparent meaning of the no-difference response—that for many Americans anti-Semitism in a political candidate would not by itself be a reason for voting against him.

anti-Semitic prejudice. Favoring the anti-Semitic candidate increases with anti-Semitic prejudice from a negligible 1 per cent to 16 per cent among extreme anti-Semites. This figure of 16 per cent stands in marked contrast to the 27 per cent of extreme anti-Semites who failed to oppose discrimination in hiring, the 53 per cent who would be disturbed by a Jewish President, and the 42 per cent who defended social club discrimination. However, indifference rises, from 28 to 43 per cent, as anti-Semitism increases, supporting the supposition that anti-Semitic prejudice is one source of indifference. The net result is that two-thirds of extreme anti-Semites and half of those high in anti-Semitic prejudice either favor the anti-Semitic candidate or are indifferent or opinionless.

For extreme anti-Semites, indifference to political anti-Semitism is understandable. Perhaps what needs to be explained is why they do not favor the anti-Semitic candidate as often now as they evidently did in 1945. Probably the main reason is the changing content of anti-Semitism away from a preoccupation with and fear of Jewish power, as indicated by the decline in the belief that Jews have too much power in the United States (from 58 per cent in 1945 to 11 per cent in 1964). When Jews are not seen as a political threat, one would expect support for political action against Jews to decline, even among the extremely prejudiced.[4]

Although indifference is greater among anti-Semites, it is high even among the least prejudiced third of the population (28 per cent gave the no-difference response, another 5 per cent had no opinion). Barring other values and commitments, the extreme anti-Semite has no reason to be concerned for the fate of a group about whom he holds so many unfavorable opinions. The unprejudiced, however, have no reason in their beliefs about Jews to be indifferent to their fate. Yet about a third failed to oppose the anti-Semitic candidate.

What distinguishes the indifferent and apathetic from those who oppose political anti-Semitism? Before confronting this question it is necessary to recall the discussion in Chapter 2 of the don't-know response. In constructing the Index of Anti-Semitic Belief, a point was assigned only for definite acceptance of a negative belief; in effect a don't-know response and a non-anti-Semitic response were given equal weight. However, we cautioned that not all low scorers are unprejudiced with the same degree of conviction. Some of the unprejudiced (the so-called convinced) definitely rejected anti-Semitic beliefs while others (the unconvinced) achieved low scores by

[4] The data are consistent with the view that the decline in the belief that Jews have excessive power has led to a decline in support of an anti-Semitic candidate. Among extreme anti-Semites who do *not* believe that Jews have too much power, 12 per cent favored the anti-Semitic candidate; among those who hold the power belief, the figure was 18 per cent. This relation holds up among extreme anti-Semites even when they have the same numerical score on the Index of Anti-Semitic Belief.

frequently answering "don't know." In Chapter 3 the unconvinced were no more likely than the convinced to hold discriminatory attitudes, and there was no need to analyze them separately.[5] But we now find that degree of conviction is a crucial factor when the issue of political anti-Semitism is raised.

In Table 16 attitudes toward the anti-Semitic candidate are analyzed in relation to anti-Semitic prejudice and opinionlessness. There are three columns of percentages: The first (F) shows the percentage favoring the anti-Semitic candidate; the second (O), the percentage opposed; the third (I), the percentage indifferent.[6] Favoring the anti-Semitic candidate continues to be a function primarily of anti-Semitic prejudice. Chronic don't-knowers are no more likely to favor the candidate than respondents with definite opinions. This further justifies our decision not to treat the don't-know response as a covert expression of anti-Semitism. Opinionlessness, on the other hand, is strongly related to indifference. For example, among the unprejudiced, indifference to the anti-Semitic candidate rises sharply from 20 per cent to 37, 51, and finally 70 per cent among those with 6 or more don't knows on the Index. This relation repeats itself at every level of prejudice, except among extreme anti-Semites. The impact of opinionlessness is of such magnitude that opposition to an anti-Semitic candidate is actually greater among extreme anti-Semites with definite opinions about Jews (38 per cent) than among the unprejudiced with 6 or more don't knows (28 per cent).

Three sources of apathy or indifference to political anti-Semitism are suggested by the data. One is anti-Semitic prejudice; among extreme anti-Semites, the modal response is indifference. Another is lack of opinion about Jews. For many people, Jews are not a salient group; these people have no contact with Jews; they have heard little about them. In explaining his no-difference response one non-anti-Semite said: "I don't know much about Jews. I have never lived around Negroes either." A lack of interest in Jews, coupled with the failure to oppose prejudice in principle, manifests itself as indifference when the issue of political anti-Semitism is raised.

A third source of indifference is a generalized incapacity or unwillingness to formulate opinions. As surveys show, some respondents consistently lack

[5] The response patterns of the unconvinced and the convinced non-anti-Semites may have been less similar had the discrimination items in Chapter 3 evoked more don't knows. But only 1 per cent said "don't know" on the hiring and neighborhood questions; 2 per cent, on the President question; 4 and 7 per cent, on the two main questions concerning social club discrimination. While more of the unconvinced than the convinced said "don't know," differences were small, and the unconvinced were not more likely to support discrimination.

[6] The 4 per cent who said "don't know" are combined with the 33 per cent who gave the no-difference response. Analysis showed that both related to don't knows on the Index in the same way.

Table 16. ATTITUDES TOWARD AN ANTI-SEMITIC CANDIDATE BY ANTI-SEMITIC BELIEF AND OPINIONLESSNESS

Number of Don't Knows[a]	Level of Anti-Semitic Belief											
	Unprejudiced			Low			High			Extreme		
	F[b]	O[b]	I[b]	F[b]	O[b]	I[b]	F[b]	O[b]	I[b]	F[b]	O[b]	I[b]
0–1	1%	79% (351)	20%	2%	72% (352)	26%	6%	63% (232)	31%	16%	38% (255)	46%
2–3	0	63 (107)	37	4	63 (120)	33	8	39 (132)	53	15	38 (40)	47
4–5	3	46 (59)	51	1	47 (74)	52	9	20 (44)	71	c	c (0)	c (0)
6+	2%	28% (84)	70%	0%	33% (55)	67%		c (3)		c	c (0)	c (0)
Total	1%	66% (601)	33%	2%	63% (601)	35%	7%	51% (411)	42%	16%	38% (295)	46%

[a]Number of don't-know responses to items making up the Index of Anti-Semitic Belief.
[b]F=favor; O=opposed; I=indifferent and includes both no-difference and don't-know responses. The inclusion of the relative handful who said "don't know" does not alter the basic findings.
[c]Either empty cell or too few cases to compute percentage.

opinions on virtually any topic. When don't knows on non-Jewish items were examined, it was found that these, too, increased the no-difference response. Characteristically, a generalized disposition to be opinionless is not a sign of objectivity; nor is it merely indicative of lack of knowledge. That people have no opinions about Jews might be interpreted as a healthy sign. Since there are only 6 million Jews in the United States, most Americans have little contact with Jews and should, therefore, have few definite beliefs about them. The difficulty is that opinionlessness entails more than lack of opinion. Especially where ethical issues are involved, the person who answers "don't know" signifies that he lacks a principle—a norm—to guide his response. The person who consistently says "don't know" to anti-Semitic statements reveals that he does not reject prejudice in principle. If in addition he is indifferent to an anti-Semitic candidate, he is saying that he also has no principled objection to political anti-Semitism. When humane and democratic values are at stake, opinionlessness may have grave consequences. Our findings suggest that many Americans lack an adequate defense in their attitudes and principles to resist political anti-Semitism. Resistance would be further weakened were an anti-Semitic candidate to appeal to their self-interests. The political dangers of opinionlessness are real since, as we shall see, anti-Semitism, opinionlessness, and indifference to political anti-Semitism are all concentrated among the lower socio-economic groups of our society.

We do not suggest that political anti-Semitism is a serious possibility in the United States. If anything, a candidate for public office would lose far more support than he would gain by running on an anti-Semitic plank. On the other hand, one out of every three in our sample say they would be indifferent. So long as Americans fail to take a principled stand against political anti-Semitism, its occurrence in the future cannot be ruled out. Nor can the occurrence of other forms of antidemocratic politics.

The Immigration Law

The second question bearing on political anti-Semitism asked: "If the United States government wanted to pass a law to stop more Jews from immigrating to this country, would you be in favor of this or against it?" To this question only 19 per cent volunteered the no-difference response; another 6 per cent said "don't know." However, unlike the question about the anti-Semitic candidate, a sizable minority—20 per cent—said they would favor an anti-Jewish immigration law. Little more than half the sample were opposed.

A few respondents explained that they oppose *all* further immigration and were not singling out Jews. Nevertheless, as anti-Semitic prejudice increases, so does the proportion favoring the anti-Jewish immigration law (Total row, Table 17). Among the unprejudiced third only 6 per cent favor the anti-Jewish immigration law. This figure increases with greater anti-Semitism to 15, 29, and finally 49 per cent among extreme anti-Semites. As before, indifference to political anti-Semitism is strongly a function of opinionlessness. Among the unprejudiced, for example, indifference ranges from 12 per cent to 63 per cent as opinionlessness increases. In short, failure to oppose the immigration law has two sources: anti-Semitic prejudice and opinionlessness.[7]

Because the two questions concerning political anti-Semitism produced somewhat different response patterns, they have been analyzed separately. This results in an overestimation of the extent of principled opposition to political anti-Semitism. While 58 per cent opposed the anti-Semitic candidate and 55 per cent opposed the immigration law, only 40 per cent opposed both.

Sympathy with the Jewish Plight

One obstacle to the elimination of prejudice is that its very existence inhibits the development of sympathy for its victims. By assigning undesirable traits to whole groups, prejudice provides itself with a built-in justification for the mistreatment of minorities. Moreover, even when they are not prejudiced, members of the majority group are not apt to keep before them as a living reality the harm done by prejudice to its victims. Certainly the situation of the American Negro, compounded of frank discrimination and frequent terror, has never deeply penetrated the collective conscience of the American people. Nor, apparently, did the crimes of Nazi Germany against the Jews.

In April 1938, a Gallup poll asked a cross section of the American population the following question: "Do you think the persecution of the Jews in Europe has been their own fault?"[8] While only 10 per cent said "entirely the Jews' fault," a startling 48 per cent answered "partly their own fault." One is tempted to attribute this low level of sympathy to flaws in the wording of the question; conceivably some people might blame the Jews for not having fled the path of the Nazis. However, results of other surveys conducted during the same period do not support this interpretation. Another poll six months later phrased the question in the following

---

[7] As with the anti-Semitic candidate, a greater number of don't knows generally does not increase support for the immigration law. This once again suggests that don't knows are not a form of deliberate dissimulation.

[8] All poll data cited in this section are reported in Hadley Cantril, *Public Opinion 1935–1946* (Princeton, N.J.: Princeton University Press, 1951).

Table 17. ATTITUDES TOWARD AN ANTI-JEWISH IMMIGRATION LAW BY ANTI-SEMITIC BELIEF AND OPINIONLESSNESS

	Level of Anti-Semitic Belief											
	Unprejudiced			Low			High			Extreme		
Number of Don't Knows[a]	Fᵇ	Oᵇ	Iᵇ	Fᵇ	Oᵇ	Iᵇ	Fᵇ	Oᵇ	Iᵇ	Fᵇ	Oᵇ	Iᵇ
0–1	6%	82% (352)	12%	13%	69% (352)	18%	30%	47% (232)	23%	48%	35% (255)	17%
2–3	8	59 (107)	33	18	59 (120)	23	25	41 (132)	34	58	30 (40)	12
4–8	3	51 (59)	46	20	42 (74)	38	39	25 (44)	36		c (0)	
6+	7	30 (84)	63	13	40 (55)	47		c (3)			c (0)	
Total	6%	68% (602)	26%	15%	61% (601)	24%	29%	43% (411)	28%	49%	35% (295)	16%

[a]Number of don't-know responses to items making up the Index of Anti-Semitic Belief.
ᵇF=favor; O=opposed; I=indifferent (combines no-difference and don't-know responses; the inclusion of the relative handful who said "don't know" does not alter the basic findings).
cEither empty cell or too few cases to compute percentage.

way: "Do you think the persecution of Jews in Europe has been chiefly due to unreasoning prejudice, or do you think it has been largely their own fault?" One out of every three (32 per cent) answered that it was their own fault.

The logic behind blaming the victims was made apparent in a 1939 *Fortune* poll which asked a national sample what they felt was "the reason for hostility toward Jewish people here or abroad." Forty-two per cent gave reasons unfavorable to Jews, such as excessive control of business, too much power in the country, unethical business practices, and the like. Another survey, in 1942, asked specifically why Hitler took away the power of the Jews in Germany. Forty-six per cent were classified as saying either that Jews were too powerful or that the Jews were running the economy. The results of these polls show little growth of sympathy from 1938 to 1942. In each poll, at least one-third blamed Jews or saw the Nazi persecutions as rooted in Jewish faults.

Not only did Americans accept the claims of Nazi propaganda that Jews were excessively powerful in Germany, large numbers believed this to be true in America as well. In 1942, 44 per cent of a national sample said that Jews have too much power and influence in this country. A year later, 50 per cent said that American Jews have too much influence in the business world. Two years later 58 per cent held this belief. Far from evoking sympathy, the Nazi persecutions apparently sparked a rise in anti-Semitism in this country.

The results of public opinion polls also show that, as late as 1943 and 1944, when millions had already been put to death in concentration camps, many Americans did not believe reports of what was happening. In November 1944, one-quarter of a national sample either indicated they did not believe the reports or had no opinion. Moreover, among those who accepted the reports, 27 per cent estimated the number of Jews killed to be 100,000 or less; another 25 per cent had no opinion. At best only 24 per cent gave a realistic estimate. Whether these figures reflect simple ignorance of the facts, genuine incredulity, or a tendency not to want to believe the reports is impossible to say. There can be no doubt, though, that in 1944 most Americans did not comprehend the extent of the tragedy.[9]

Our data also show that many Americans are unsympathetic to the history of Jewish suffering. Respondents were asked the following question:

[9] One study in the present series, which sought to assess the impact of the Eichmann trial on public opinion, found that knowledge of the number of Jews killed by the Nazis was confined to a minority. When offered a card with various figures, only a third correctly chose 6 million, a figure highly publicized throughout the trial. Even after being informed of the official estimate, 24 per cent insisted it was too high. [Charles Y. Glock, Gertrude J. Selznick, and Joe L. Spaeth, *The Apathetic Majority* (New York: Harper and Row, 1966), pp. 138–139.]

"Some people say that Jews have suffered a great deal in the past. Which of these statements comes closest to your own feelings about this? The Jews have suffered no more than anybody else; the Jews have suffered but they generally brought it on themselves; the Jews have suffered through no fault of their own." One-third of the sample chose the statement that the Jews have suffered no more than anybody else; 17 per cent said that the Jews have suffered but they generally brought it on themselves. Seven per cent answered "don't know," leaving 43 per cent who chose the unequivocally sympathetic response that Jews have suffered through no fault of their own. Another question revealed that many Americans do not wish to be reminded about the past: 43 per cent of the sample agreed with the statement that Jews should stop complaining about what happened to them in Nazi Germany.

It might be argued that little importance should be attached to these findings. Many respondents may feel, as a matter of objective reality, that Jews have not suffered more than other persecuted groups, for example, Negro Americans. Moreover, one-third of the Jewish respondents agreed that Jews should stop complaining, as did 27 per cent of the unprejudiced. Nevertheless, lack of sympathy for Jewish suffering is related to anti-Semitic prejudice. Although a quarter of the unprejudiced say that Jews should stop complaining about what happened in Nazi Germany, this figure is 68 per cent among extreme anti-Semites. While 8 per cent of the unprejudiced blame Jews for bringing their past suffering on themselves, 40 per cent of extreme anti-Semites do so. Lack of special sympathy for Jews is not always grounded in anti-Semitism, but often it is.

Along with past polls the present study indicates that, despite their frequent lack of sympathy with Jews, Americans are almost unanimous in their disapproval of Hitler's treatment of the Jews. The following question was asked: "Which of these statements about Hitler comes closest to what you believe: Sometimes I think that Hitler was right in getting rid of the Jews; Hitler was partly right in trying to get rid of the Jews, but he went too far; Hitler was wrong in treating the Jews as he did." Nine out of ten respondents—89 per cent—chose the statement that Hitler was wrong in treating the Jews as he did. Four per cent had no opinion. Only 1 per cent said Hitler was right; another 6 per cent said he was partly right but went too far. A 1938 Gallup poll reported roughly the same result. At that time, when asked whether they approved or disapproved of the Nazi treatment of Jews in Germany, 6 per cent of those with opinions approved and 94 per cent disapproved. Despite the high level of anti-Semitism before and during World War II, few Americans went so far as to condone Hitler, even when they were extremely prejudiced against Jews. This must be interpreted in proper perspective, however. Had an analogous poll been conducted in Germany in 1938, one might have found only 6 per cent in favor of genocide and 94 per cent opposed. But Hitler did not have to depend on the active support of the German people; all that was required was the acquiescence of the 94 per cent to the acts of the 6 per cent. As was said in the introduction, political anti-Semitism, like all repression, depends less on open support than on lack of principled opposition.

Evaluation of the Findings

This chapter provides additional evidence that, despite the persistence of many anti-Semitic beliefs, political anti-Semitism is at minimal levels. No more than a handful of the population can be said to be political anti-Semites: only 5 per cent said they would be inclined to vote for an avowed anti-Semite; only 7 per cent expressed approval of Hitler; not reported earlier is that only 3 per cent identified Jews as more likely than other Americans to be Communists.[10] These figures are consistent with the figure of 11 per cent who believe that Jews have too much power in the United States; the 8 per cent who say that something should be done to take power away from the Jews; the 13 per cent who said that Jews have stirred up a lot of the trouble between whites and Negroes.

If there is any danger of political anti-Semitism in this country, it stems not from virulent anti-Semitic prejudice but from widespread indifference. Because of indifference, only 60 per cent of the national sample indicated they would vote against an anti-Semitic political candidate. Even this figure probably overestimates the extent to which Americans are prepared to oppose political anti-Semitism. Some opposition to the candidate came from people who hold many anti-Semitic beliefs. How firm their opposition would be under the pressures of an actual anti-Semitic campaign is open to question. Some opposition came from people who are opinionless and do not reject anti-Semitism on principled grounds. The danger is that in a period of heightened anti-Semitic propaganda they would take on beliefs they do not now hold, or might be convinced to vote for an anti-Semitic candidate on grounds other than anti-Semitic prejudice. Though few Americans now openly advocate political anti-Semitism, their ranks might easily be swelled by the already prejudiced and by those who, while not intolerant of Jews, are tolerant of anti-Semitism.

The implications of this chapter go beyond political anti-Semitism. Fail-

[10] The following question has been asked of past national samples: "In this country, do you think any of the people listed here are more likely to be Communists than others?" The proportion naming Jews declined from 11 per cent in 1950 to 9 per cent in 1953 and to 6 per cent in 1954. [Stember, *Jews in the Mind of America*, "Recent History of Public Attitudes" (New York: Basic Books, 1966), p. 162.]

ure to reject anti-Semitic beliefs and indifference to political anti-Semitism are both symptomatic of a weak commitment to democratic principles. Past research has shown that support for totalitarian movements is strong among the kinds of people who in normal times are politically uninformed and apathetic.[11] Our data parallel this on an individual level. Respondents who lack opinions typically fail to oppose political anti-Semitism.

[11] ". . . the underlying disaffection of which apathy may be an expression readily leads to activism in times of crisis, as when people who have previously rejected politics turn out in large numbers to support demagogic attacks on the existing political system" [William Kornhauser, *The Politics of Mass Society* (New York: Free Press of Glencoe, 1961), p. 61].

"The same underlying factors which predispose individuals toward support of extremist movements under certain conditions may result in total withdrawal from political activity and concern under other conditions. In 'normal' periods, apathy is most frequent among such individuals, but they can be activated by a crisis, especially if it is accompanied by strong millennial appeals" [Seymour Martin Lipset, *Political Man* (New York: Anchor, 1963), p. 116].

PART II LOCUS

"*Some studies reveal college-educated people to be the most prejudiced, others show quite the opposite. Similarly, the factor of income and class status is not clear in its impact. For sometimes the lowest classes, at other times the highest classes, are reported as most anti-Semitic. . . . Some say that Southerners are most prejudiced; others say Easterners are, or Northerners. Vague, too, is the significance of contact with Jews.*"

MELVIN M. TUMIN
An Inventory and Appraisal of Research
on American Anti-Semitism, 1961.

5 : Education, Occupation, and Income

In most social research, education, occupation, and income are routinely combined to form a single index of socio-economic status. When this was done in the present study, acceptance of anti-Semitic beliefs was found to vary inversely with socio-economic status: the lower the status, the greater the incidence of anti-Semitic beliefs; the higher the status, the less frequent the acceptance of anti-Semitic beliefs.[1] This finding is worth noting since some social scientists continue to see anti-Semitism as primarily a middle-class phenomenon.

A recent statement asserts, as a general proposition, that "prejudice is most commonly found where a competitive threat is most acutely perceived." Hence, anti-Negro sentiment is "strongest among Caucasians of social status similar to that of most Negroes" while anti-Semitism "tends to be particularly intense among Christians of social status similar to that of most Jews."[2] Along with past findings, the present study confirms the observation that anti-Negro prejudice is most prevalent among the lower classes (these data are presented in Chapter 9). But it does not support the contention that anti-Semitism is "particularly intense" in the middle class where Jews

[1] The measure of social class is a cumulative index scoring one point for each of the following characteristics: at least four years of high school, a family income of $8,000 or more, and a white-collar job (occupation of the head of household is used). When correlated with anti-Semitic prejudice, the following result is obtained.

Per Cent Anti-Semitic		
Score 0	62%	(495)
Score 1 or 2	38	(733)
Score 3	23	(289)

[2] Thomas F. Pettigrew, "Parallel and Distinctive Changes in Anti-Semitic and Anti-Negro Attitudes," Charles Herbert Stember, *et al., Jews in the Mind of America* (New York: Basic Books, 1966), p. 388.

are disproportionately located. On the contrary, the data show that anti-Semitism is far more characteristic of the working class who rarely come into direct competition with Jews.[3]

This is not to say that *all* manifestations of anti-Semitism are most prevalent among the lower classes. The question of whether contemporary anti-Semitism is basically lower class or basically middle class is not entirely misguided. But it is too broad to admit of a single unqualified answer. The answer depends in part on which dimension or manifestation of anti-Semitism is examined. From the evidence to be presented in this chapter, it is clear that there is at least one sense in which anti-Semitism is a middle-class phenomenon. On the whole, however, anti-Semitism is strongly associated with lower socio-economic status.

A still more basic question is whether anti-Semitism is a social-class phenomenon at all. This issue is not resolved by showing that anti-Semitic beliefs are more prevalent in the working class than in the middle class. The more important question is why this is so. Writers who correctly locate anti-Semitic prejudice in the lower strata of society sometimes attribute this to the greater incidence of frustration and insecurity among the less privileged.[4] But are anti-Semitic beliefs actually rooted in the exigencies and frustrations of working class life? Or are they mainly a function of the

---

[3] Pettigrew found support for his theory of middle-class anti-Semitism in Stember's examination of the relation between income and responses to nine questions about Jews in a 1962 national survey. "Stember shows . . . that anti-Semitism is relatively widespread among individuals of higher status, especially when measured by questions which paint Jews as a 'race,' 'more radical than others' or having 'objectionable qualities' " (Pettigrew, *loc. cit.*).

Let us examine Stember's data for 1962 (*op. cit.*, p. 227). (1) On the three items singled out by Pettigrew—Jews as a race, as radical, and as having objectionable qualities—higher income is indeed positively associated with greater anti-Semitism (as measured by these three items). But the percentage differences range from 8 to 11, hardly a firm basis for generalization. On the other six items, higher income is negatively associated with anti-Semitism, though the differences are again small, ranging from −1 to −11. When an average percentage difference is calculated for all nine items, it is less than 1 percentage point. On the basis of Stember's data, either there is no relation, or at best no consistent relation, between income level and anti-Semitism. (2) It might be argued from Stember's data that, while the middle class is no more anti-Semitic than the working class, it is certainly not less so. However, the highest of Stember's income categories is only $7,000 or over. This is so low that it includes many respondents who by a more realistic definition would be classified as working class. In other words, an income as low as this does not separate out higher-status respondents, and thus warrants no inference about the prevalence of anti-Semitic prejudice in higher-status groups.

[4] For example, the authors of a 1945 study observed that anti-Semitism among Protestants increases as income and education decline, and drew the following conclusion: "In this group there are many persons whose positions in the dominant religious group, and perhaps as native-born 'Americans,' contrast painfully with the economic disadvantage and insecurity which they experience. Such a position might lead to feelings of frustration and antagonism which could be channelized readily into anti-Semitic views" (Duane Robinson and Sylvia Rhode, "A Public Opinion Study of

relative lack of education of the lower classes? In other words, are working class people more apt to be anti-Semitic because they are generally less advantaged or more specifically because they are less educated?

These are basic questions for identifying the origins and understanding the etiology of contemporary anti-Semitism, and much of Part III is devoted to their further exploration. Once posed, however, such questions make it mandatory to abandon our composite index of social class and to examine the separate and independent effects of education, occupation, and income on anti-Semitic prejudice. Analysis may show that an individual's occupation and income are more important determinants of his anti-Semitism than are the years he spent in school. In that case, one would be justified in conceiving of anti-Semitism as rooted in the existential concomitants of social class. On the other hand, if education is the more basic determinant, then this would argue for seeing contemporary anti-Semitism as rooted in the cognitive and cultural concomitants of social class.

Education

Table 18 shows the relation of education to each of the eleven beliefs in the Index of Anti-Semitic Belief. Without exception, the less educated are more likely to accept every belief in the Index regardless of its content.

Table 18.   ACCEPTANCE OF INDIVIDUAL ANTI-SEMITIC BELIEFS
BY EDUCATION

Beliefs in Index	Grade School	High School	Some College	College Graduate
Too much power in U.S.	18%	10%	4%	5%
Care only about own kind	41	24	15	7
Not as honest as other businessmen	34	28	24	14
Too much power in business world	39	28	22	16
More loyal to Israel than to America	46	29	19	12
Control international banking	41	25	27	26
Shrewd and tricky in business	50	34	24	13
Have a lot of irritating faults	46	39	39	30
Use shady practices to get ahead	54	42	36	21
Stick together too much	62	52	43	37
Always like to head things	61	52	53	44
100% (N) =	(535)	(957)	(226)	(193)

Anti-Semitism in New York City," *American Sociological Review*, August 1945, p. 514). Emphasis on the role of frustration and insecurity also appears in theories relating prejudice to social mobility.

Table 19 shows the relation of education to the Index as a whole. Among persons with only a grade school education, half (52 per cent) score as High or Extreme. This proportion steadily decreases with every increase

Table 19.   ANTI-SEMITIC BELIEF BY EDUCATION

	Grade School		High School		Some College		College Graduates	
Anti-Semitic[a]	52%		36%		24%		15%	
Extreme		24%		15%		8%		3%
High		28		21		16		12
Non-anti-Semitic[a]	48		64		76		85	
Unconvinced		21		14		8		4
Convinced		27		50		68		81
100% (N) =	(535)		(957)		(226)		(193)	
Per cent convinced among non-anti-Semites	56%		78%		90%		95%	
100% (N) =	(254)		(617)		(171)		(164)	
Per cent anti-Semitic excluding the unconvinced[b]	66%		41%		26%		16%	
100% (N) =	(423)		(822)		(209)		(185)	

[a]Based on the Index of Anti-Semitic Belief. Anti-Semitic = score of 5–11; extreme = score of 8–11; high = score of 5–7. Non-anti-Semitic = score of 0–4; non-anti-Semites with four or more don't-know responses are called "unconvinced"; those with less than four don't-knows, "convinced" non-anti-Semites.

[b]In subsequent tables the per cent anti-Semitic excludes the unconvinced, unless otherwise indicated.

in education—to 36 per cent among high schoolers, 24 per cent among those with some college, and 15 per cent among college graduates.[5] The strength and consistency of this relation should leave no doubt that it is the less and not the more educated who are most likely to hold traditional anti-Semitic beliefs.[6] Furthermore with greater education the proportion of both high scorers and extreme scorers decreases. Among college graduates extreme anti-Semitism is virtually nonexistent; a mere 3 per cent score as Extreme.

The full strength of the relation between education and anti-Semitism is not apparent until one examines the relation of education to actual *rejec-*

[5] College graduates include postgraduates as well as those with four years of college. Among the latter, the rate of anti-Semitism is 20 per cent; among postgraduates it is just 9 per cent.

[6] The consistency of the relation between education and anti-Semitism is such that, with every yearly increment in amount of schooling, there is a corresponding decrease in the proportion anti-Semitic (except among those with six years of education or less).

tion of anti-Semitic beliefs. As noted before, some respondents scored as non-anti-Semitic because they frequently answered "don't know." A disproportionate number of grade schoolers are unconvinced non-anti-Semites, having received their low scores largely because of chronic don't knowism. In fact, only a quarter (27 per cent) of grade schoolers consistently rejected anti-Semitic beliefs and could be called convinced non-anti-Semites, as compared to 50 per cent of high schoolers and 81 per cent of college graduates. Thus a difference of 54 percentage points separates grade schoolers and college graduates when the greater opinionlessness of the less educated is taken into account.

Public opinion polls regularly show that the less educated more often say "don't know" on virtually every kind of issue and, when they do have opinions, tend to have unenlightened ones. Much the same is true of anti-Semitism. Among grade schoolers as a whole, 52 per cent score as anti-Semitic. But when unconvinced non-anti-Semites are excluded, 66 per cent of grade schoolers score as anti-Semitic. Opinionlessness is less of a factor at higher levels of education. Among all high schoolers, 36 per cent score as anti-Semitic; among those with firm opinions, 41 per cent do so. Virtually all college graduates had firm opinions, and therefore the percentage anti-Semitic is about the same whether the opinionless are excluded or not.

We have just reported two sets of percentages. If one is interested in a descriptive estimate of anti-Semitism among all grade schoolers, then the figure of 52 per cent is the more appropriate one. If one is interested in the extent to which grade schoolers *accept rather than reject* anti-Semitic beliefs, then the figure of 66 per cent is more meaningful since it eliminates the influence of lack of education on opinionlessness. In the subsequent analysis, we shall have occasion to use both kinds of figures. Whichever is used, however, there is no doubt that accepting anti-Semitic beliefs is consistently and strongly associated with lack of education.

The question was raised at the beginning of this chapter as to which was more fundamentally related to anti-Semitism—education or the distinctively social-class variables of occupation and income. In pursuing this issue we turn first to occupation. If the material aspects of social class are basic factors in acceptance of anti-Semitic beliefs, then education should have little effect when occupation is controlled. On the other hand, if education is the important factor, then occupation should have little effect when education is controlled.

Occupation

Education is so closely associated with occupation that, at the extremes of education, a person's occupational level can be predicted with virtual certainty. Among grade schoolers in the sample, 85 per cent are in blue-collar jobs; among college graduates, just 3 per cent are. (The figure for high school graduates is 52 per cent.) This close empirical relation raises the possibility that lack of education is associated with anti-Semitism because it is associated with occupation.

However adequate in other respects, a sample of 2,000 cases is too small for precise distinctions to be made within the vast array of present-day occupations. Following common practice, this study uses the abbreviated classification of the United States Census Bureau which divides the nation's occupations into eleven categories. These categories are extremely broad. Policemen and maids are classified together as service workers, and the proprietor of a local cigar store is grouped with the president of a large corporation. Such incongruities are unavoidable if, in a moderate-sized sample, there are to be enough cases in each category to permit analysis. However, they are not so serious as to obscure the empirical association between broad occupational category and attitudes toward Jews (Table 20). When occupations are classified as blue collar or white collar, the proportion anti-Semitic is 56 per cent among blue-collar workers and 31 per cent among white-collar workers.[7]

When finer distinctions are made, specific occupation has little effect. With one exception white-collar workers show virtually no variation in anti-Semitism. Only professionals stand out as comparatively low, with 19 per cent scoring as anti-Semitic compared to a third in all other white-collar categories. Among those in blue-collar occupations, rates of anti-Semitism range from 50 per cent among laborers to 60 and 63 per cent among farmers and the semiskilled. However, every blue-collar occupation shows a higher rate of anti-Semitism than every white-collar occupation.

Two attempts were made in this study to refine the Census classification. One distinguished between two kinds of professional—the *self-employed* professional (for example, most doctors and lawyers) and the *salaried* professional (primarily teachers and social workers). When this distinction is made only salaried professionals stand out as particularly low on anti-Semitism; 14 per cent scored as anti-Semitic. Of the few self-employed professionals in the sample 26 per cent scored as anti-Semitic.

A second modification of the Census classification distinguished three ranks within the general category of service worker. The proportions anti-Semitic are as follows:

[7] In the above analysis, we examine occupation of respondent only on the ground that it would be conceptually weak to relate the anti-Semitism of housewives to the occupation of their husbands. However, the results are essentially the same when occupation of head of household is used.

	Number	
Rank 1 (policemen, firemen, hairdressers, practical nurses, etc.)	32%	(43)
Rank 2 (hospital attendants, bartenders, waiters, etc.)	38%	(29)
Rank 3 (domestics, janitors, guards, etc.)	63%	(73)

Ranks 1 and 2 are about as low in anti-Semitism as white-collar workers. On the other hand, Rank 3 is the most anti-Semitic of all occupational groups.

The effect of these two refinements has been to show the full range of anti-Semitism—from 14 per cent among salaried professionals (one of the most educated groups in the sample) to 63 per cent among domestic and kindred workers (one of the least educated groups in the sample). This almost exactly duplicates the association of education with anti-Semitic prejudice, and returns us to the question of whether the generally greater

Table 20.   ANTI-SEMITIC BELIEF BY OCCUPATION

	Anti-Semitic	
	Per Cent	Number
Blue collar[a]		
Semiskilled workers (mostly machine operators)	63%	171
Farmers (mostly small proprietors)	60	86
Skilled workers (craftsmen, foremen, etc.)	52	193
Service workers (barbers, policemen, etc.)	51	146
Laborers (lumbermen, fishermen, etc.)	50	36
Total blue collar	56%	632
White collar[a]		
Managers, officials, and proprietors (shop owners, executives, etc.)	35%	113
Sales workers (insurance agents, sales clerks, etc.)	33	78
Semiprofessional workers (technicians, nurses, etc.)	34	65
Clerical workers (secretaries, clerks, etc.)	34	148
Professionals (teachers, doctors, etc.)	19	103
Total white collar	31%	507

[a]Refers to present occupation of the respondent or past occupation if retired or unemployed; housewives are excluded.

anti-Semitism of blue-collar workers is an artifact of their lesser education. To a large extent it is. We reported earlier that 56 per cent of blue-collar and 31 per cent of white-collar workers scored as anti-Semitic, a difference of 25 percentage points. When education is introduced as a control variable (Table 21), this difference is either reduced or reversed.[8] In short, there is

Table 21.   ANTI-SEMITIC BELIEF BY OCCUPATION AND EDUCATION

(per cent anti-Semitic)

	Grade School	High School	Some College	College Graduate	Total
Blue collar[a]	71%	48%	26%	b	56%
	(249)	(348)	(31)	(2)	(631)
White collar[a]	58	35	31	17	31
	(50)	(203)	(110)	(144)	(507)
Total	68%	43%	30%	17%	
	(299)	(551)	(141)	(146)	
Percentage difference[d]	+13	+13	-5	c	+25

[a]Refers to present occupation of the respondent or past occupation if retired or unemployed; housewives are excluded.
[b]Too few cases to compute percentage.
[c]No comparison possible.
[d]Between blue-collar and white-collar workers.

little difference in the anti-Semitism of blue- and white-collar workers when their education is taken into account. Even the remaining differences between blue- and white-collar workers are to some extent a "residual effect" of education.[9] It is evident that the tendency of blue-collar workers to be anti-Semitic is largely a function of their lesser education.

In contrast, the effect of education continues to be powerful among both blue- and white-collar workers, as can be seen from the horizontal compari-

[8] At both the grade school and the high school level, the impact of occupation is reduced from 25 to 13 percentage points; at the some-college level it is slightly reversed; at the college graduate level no comparison is possible since so few college graduates are in blue-collar occupations. When the percentage differences at each level of education are totaled and divided by three (the number of categories between which comparisons are possible), the average percentage difference produced by occupation is 7 instead of the original 25. Such an average is a crude but nevertheless useful way of summarizing the explanatory power of a control variable, in this case, the capacity of education to account for the statistical relation of occupation to anti-Semitism.

[9] Table 21 does not distinguish between those with some high school and high school graduates, and therefore does not take into account the fact that fewer blue-collar workers than white-collar workers have actually graduated from high school. When this is taken into account, the difference between blue- and white-collar workers with some high school is only 7 percentage points.

sons in Table 21. Among blue-collar workers, 71 per cent of grade schoolers are anti-Semitic compared to 26 per cent among those with some college. Similarly, among white-collar workers, anti-Semitism ranges from 58 per cent at the grade school level to 17 per cent among college graduates. The impact of lack of education on anti-Semitic prejudice is affected hardly at all by the introduction of occupation as a control variable.[10]

Table 21 suggests that the reason for the greater anti-Semitism of blue-collar workers is to be sought in their lack of education, not in circumstances connected with their jobs or the material exigencies of their social-class position. In our society, lack of education and economic deprivation are so frequently conjoined that the former rarely exists without the latter: most uneducated people are in low-status occupations. But it matters little whether the uneducated are in relatively low- or relatively high-status occupations: they tend to be anti-Semitic in either case.

Occupational Mobility

One social-class interpretation of prejudice holds that upward or downward mobility in the class structure is a key factor in prejudice.[11] This study does not have data on the mobility of the individual during his occupational career. However, we can compare respondent's occupation with his father's occupation. Thus among blue-collar workers we can distinguish between those whose fathers were also blue-collar workers and those whose fathers were white-collar workers. The former we call blue-collar stationaries; the latter, downwardly mobile. Among white-collar workers we distinguish between the stationaries and the upwardly mobile—those whose fathers were blue-collar workers.

According to one version of the mobility theory, mobility makes for

[10] It is sometimes claimed that status discrepancy makes for status anxiety and therefore greater prejudice. In Table 21 white-collar grade schoolers and blue-collar workers with some college might be said to be status discrepant. Both groups are, if anything, relatively low on anti-Semitism. It should be pointed out, however, that such comparisons are always precarious. Grade schoolers occupying white-collar positions are on the lowest levels of the white-collar hierarchy, the converse holding for blue-collar workers with some college education.

[11] Bruno Bettelheim and Morris Janowitz, *Social Change and Prejudice* (New York: Free Press of Glencoe, 1964), pp. 25–43 and 101–331; Joseph Greenblum and Leonard I. Perlin, "Vertical Mobility and Prejudice," in Reinhard Bendix and Seymour M. Lipset (eds.), *Class, Status and Power: A Reader in Social Stratification* (New York: Free Press of Glencoe, 1953), pp. 480–491; Peter M. Blau, "Social Mobility and Interpersonal Relations," *American Sociological Review*, June 1956, pp. 290–295. For another view, see Fred B. Silberstein and Melvin Seeman, "Social Mobility and Prejudice," *American Journal of Sociology*, November 1959, pp. 258–264.

greater prejudice regardless of its direction. It is reasoned that mobility creates status anxiety: the upwardly mobile are fearful lest their new status be impugned; the downwardly mobile are resentful of their loss of status. This theory is not supported by our data. The group highest in anti-Semitic prejudice is not a mobile one but the blue-collar stationaries (Table 22, Total column).

Table 22.   ANTI-SEMITIC BELIEF BY OCCUPATIONAL MOBILITY
AND EDUCATION
(per cent anti-Semitic)

Mobility[a]	Grade School	High School	Some College	College Graduate	Total
Blue collar					
Stationary	70%	52%	33%	b	59%
	(212)	(265)	(21)	(1)	(500)
Downwardly mobile	74	28	b	b	37
	(19)	(50)	(7)	(1)	(78)
White collar					
Upwardly mobile	57	38	31	17	34
	(37)	(130)	(55)	(66)	(288)
Stationary	60	25	31	16	25
	(10)	(60)	(48)	(74)	(192)

[a]Blue-collar stationary = Respondent in blue-collar occupation, father in blue-collar occupation; Downwardly mobile = Respondent in blue-collar occupation, father in white-collar occupation; Upwardly mobile = Respondent in white-collar occupation, father in blue-collar occupation; White-collar stationary = Respondent in white-collar occupation, father in white-collar occupation.
[b]Too few cases to compute percentage.

At first glance the data are not totally incompatible with a mobility theory of prejudice, since the upwardly mobile are slightly more anti-Semitic than white-collar stationaries. But they are also less educated; 20 per cent are college graduates compared with 34 per cent of the stationaries. When education is controlled, generational mobility, whether upward or downward, has little if any systematic relation to acceptance of anti-Semitic beliefs. In other words, the reason that upwardly mobile workers are higher in anti-Semitic prejudice than white-collar stationaries is that they have less education. Correspondingly, the reason that downwardly mobile workers are less anti-Semitic than blue-collar stationaries is that they have more education: 35 per cent had at least some college compared to 6 per cent for blue-collar stationaries. One implication of the above analysis is that it is hazardous to observe the effects of mobility without holding education constant since occupational mobility typically masks educational differences.

Our findings do not contradict the argument that intergroup hostilities tend to increase during economic depressions. For one thing, we have examined generational, not personal, mobility. For another, our data measure acceptance rather than expression of anti-Semitic prejudice. Finally, we are dealing with anti-Semitism in a period of relative prosperity, not one of economic crisis and widespread unemployment when whole groups would be threatened by downward mobility. If under such circumstances there were an increase in anti-Semitic propaganda and the Jewish question became salient, widespread downward mobility would undoubtedly be accompanied by an increase in both the incidence and the acting out of anti-Semitic prejudice. However, education would be an important determinant of how individuals respond to their downward mobility. The educated among the downwardly mobile would be less apt than the uneducated to use Jews as scapegoats, in part because they accept

Table 23.   ANTI-SEMITIC BELIEF BY INCOME AND EDUCATION
(per cent anti-Semitic)

Annual Family Income[a]	Grade School	High School	Some College	College Graduate	Total
Less than $5,000	69%	48%	33%	11%	54%
	(279)	(261)	(60)	(27)	(628)
$5,000–$9,999	60	37	25	15	37
	(100)	(387)	(76)	(61)	(624)
$10,000–$14,999	50	40	20	14	30
	(18)	(116)	(51)	(65)	(250)
$15,000 or more	b	22	33	28	31
	(4)	(23)	(15)	(25)	(67)

[a]Roughly 4 per cent at each educational level refused to report their income; these 93 cases are excluded.

[b]Too few cases to compute percentage.

economic stereotypes less often, in part because they would be less likely to accept anti-Semitic ideology as a credible explanation of events.

Income

The overwhelming majority of grade schoolers (72 per cent) report an annual family income of less than $5,000; only 4 per cent had incomes of $10,000 or more. The situation is reversed among college graduates. Sixty-one per cent reported family incomes of $10,000 or more; only 12 per cent had incomes of less than $5,000.[12] Because of its close relation to education, it is not surprising that on the whole low income is associated with greater anti-Semitism (Total column, Table 23).

[12] To show the full strength of the relation between education and income in the national population, respondents under 25 years of age are excluded from these comparisons.

Despite its relation to both education and anti-Semitism, low income does not explain the link between lack of education and anti-Semitism. At the first three levels of income, where the overwhelming majority of the sample are concentrated, education continues to be systematically and strongly related to anti-Semitism. College graduates are comparatively low on anti-Semitism even when they have low annual incomes, and grade schoolers are comparatively high on anti-Semitism even when they have fairly high incomes. In short, the reason that the uneducated are much higher on anti-Semitism is not to be found in their low incomes.[13]

The picture is quite different among the handful of respondents in the highest income category of $15,000 or more. Although higher income is generally associated with decreasing anti-Semitism, at the two college levels (Some College or College Graduate) persons earning $15,000 or above are more likely to be anti-Semitic than their educational counterparts at lower levels of income. Though higher income is generally associated with a decline in anti-Semitism, a *combination* of college education and a very high income tends to increase acceptance of anti-Semitic beliefs. The average rate of anti-Semitism among college graduates is 16 per cent, but among the twenty-five college graduates with incomes of $15,000 or more it is 28 per cent. Thus, we seem to have come upon an enclave of middle-class anti-Semitism. While anti-Semitism is generally low among college graduates, it is disproportionately high among college graduates with high incomes.[14]

It is important to remember that only 6 per cent of the national population have family incomes of $15,000 or more. Thus only a minute proportion of the total anti-Semitism in the population can be attributed to the effects of high income. In the sample, of the 706 respondents who scored as anti-Semitic, only 21 earned $15,000 or more. The finding that high income is associated with anti-Semitism among the college educated has little bearing, therefore, on the incidence of anti-Semitism in the country as a whole. The effect of high income does have bearing, however, on the

[13] As can be seen from Table 23, education explains a good deal but not all of the statistical association between low income and anti-Semitic prejudice. However, the remaining income effect is not necessarily evidence that lower-class anti-Semitism is a response to existential frustration. Other factors are associated with low income, including degree of intellectual sophistication not measured by years of schooling. At every level of education, except among college graduates, higher income is associated with greater intellectual and cultural sophistication as measured by indexes to be introduced later (the writers test and the Index of Simplism).

[14] Anti-Semitism is also disproportionately high (33 per cent) among the 15 respondents with some college education and incomes of $15,000 and above. This small group is ignored in the following discussion. Analysis showed that the same factors did not operate to increase anti-Semitism in this group as among college graduates, and it is too small to permit separate analysis.

issue of middle-class anti-Semitism. Insofar as anti-Semitic beliefs increase among the college educated when their income is very high, the connection of anti-Semitism with greater privilege does seem to be borne out. However, it is still not certain whether income per se or some noneconomic factor associated with income is producing this greater anti-Semitism.

One consideration is whether the education of high-income college graduates has been of a different kind from that of low-income graduates. There is some indication that this is true. College graduates at higher levels of income are apt to be either businessmen or self-employed professionals, such as doctors and lawyers. Those at lower levels of income are more often salaried professionals, such as teachers and social workers. Thus the greater anti-Semitism of high-income college graduates may have less to do with their incomes than with the kind of education they received (or sought) in college. We know from a number of past studies that college students in different fields of specialization vary in prejudice and civil libertarianism. Broadly speaking, students majoring in the humanities or the social sciences tend to be more libertarian and less prejudiced than those in business administration or the natural sciences.[15] This suggests that if we test college graduates in our sample for the kind of "cultural sophistication" traditionally associated with a liberal arts education, this factor may explain the relatively high rate of anti-Semitism found among high-income college graduates.

In the interview, respondents were presented with the names of sixteen notables and asked to identify each as a writer, a politician, an entertainer, or a sports figure. The four writers were Robert Frost, William Faulkner, Mark Twain, and Herman Melville. Knowledge of these writers is, of course, highly dependent on amount of schooling. On the average, respondents knew slightly more than two of the four writers. Grade schoolers were well below average, with a score of 1.2; college graduates, well above average, with a score of 3.5. Sixty per cent of college graduates recognized all four writers; only 10 per cent knew fewer than three. Consequently, we are obliged to make a distinction between college graduates who had a perfect score and those who did not. This apparently trivial distinction turns out to be helpful for understanding anti-Semitism among college graduates.

In the total sample, 16 per cent of college graduates scored as anti-

---

[15] A very early study of college students found students in business subjects "above average," in anti-Semitic prejudice, social science majors "below average" (H. H. Harlan, "Some Factors Affecting Attitudes Toward Jews," *American Sociological Review*, December 1942, pp. 816–827). A more recent study reports similar results for civil libertarian attitudes: students in business administration or the natural sciences were less libertarian than those majoring in the social sciences or in the humanities (Hanan C. Selvin and Warren O. Hagstrom, "Determinants of Support for Civil Liberties," *British Journal of Sociology*, April 1960, pp. 51–73).

Semitic. Of those with perfect scores on the writers test only 6 per cent scored as anti-Semitic in contrast to 31 per cent of those with less than perfect scores (bottom row, Table 24).[16] Thus among culturally sophisti-

Table 24.   ANTI-SEMITIC BELIEF AMONG COLLEGE GRADUATES BY INCOME AND CULTURAL SOPHISTICATION

(per cent anti-Semitic)

| Annual Family Income | Cultural Sophistication[a] | | Total |
	Perfect Score	Less than Perfect Score	
Less than $5,000	6% (17)	20% (10)	11% (27)
$5,000–$9,999	8% (51) — 9 (34)	22% (37) — 21 (27)	15 (61)
$10,000–$14,999	5 (42)	30 (23)	14 (65)
$15,000 or more	4 (56) — 0 (14)	41 (34) — 64 (11)	28 (25)
Total	6% (113)	31% (72)	16% (185)
Percentage difference[b]	−6	+44	+17

[a]As measured by the writers test.
[b]Between those in the highest income category and those in the lowest income category.

cated or "better educated" college graduates, anti-Semitic prejudice appears to be virtually nonexistent. What anti-Semitic prejudice there is among college graduates comes largely from the minority who are relatively unsophisticated. Only 29 college graduates scored as anti-Semitic but, of these, 22 had less than perfect scores on the writers test. Just as differences in amount of schooling predict anti-Semitism in the general population, so more subtle differences in the substance and quality of a college education predict anti-Semitism among college graduates. Thus education continues as the overriding factor in acceptance of anti-Semitic beliefs.

Table 24 also shows that when college graduates are culturally sophisti-

[16] Since Melville was the main stumbling block, in effect the distinction is between college graduates who recognized the name of Melville and those who did not. This is a good example of what an indicator does and does not do. Certainly, one would not want to argue that distributing copies of *Moby Dick* would reduce anti-Semitism. Needless to say, recognizing the name of Melville is indicative of a more general factor.

cated, greater income is *not* associated with an increase in anti-Semitic prejudice. Of the 25 college graduates with incomes of $15,000 or more, 14 had perfect scores on the writers test. Of these 14, none scored as anti-Semitic. Income continues to have an effect, however, among less sophisticated college graduates. At income levels below $10,000, 22 per cent of the less culturally sophisticated score as anti-Semitic; this rate doubles to 41 per cent among those with incomes of $10,000 or more. Indeed, of the 11 relatively unsophisticated college graduates earning $15,000 or more, 7 (or 64 per cent) scored as anti-Semitic. The conclusion suggested by Table 24 is that what increases anti-Semitism is not income per se, but income conditioned by a relative lack of cultural sophistication.[17]

The same results obtain when occupation is examined (Table 25). Past research has sometimes shown that the self-employed tend to hold illiberal attitudes.[18] This is confirmed by our data. Among college graduates the self-employed are twice as likely to score as anti-Semitic as the salaried. But this relation holds only among the relatively unsophisticated. Of the 12 self-employed in this group, 8 (or 67 per cent) scored as anti-Semitic compared to 31 per cent of salaried businessmen and 22 per cent of salaried professionals. Like income, occupation makes no difference among the culturally sophisticated. Of 11 self-employed college graduates who knew all four writers, none scored as anti-Semitic.

The preceding analysis is based on a small number of cases. Occupation and income could not be controlled simultaneously, and some of the findings may not meet rigorous standards of statistical significance. However, the results fall into a consistent pattern. When college graduates are culturally sophisticated, it does not matter what their occupation is or how much money they earn; virtually none are anti-Semitic. Income and occupa-

---

[17] A number of factors are probably at work to create the syndrome consisting of lack of cultural sophistication, high income, and anti-Semitism among college graduates. First, the already illiberal student may view a college education in instrumental terms, and therefore choose the more remunerative fields, such as business administration or medicine, while avoiding the less remunerative ones, such as the social sciences or the humanities. The second is the differential degree to which the various curriculums emphasize libertarian values or impart facts relevant to prejudice. These two factors reinforce one another. The student who is less liberal to begin with tends to select precisely those curriculums in which he is least likely to obtain a liberal arts education or be disabused of prejudice through relevant knowledge (for example, in anthropology or sociology courses). Thus, even without consciously—or unconsciously —desiring to protect his attitudes, the less liberal student probably has a good chance of isolating himself from countervailing influences. At the same time, his college specialization is apt to propel him into the higher-income brackets. The result is an empirical configuration in which high income, lack of cultural sophistication, and prejudice are apt to be found together among college graduates.

[18] For example, Martin Trow, "Small Businessmen, Political Tolerance, and Support for McCarthy," *American Journal of Sociology*, November 1958, pp. 270–281.

Table 25.   ANTI-SEMITIC BELIEF AMONG COLLEGE GRADUATES BY
OCCUPATION AND CULTURAL SOPHISTICATION

(per cent anti-Semitic)

| | Cultural Sophistication[a] | | |
	Perfect Score	Less than Perfect Score	Total
Salaried[b]			
Professionals	8%	22%	14%
	(35)	(23)	(58)
Business employees[c]	7	31	18
	(15)	(13)	(28)
Self-employed[b]			
Professionals and proprietors	0%	67%	35%
	(11)	(12)	(23)
Percentage difference[d]	−9	+45	+21

[a]As measured by writers test.

[b]Refers to present occupation of the respondent or past occupation if retired or unemployed; housewives are excluded.

[c]Includes semiprofessionals, managers, and officials.

[d]Between self-employed professionals and salaried professionals.

tion have an effect on anti-Semitism only among college graduates who are relatively unsophisticated. Indeed, most of the anti-Semitism among college graduates comes from the relatively unsophisticated.

Discriminatory Attitudes

Insofar as anti-Semitic prejudice predicts discriminatory attitudes (Chapter 3), it can be assumed that a group high in anti-Semitic prejudice is relatively high on discriminatory attitudes. One must always be prepared to discover that, in certain subgroups of the population, special circumstances intervene to render such an assumption invalid. (A good example of this appears in Chapter 7.) But on the whole, the inference from prejudice to support of discrimination is a reliable one.

However, previous analysis showed that two behavioral orientations—support of social club discrimination and indifference to political anti-Semitism—are not highly correlated with anti-Semitic prejudice. For this reason we single these issues out for special attention. There is another reason, however. Political anti-Semitism, while presently a remote concern, is nevertheless the ultimate expression of anti-Semitism. Social club discrimination, while scarcely an ultimate injustice, is one of the last barriers to be overcome and in this sense is of immediate concern. Finally, these two issues cover the full range of discrimination, encompassing both the public and the more private spheres of behavior.

Political Anti-Semitism

We have seen that lack of education is related to both anti-Semitic prejudice and opinionlessness. The uneducated are thus more likely than the educated both to support political anti-Semitism and to be indifferent to it. The result is a considerable gap between the least and the most educated in the extent to which they oppose an anti-Semitic candidate. Whereas 76 per cent of college graduates oppose the candidate, only 42 per cent of grade schoolers do so. The figures are virtually identical for opposition to an anti-Jewish immigration law.

The tendency of the uneducated to lack opinions is sometimes interpreted as reflecting a general lack of knowledge or a lack of self-confidence in asserting opinions. But, as was suggested in Chapter 4, saying "don't know" to a belief about Jews is more than an expression of ignorance; it reflects a failure to reject prejudice in principle. The greater opinionlessness of the uneducated, whatever its sources, is not inconsequential. It manifests itself in greater indifference to the anti-Semitic candidate. The proportion saying they would be indifferent rises from 21 per cent among college graduates to 33 per cent among high schoolers, to 44 per cent among grade schoolers.

While relatively low, the figure of 21 per cent for college graduates represents a sizable minority. Some of this indifference to political anti-Semitism stems from anti-Semitic prejudice, some from opinionlessness. However, as we saw in Chapter 4, even convinced non-anti-Semites sometimes gave the no-difference response. Thus, while a large majority (76 per cent) of college graduates opposed the anti-Semitic candidate, and are the most likely of all educational groups to do so, opposition to political anti-Semitism still falls short of unanimity within one of the most unprejudiced segments of the society.

Social Club Discrimination

Despite their low level of anti-Semitic prejudice and general opposition to political anti-Semitism, college graduates are the most likely of all educational groups to defend social club discrimination (Table 26). Four out of ten said that members of a social club have the right to exclude Mr. Cohen "just because he is Jewish." That a college education is associated with defending social club discrimination is highlighted when a distinction is made between those with four years of college and postgraduates. Among

Table 26.   ATTITUDES TOWARD SOCIAL CLUB DISCRIMINATION
BY EDUCATION

Attitudes[a]	Grade School	High School	Some College	College Graduate
Defenders	30%	24%	29%	40%
Token opponents	30	32	29	16
Militant opponents	29	38	38	39
Unclassifiable	11	6	4	5
100% (N) =	(533)	(955)	(224)	(191)
Among opponents, per cent militant	49% (310)	54% (667)	57% (150)	70% (105)

[a]Defenders said the members of a social club have the right to exclude Jews. Token opponents denied the right to exclude Jews but said Smith should stay in and forget the whole thing. Militant opponents denied the right to exclude Jews and said Smith should either quit the club or stay in and keep trying.

the former, 37 per cent are defenders; among postgraduates, the figure is 45 per cent. Thus the educational groups lowest in anti-Semitic prejudice, as measured by derogatory beliefs about Jews, are highest in defense of social club discrimination.

This finding is significant for several reasons. The educated are the joiners in our society and belong to the kinds of clubs that are appropriate to the socio-economic status of a majority of Jews. They are the kind of people with whom Jews, largely middle class themselves, come into contact in their communities and occupations. This is undoubtedly one reason that the educated middle class are often thought to be more anti-Semitic than the less educated working class. Even a small amount of social discrimination within the middle class would be visible and salient to Jews, and might lead to the misconception that the educated middle class is *in general* more anti-Semitic than the uneducated lower classes. Our data leave no doubt that traditional anti-Semitic beliefs and most discriminatory attitudes are most prevalent among the uneducated. Support for social club discrimination is nevertheless most characteristic of the educated.

Opinion among college graduates does tend to be polarized, however—between principled defense and militant opposition. If 40 per cent are defenders of social club discrimination, an equal number (39 per cent) are militant opponents.[19] Relatively few college graduates (16 per cent) are

[19] Militant opponents and token opponents both denied that the members of our hypothetical club had a right to exclude Mr. Cohen. But token opponents said that Mr. Smith should "stay in and forget the whole thing" while militant opponents said that Mr. Smith should either quit the club or stay in and keep trying.

token opponents. Thus, among people who do not defend social club discrimination, militant opposition increases with education, from 49 per cent among grade schoolers to 70 per cent among college graduates (bottom row, Table 26). The relation of a college education to social club discrimination is double-edged: college graduates are high both on defense of social club discrimination and on militant opposition to it.

Table 27 examines defense of social club discrimination by both education and anti-Semitic prejudice. Two facts stand out. First, roughly four

Table 27.   DEFENSE OF SOCIAL CLUB DISCRIMINATION BY EDUCATION AND ANTI-SEMITIC BELIEF

(per cent defenders of social club discrimination)

Level of Anti-Semitic Belief	Grade School	High School	Some College	College Graduate
Unprejudiced	25%	19%	18%	32%
	(106)	(325)	(78)	(90)
Low	25	22	34	46
	(146)	(291)	(92)	(72)
High	29	25	36	43
	(151)	(199)	(36)	(23)
Extreme	42	42	39	a
	(130)	(141)	(18)	(5)

[a]Too few cases to compute percentage.

out of ten extreme anti-Semites defend social club discrimination, no matter what their level of education. Second, roughly four out of ten college graduates defend social club discrimination, no matter what their level of prejudice. There is an apparent irony in this finding. If the data are taken at face level, being a college graduate seems to be as conducive to social club discrimination as being an extreme anti-Semite.

As the discussion in Chapter 3 emphasized, discrimination has sources other than anti-Semitic prejudice. If not anti-Semitic prejudice, what does lead college graduates to defend social club discrimination? Part of the reason can be found in their higher incomes. At every level of education, the higher the income the larger the proportion of defenders (Table 28). Since more college graduates have higher incomes, more of them defend social club discrimination. In other words one reason that a college education is associated with defense of social club discrimination is that it is associated with a high income. However, *both* education *and* income increase defense of social club discrimination, and college graduates earning $15,000 or more are the most discriminatory of all groups. Among the

Table 28.   DEFENSE OF SOCIAL CLUB DISCRIMINATION BY
EDUCATION AND INCOME

(per cent defenders of social club discrimination)

Annual Family Income	Grade School	High School	Some College	College Graduate	Total
Less than $5,000	30% (358)	23% (322)	22% (65)	30% (30)	26% (775)
$5,000–$9,999	30% (115)	23% (436)	30% (84)	33% (64)	26% (699)
$10,000–$14,999	45% (20)	32% (130)	35% (52)	44% (66)	36% (268)
$15,000 or more	a (5)	31% (26)	40% (15)	52% (25)	41% (71)
Total	30% (533)	24% (955)	29% (224)	40% (191)	

[a]Too few cases to compute percentage.

twenty-five people in this category, 52 per cent are principled defenders of social club discrimination as compared to 40 per cent of the entire college graduate group and 28 per cent of the sample.

This small group of high-income college graduates is by now familiar to us. Earlier we saw that they are high on anti-Semitic prejudice, at least when they are relatively unsophisticated. The question now arises whether high-income college graduates are discriminatory because they are more prejudiced or whether income is a factor in its own right.[20] Table 29 shows that when college graduates are unprejudiced, high income ($10,000 or above) does not produce a much higher incidence of discriminatory atti-

Table 29.   DEFENSE OF SOCIAL CLUB DISCRIMINATION AMONG COLLEGE
GRADUATES BY ANTI-SEMITIC BELIEF AND INCOME

(per cent defenders of social club discrimination)

| Annual Family Income | Level of Anti-Semitic Belief | | | | Total |
	Unprejudiced	Low	High	Extreme	
Less than $10,000	28% (42)	38% (40)	20% (10)	a (2)	32% (94)
$10,000 or more	34 (47)	54 (28)	67 (12)	a (4)	46% (91)

[a]Too few cases to compute percentage.

[20] Cultural sophistication is unrelated to social club discrimination among college graduates.

tudes. On the other hand, when high-income college graduates are even *slightly* prejudiced, large proportions defend social club discrimination. Among unprejudiced college graduates, about 3 out of 10 defend social club discrimination, regardless of their income. Similarly, among low-income college graduates about 3 out of 10 defend it, regardless of their scores on the Index of Anti-Semitic Belief. However, among high-income college graduates even a low score on the Index of Anti-Semitic Belief suffices to raise principled defenders to a majority (54 per cent), while a high score brings this figure still higher. In short, a college education, a relatively high income, and even a small degree of anti-Semitic prejudice combine to make for an exceptionally high rate of support for social club discrimination.

Private vs. Public Discrimination

If social club discrimination stands out as a particularly ambiguous issue, this is partly because the social club so often stands on the borderline between the private and the public. Especially at higher socio-economic levels, the private social club can control access to social status, to business opportunities, to power and influence. That democratic principles frequently exist in tension with one another is well exemplified by the restricted social club. Here the principle of freedom of private association comes into conflict with the principle of equal opportunity.

In most areas of discrimination there is less room for ambiguity. The more private the context, the more defensible the discriminatory practice; the more public the context, the less legitimate does all discrimination become. An example of a relatively legitimate form of discrimination is opposition to religious intermarriage (provided, of course, opposition remains personal and does not seek legal sanction). At the other extreme is political discrimination on religious, racial, or ethnic grounds.

In Chapter 3 it was shown that anti-Semites do not distinguish between objecting to religious intermarriage and objecting to a Jewish candidate for President: the extreme anti-Semite was about as likely to object to a Jewish candidate for President as he was to object to religious intermarriage. In contrast, unprejudiced respondents disapproved of intermarriage more often than they did of the Jewish candidate. To what extent is this ability to distinguish between the private and public a function of education?

The first thing to be observed is that education is unrelated to attitudes toward intermarriage (Table 30).[21] At every educational level about 4 out

[21] A relation does appear when only those who strongly object are considered: 27 per cent of grade schoolers would strongly object versus 16 per cent of college graduates. However, this relation is a function of the greater anti-Semitic prejudice of the less educated.

Table 30. DISAPPROVAL OF INTERMARRIAGE AND OF A JEWISH PRESIDENT
BY EDUCATION

	Grade School	High School	Some College	College Graduate
Part A				
Disapprove of intermarriage	41%	42%	45%	40%
Disapprove of Jewish President	34	27	27	18
Part B				
Disapprove of neither	39%	44%	44%	52%
Disapprove of both	19	17	21	11
Disapprove only of Jewish President	14	10	6	6
Disapprove only of intermarriage	21	24	24	29
Opinionless	7	5	5	2
100% (N) =	(533)	(956)	(224)	(191)
Part C				
Among those who disapprove only of one or the other, how many disapproved of the Jewish President?	41%	28%	20%	17%
	(187)	(324)	(68)	(66)

of 10 would object strongly or somewhat to their child marrying a Jew. However, education *is* associated with attitudes toward political discrimination; whereas 34 per cent of grade schoolers disapprove of a Jewish presidential candidate, only half as many college graduates (18 per cent) do so. Thus almost as many grade schoolers disapprove of a Jewish President as disapprove of intermarriage. College graduates, on the other hand, disapprove of a Jewish President far less often than they disapprove of intermarriage.

The impact of education is more clearly shown in the bottom row of Table 30, which reports the percentage who disapprove of the Jewish President *among those who support only one of the two forms of discrimination.* Among grade schoolers 41 per cent disapprove of the Jewish candidate but not of intermarriage; in other words, when they make a choice, 41 per cent choose the less legitimate form of discrimination. As education increases, there is a greater tendency to choose private over public forms of discrimination. Among college graduates who are discriminatory in one way but not the other, only 17 per cent chose the less legitimate form of discrimination. Even when they score as anti-Semitic they tend to limit themselves to private forms of discrimination.

Considering their frequent acceptance of anti-Semitic beliefs, the uneducated are relatively tolerant in the private areas of intermarriage and social clubs. But this must be set against their greater tendency to express their anti-Semitism in the political realm. On the other hand, the failure of the college educated to be especially tolerant in private areas must be set against their greater rejection of traditional anti-Semitic beliefs and greater opposition to political discrimination and political anti-Semitism.

Evaluation of the Findings

This chapter dealt with a single major issue: To what extent and in what ways is anti-Semitism a social-class phenomenon? Income and occupation were used to define social-class position, with the implication that whatever independent relation these variables bear to anti-Semitism reflects the operation of some distinctively social-class factor. Education was treated separately on the ground that, while education is a major determinant and excellent predictor of social-class position, it is not a defining attribute of it. Thus, instead of using education as a component of social-class position, the analysis focused on separating out the influence of social class from that of education. The results may be summarized as follows:

1. For the most part whether or not a person holds traditional anti-Semitic beliefs and discriminatory attitudes is a function of how much education he has had, not his social-class position. Low income and low occupational status are statistically associated with holding anti-Semitic beliefs. But the effects of these two social-class variables largely vanish when education is brought into the picture. The less educated are consistently higher on anti-Semitic prejudice than the more educated, no matter what their income or occupational status.

2. An important exception to this pattern is found among the college educated. Here high income and high occupational status are associated with acceptance of anti-Semitic beliefs, suggesting that distinctive social-class factors are at work. However, this is true only among the culturally unsophisticated. College-educated persons who are culturally sophisticated are unlikely to hold anti-Semitic beliefs, no matter what their income or occupational status.

3. Social-class factors again come into play with respect to social club discrimination. Support for social club discrimination generally rises as income rises, and is highest among college graduates in the highest income group. Thus, despite their low level of prejudice, and largely because of their higher incomes, college graduates are not the least but the most likely of all educational groups to support discrimination in social clubs.[22] Speak-

---

[22] It is possible that status anxiety and social snobbery intervene in the relation between high income and anti-Semitism. An attempt was made to measure status anxiety by asking respondents whether they were satisfied with their neighborhoods,

ing very generally, the data suggest that social club discrimination is a social-class phenomenon, whereas holding anti-Semitic beliefs and most discriminatory attitudes is largely a function of lack of education.

Part III of this book explores further the systematic relation between education and anti-Semitic prejudice. It is not too early, however, to introduce several qualifications. First of all, it should not be overlooked that this finding, as all others in this study, is a comparative one. To say that anti-Semitic prejudice is more common among the less educated is not to say that it is absent among the educated. Indeed, our data show that a minority of the most educated in our society hold anti-Semitic beliefs. Furthermore, to assert that anti-Semitic prejudice is comparatively high among the less educated is not to deny the significance of what little anti-Semitism there is among the educated. Because the educated have greater access to positions of power and because they constitute a social elite, any degree of anti-Semitism among them is significant. Their contamination with anti-Semitism, and especially their support of social club discrimination, may help to validate and reinforce the anti-Semitic attitudes of the less educated. Nevertheless, these considerations should not divert attention from the brute empirical fact that anti-Semitic beliefs are far more prevalent among the less educated segments of the population.

It should also be emphasized that we are concerned with acceptance of anti-Semitic beliefs by the contemporary individual, not with the historic origins of the beliefs themselves. We have said that degree of education, rather than social-class position, is the basic factor in determining whether or not the individual holds anti-Semitic beliefs. This is not to say that social-class factors were irrelevant in the historic genesis of modern anti-Semitism, whose content is sometimes linked to the emergence of a commercial middle class. Nor is it to say that anti-Semitism originated among, or was "invented" by, the uneducated. Factors that account for the innovation

---

their incomes, their jobs, and their success in life. The relation is consistently small, but at every level of education, it is the more rather than the less satisfied who defend social club discrimination. Nor was there any systematic relation when generational mobility was examined. Among the two stationary groups and the upwardly mobile, about a third in each case defended social club discrimination. While the downwardly mobile are sometimes thought to be especially susceptible to status anxiety, only 18 per cent of the downwardly mobile in our sample scored as defenders. Finally, respondents were presented with the statement: "I worry quite a bit about what people think of me." At every level of education, those who agreed and those who disagreed were defenders of social club discrimination in about equal proportions.

Both status anxiety and social snobbery are difficult to measure, especially in a cross-sectional sample. The status anxiety of an uneducated worker is quite different from that of a middle-class social climber, and the same measure would obviously not do for both. A national sample is handicapped in exploring the role of status concerns in anti-Semitic prejudice and social club discrimination.

and promulgation of a belief system may be quite different from the factors that account for its acceptance.[23] The educated elite are usually the leaders and the innovators, even though the ideas they innovate may remain minority opinion in their own group. The construction and promulgation of anti-Semitic ideology is typically the work of the half-educated—those who are able to give some semblance of intellectual articulation to an essentially primitive and unsophisticated belief system. By and large, however, whether or not an individual accepts the anti-Semitic beliefs promulgated by others appears to be largely a function of how much education he has had.

The finding that education, not the social-class variables of income and occupation, is the crucial factor in predicting anti-Semitic prejudice has two implications for theory. First, it casts a shadow on theories that attempt to account for working class anti-Semitism by pointing to conditions of working class existence, such as material deprivation, lack of opportunity, and general frustration and despair. Secondly, the importance of education raises the question of what it is about education that makes it so powerfully related to anti-Semitism. Numerous factors could plausibly intervene in this relationship. Education is a learning process through which people acquire knowledge, are exposed to values, and develop modes of thinking and acting. Secondly, education is a social process through which individuals come into contact with different kinds of people and are exposed to an environment generally committed to norms of tolerance. Third, education has many consequences for the existential situation of the individual after he has broken his ties with educational institutions. Finally, education involves a self-selection process whereby certain kinds of individuals choose and are encouraged to continue their education. Any of these factors could explain why the more educated segments of our society exhibit comparatively low rates of anti-Semitism. Much of the analysis in Part III is devoted to assessing which of these factors are most crucial for understanding the relation between education and acceptance of anti-Semitic beliefs.

[23] For example, in *Young Man Luther* (New York: Norton, 1958) Erik H. Erikson proposes through psychoanalytic concepts to throw light on Luther's "discovery" of the doctrine of salvation by faith. It goes without saying that factors determining Luther's elaboration of a Protestant belief system may be totally irrelevant for understanding its acceptance by his contemporaries, not to mention its acceptance centuries later.

6 : Age, Sex, and Nativity

Of the three variables considered in this chapter, age is of particular interest for the light it may throw on the trend of anti-Semitism. Partly under the impact of the Nazi holocaust, official opinion in the United States has gone on record against anti-Semitism. One may question the quality and depth of official pronouncements, but there is little doubt that anti-Semitism is no longer respectable, that efforts have been made—in the schools, the mass media, the churches, and elsewhere—to combat it. For this and other reasons the climate of opinion with respect to Jews is different now from what it was in the 1940s and before. However, the question remains whether elite opinion, and the many social changes that have occurred in recent decades, have affected the beliefs and attitudes of the rank-and-file of Americans.

If a long-term downward trend in anti-Semitism has occurred, then the young should be less anti-Semitic than the old. While our sample is composed only of adults, those who are relatively young are considerably less anti-Semitic than the elderly. This finding may be misleading, however. For one thing, younger people may be less anti-Semitic simply because they are more educated. If this is so, we cannot speak of a downward trend in anti-Semitism beyond what can be attributed to the upward trend in education.[1] Nor can we speak of a downward trend in anti-Semitism if people become more anti-Semitic as they grow older. If the unprejudiced young person gradually becomes the prejudiced oldster,

[1] The upward trend in education is shown in Census figures. In 1940 only 24.1 per cent of the adult population (25 years or older) were at least high school graduates. By 1964, when our data were gathered, this figure had doubled to 48.0 per cent. During the same period the proportion who had completed four or more years of college also doubled—from 4.6 per cent to 9.1 per cent (*Statistical Abstract of the United States, 1965*, U.S. Dept. of Commerce, Bureau of the Census, p. 112).

then the present attitudes of the young signify little either for the past or the future trend of anti-Semitism.[2]

Age

For the initial examination of age and anti-Semitism, respondents were coded into eleven age categories. Analysis revealed that rates of anti-Semitism are fairly uniform within three broad age categories: less than 35, 35 to 54, and 55 and older.[3] Among these categories, however, greater age is related to greater anti-Semitism. As we move from the youngest to the oldest age group, anti-Semitism increases from 31 to 40 to 59 per cent. Thus people 55 or older are almost twice as likely to be anti-Semitic as those under 35.

Since the educational level of the nation has been steadily rising, age is highly associated with education. A majority (56 per cent) of the oldest age group have no more than a grade school education, as compared to 20 per cent of the middle age group and just 9 per cent of the youngest age group. The educational gap between the old and the young is so great that the observed effect of age seems almost certainly to be an artifact of education. Are the elderly more anti-Semitic, then, simply because they are less educated?

This question is answered in Table 31. Some of the effect of age is accounted for by the lesser education of the elderly. When education is taken into account, the effect of age is reduced from 28 percentage points to an average of 15 (bottom row, Table 31). One reason that the old are more anti-Semitic is that as a group they are far less educated.[4] But

[2] An age effect is always subject to different interpretations. It may signify changes over time in the larger society, or it may signify changes over time in the individual. In other words, an age difference in anti-Semitism may reflect either a historic trend or something in the aging process that leads people to take on anti-Semitic beliefs as they grow older.

[3] Rates of anti-Semitism (excluding the opinionless) are as follows:

Less than 25	25–29	30–34	35–39	40–44	45–49
36%	31%	27%	39%	39%	43%
(146)	(159)	(175)	(207)	(184)	(145)

50–54	55–59	60–64	65–69	70–74	75+
40%	50%	58%	58%	61%	71%
(126)	(113)	(123)	(92)	(77)	(94)

[4] If the elderly were as educated as the young, their rate of anti-Semitism would be 49 per cent instead of the 59 per cent that actually occurs in the data. We arrived at this adjusted rate by applying the rate of anti-Semitism exhibited by the elderly at each educational level to the educational distribution of the young. This procedure is similar to the standardization of rates employed by demographers to compare disparate populations. For further details, see Morris Rosenberg, "Test Factor Standardization as a Method of Interpretation," *Social Forces*, October 1962, pp. 53–61.

age differences persist, indicating that education and age are independently related to holding anti-Semitic beliefs. Their combined effect is powerful: among college graduates under 35 the rate of anti-Semitism is only 10 per cent; among grade schoolers 55 or older it is 68 per cent.

Though age continues to be related to anti-Semitism, its effect should not be overemphasized. For one thing, it begins clearly to manifest itself only at age 55. For another, the independent effect of age is not nearly as great as that of education. Nonetheless, age differences are worth pursuing since they may have implications for the future trend of anti-Semitism.

Table 31.   ANTI-SEMITIC BELIEF BY AGE AND EDUCATION

(per cent anti-Semitic)

	Grade School	High School	Some College	College Graduate	Total
Less than 35	64%	35%	20%	10%	31%
	(39)	(280)	(87)	(73)	(480)
35–54	63	40	27	17	40
	(114)	(394)	(78)	(76)	(662)
55 or older	68	57	39	25	59
	(270)	(148)	(44)	(36)	(499)
Percentage difference[a]	4	22	19	15	28

[a]Between those 55 or older and those under 35.

The first avenue to be explored is whether remaining age differences reflect hidden educational differences. Not only are young people getting more education, but the content and quality of education have changed in ways directly relevant to prejudice. A generation ago it was possible to learn that social differences are the result of innate biological traits. The modernization of education may be one reason why, even when they have had the same amount of schooling, the old are more anti-Semitic than the young.

There is some evidence in the data that the young in fact obtain a superior education. In Chapter 5 we used the writers test as an indirect indicator of quality of education. We now find that at every level of education the young are more culturally sophisticated than the old. Among college graduates the difference is especially striking: 78 per cent of the youngest group' knew all four writers as opposed to 35 per cent of the oldest group. However, even when their relative lack of sophistication and their relative lack of schooling are both taken into account, the elderly continue to exhibit higher rates of anti-Semitism.[5]

The writers test can hardly be defended as a good measure of the modernization of education over recent decades. Hence its failure to account for age differences does not rule out the possibility that the greater anti-Semitism of the elderly is directly traceable to the content and quality of an older system of education. However, presuming that age differences represent more than educational differences, why should the elderly be more likely than the young to accept anti-Semitic beliefs? There are at least three possible explanations. One is that the aging process leads to greater insecurity, rigidity, and withdrawal, and thus to greater ethnocentrism, intolerance, and prejudice. But a developmental process may not be involved at all. The elderly may score as more anti-Semitic simply because they have had more time to be exposed to the full repertory of anti-Semitic beliefs. Both these hypotheses assume that as people become older they take on anti-Semitic beliefs they did not hold in their youth.

A third possible explanation is that compared to the young of today the elderly were already more anti-Semitic in their youth. In other words, their greater anti-Semitism may be traceable to their having spent their formative years in an era more outspokenly anti-Semitic than our own. For example, a 55-year-old respondent in our sample was an adolescent in the 1920s and a young adult in the 1930s. This was a period of widespread and unabashed discrimination against Jews in residential areas, in resorts, in colleges and professional schools. It was in the 1920s that Henry Ford distributed *The Protocols of the Elders of Zion* and the Ku Klux Klan became a large-scale movement, even outside the South. The early 1930s saw the advent of the Nazi era, the German-American Bund, and the radio broadcasts of Father Coughlin. The prevalence of anti-Semitism in earlier decades makes plausible the view that the greater anti-Semitism of the elderly is a carry-over from their past, not something acquired as they grew older.

Lacking longitudinal data in which the same respondents are interviewed at different points in their life span, no theory about the effect of age can be satisfactorily tested and confirmed. However, data collected at a single point in time may throw some light on the question. So far we have compared the elderly and the young only with reference to their scores on the Index of Anti-Semitic Belief. We turn now to an examination of the independent effect of age on each of the eleven beliefs in the Index.

---

[5] One exception is the twelve older people in the sample who were college graduates and knew all four writers; none is anti-Semitic. As observed in Chapter 5, if a college graduate is sophisticated, there is little chance he will be anti-Semitic, no matter what other characteristics describe him.

In observing the kinds of beliefs that are "favored" by the elderly, we shall be in a better position to judge whether they became more anti-Semitic with increasing age or whether their greater anti-Semitism is due to their having grown up in a more anti-Semitic era.

Table 32 shows that on each of the eleven beliefs in the Index acceptance is higher for the elderly than for the young. On ten of the beliefs age differences range from 13 to 29 percentage points (column 4). The size of these differences is misleading, however; when education is held constant, the effect of age is considerably reduced (column 5). On five beliefs the remaining age differences are between 2 and 6 percentage points; on another five they are between 11 and 13 percentage points. On only one belief—that Jews control international banking—is there a substantial age difference (25 percentage points) once the effect of education is eliminated. In fact, this is the only belief in the Index whose acceptance is almost exclusively a function of age.[6]

It could hardly be argued that growing old has some peculiar relation to this belief that it does not have to others. The only plausible explanation is that the belief in Jewish control of international banking was acquired by the elderly in their younger years. If this is true, then it is a fair inference that they acquired other of their beliefs when they were young. In other words the elderly were already more anti-Semitic in their youth than the young are today. Their greater anti-Semitism seems to have nothing to do with the aging process, but reflects an era when anti-Semitism was more intense.[7]

The evidence suggests that the belief in Jewish control of international banking is dropping out of anti-Semitic ideology. Chapter 1 reported that this belief received an extraordinary number of don't-know responses (47 per cent). We now find that "don't knows" are much higher among the young than among the elderly. Among the elderly the modal response is

[6] The relation of lack of education to acceptance of the belief in Jewish control of international banking was reported in Table 18. Saying "don't know" is also higher among the less educated. As a result the proportions at each level of education rejecting this belief run from 14 per cent among grade schoolers to 39 per cent among college graduates. Controlling for age and education simultaneously shows that acceptance is more a function of age than of education, but because of don't knows, rejection is more a function of education than of age. Incidentally, on most items the young and old did not differ on don't-knowism independently of education.

[7] It is even possible that the elderly have become *less* anti-Semitic as they have grown older, but that, having started out very high, they are still higher than the present-day young. That the elderly also overaccept the relatively recent belief that Jews are more loyal to Israel involves no contradiction. If twenty years ago the elderly were already more anti-Semitic than their counterparts today, one would expect them to be more inclined to accept new anti-Semitic beliefs as they emerge.

Table 32. ACCEPTANCE OF INDIVIDUAL ANTI-SEMITIC BELIEFS BY AGE

Anti-Semitic Beliefs	Less than 35	35–54	55 or older	Average Percentage Difference, Education Not Controlled[a]	Average Percentage Difference, Education Controlled
Control international banking	17%	26%	46%	29	25
More loyal to Israel than America	23	27	42	19	13
Too much power in business world	20	28	40	20	12
Shrewd and tricky in business	27	33	47	20	12
Have a lot of irritating faults	34	39	48	14	12
Use shady practices to get ahead	36	41	51	15	11
Too much power in U.S.	5	9	18	13	6
Always like to head things	49	52	62	13	5
Stick together too much	46	51	59	13	4
Not as honest as other businessmen	24	27	32	8	4
Care only about own kind	21	23	35	14	2

[a]Difference between those 55 or older and those under 35.

acceptance (56 per cent); among the young the modal response is "don't know" (50 per cent). There is another indication in the data that the belief in Jewish control of international banking is no longer a central element in contemporary anti-Semitism. Whereas 82 per cent of extreme anti-Semites among the old hold this belief, only 55 per cent of extreme anti-Semites among the young do so. This is in marked contrast to other beliefs which are just as prevalent among young as among older anti-Semites.[8]

These findings have implications for measuring the relation between age and anti-Semitism. Whenever anti-Semitic beliefs are dying away, the old will appear to be more anti-Semitic on any index that includes outmoded beliefs, not because the old are subjectively more anti-Semitic (that is, actually more hostile toward Jews), but merely because they have lived in an era when such beliefs were more salient. Insofar as the elderly score higher on our Index because they overaccept the belief in Jewish control of international banking, to that extent the gap in anti-Semitic prejudice between the young and the old may be less significant than their Index scores would indicate. This minimizes still further the small difference found between the young and the old in degree of anti-Semitism. Some of this difference is a function of the greater education of the young; some reflects differential acceptance of the belief in Jewish control of international banking.

Discriminatory Attitudes

Earlier we pointed out that a climate of tolerance might not change people's beliefs but might inhibit the acting out of prejudice. However, while the young are somewhat less likely to hold discriminatory attitudes, age differences are small and in large part reflect educational differences. In the oldest age group, half (52 per cent), in the youngest age group, a third (35 per cent) failed to oppose the anti-Semitic presidential candidate. This difference of 17 percentage points is reduced to 10 when education is taken into account. The figures for the immigration law are virtually the same, and when education is controlled the 20 percentage point difference is reduced to 13 percentage points. These differences are hardly great enough to argue for a special development of tolerance among the young.

A higher proportion of the elderly (38 per cent) than of the young (23

[8] For example, the proportion of extreme anti-Semites agreeing that Jews stick together too much is exactly the same for the young as for the old—94 per cent. On the harsher belief that Jews are shrewd and tricky 96 per cent of extreme anti-Semites among the old and 87 per cent among the young agree.

per cent) say they would be very much or somewhat disturbed if their party nominated a Jew for the Presidency. Once again, this difference of 16 percentage points is reduced to 10 when education is controlled. The close resemblence between the young and the old is most manifest on the marginal issues of Christmas carols and intermarriage, neither of which is highly related to acceptance of anti-Semitic beliefs. The young are about as likely as the old to defend Christmas carols (68 per cent versus 74 per cent) and to object strongly or somewhat to intermarriage (38 per cent versus 43 per cent).

On social club discrimination, a third of the oldest group (33 per cent) are defenders as compared to a quarter (23 per cent) of the youngest group. The similarity of the young and the old is not surprising, since greater education is associated with greater support of social club discrimination. On the other hand, almost half the young (46 per cent) are militant opponents, a figure nearly twice that for the old (24 per cent). Only a minority of the young are token opponents (that is, said Smith should stay in the club and forget the whole thing). Compared to the old, when the young oppose social club discrimination they are willing to take steps to combat it in practice.

Is this greater "militancy" of the young a result of their greater education or is it a reflection of their youth? Table 33 shows that education and age have independent effects. Among college graduates who oppose social club discrimination, at least 6 out of 10 are militant opponents, no matter what their age. Similarly, among the young, roughly 6 out of 10 are militant opponents, no matter what their level of education. In short, either being young or being a college graduate substantially increases the likelihood of one's taking a firm stand against social club discrimination.

The data suggest that many of the elderly who now voice only token opposition to social club discrimination would have taken a firmer position in their younger days. This is consistent with the common observation that militancy, as expressed, for example, in a willingness to participate in civil rights demonstrations, is generally an attribute of youth, not of older, more established segments of the population. There is no evidence in the data that people become more anti-Semitic as they grow older. But it appears that militant opposition to discrimination attenuates with increasing age.

Sex

Men and women are pretty much alike when it comes to anti-Semitism. Men are slightly more apt to score as anti-Semitic (42 per cent versus 33 per cent), but women are less likely to have opinions. The net result

Table 33. MILITANT OPPOSITION TO SOCIAL CLUB DISCRIMINATION BY AGE AND EDUCATION

(per cent militant opponents of social club discrimination among those scoring either as token opponents or militant opponents)[a]

	Less than 35	35–54	55 or older	Total
Grade school	56% (32)	57% (102)	43% (176)	49% (310)
High school	63 (250)	54 (306)	39 (111)	55 (667)
Some college	66 (68)	55 (53)	41 (29)	57 (150)
College graduate	73 (45)	71 (41)	63 (19)	70 (105)
Total	64% (396)	56% (502)	43% (336)	

[a]Militant opponents of social club discrimination said the members of a club had no right to exclude Cohen because he is Jewish and that, if he is excluded, Smith should either quit the club or stay in and keep trying. Token opponents also denied that the members had a right to exclude Jews, but said that Smith should stay in and forget the whole thing. Defenders said the members had a right to exclude Jews.

is that the proportion of men and women who score as convinced non-anti-Semites is precisely the same—49 per cent.

One might suppose that there are "male" stereotypes and "female" stereotypes of Jews, for example, that women tend to hold clannish stereotypes, men economic stereotypes. Again the data give little or no support to such speculation. With only one exception, men and women show no differential tendency to select some beliefs more than others. The exception is the belief that Jews control international banking, accepted by 38 per cent of the men and 22 per cent of the women—a difference of 16 percentage points. Women, however, were not more likely to reject this belief, but rather said "don't know" more often.

On behavioral questions, women continue to be less anti-Semitic than men, but differences are not substantial. On only one question did this pattern reverse itself. Women are slightly more likely to disapprove of intermarriage; 45 per cent of the women and 38 per cent of the men said they would object strongly or somewhat to their child marrying a Jew. It is frequently conjectured that American women have jurisdiction over social relations in the home, and that, while they may be no more prejudiced than men, they are more apt to be discriminatory in interpersonal relations. The only evidence for this is their slightly greater disapproval of intermarriage.[9] Women were not more likely than men to defend social club discrimination.

Since they have approximately the same amount of formal education, it is not surprising that men and women exhibit roughly the same rates of anti-Semitism. Census tabulations, as well as our own data, show that men are slightly more likely than women to finish college but women are slightly more likely to finish high school. When education is controlled, men continue to be slightly more anti-Semitic than women except among college graduates, where women are slightly more anti-Semitic than men. But differences are small, and no importance can be attached to them. On the whole, men and women do not differ substantially with respect either to anti-Semitic beliefs or to discriminatory attitudes.

Nativity

Only a few decades ago the United States could be described as a nation of immigrants. Between 1880 and 1920 nearly 25 million immigrants were added to an original population of 50 million. After 1920 the flow of

---

[9] Women are more likely than men to say that their religion is very important to them (57 per cent versus 44 per cent). However, when men and women who said this are compared, women continue to disapprove of intermarriage more often than do men (50 per cent versus 41 per cent).

immigration was sharply curtailed by restrictive quotas. The decline in immigration, taken together with the natural population increase, has drastically altered the nation's ethnic composition. In 1930 about one in nine Americans was foreign born, but by 1960 the proportion had shrunk to about one in twenty-four. In our sample 6 per cent—133 respondents— were foreign born. While too few to influence our assessment of contemporary anti-Semitism, they may nevertheless contribute to our understanding of past decades when immigrants constituted a much more significant segment of the general population.

The foreign-born are more likely to be anti-Semitic than native Americans—54 per cent as compared with 42 per cent. However, a majority of immigrants (57 per cent) in the sample are at least 55 years old, compared to a minority (29 per cent) of the native-born. They are also less educated. The question is whether immigrants are more anti-Semitic simply because they are older and less educated or because many came from European countries with long histories of virulent anti-Semitism.[10] When either age or education is held constant (there are too few cases for simultaneous controls), most of the relation between nativity and anti-Semitism is explained. In other words, the higher anti-Semitism of immigrants appears to be a function of these factors, not their foreign birth.[11]

An attempt was made to measure the effect of specific ethnic background on anti-Semitism. Respondents were asked the country in which each parent and grandparent was born. It is sometimes conjectured that old-generation Americans are particularly likely to be anti-Semitic; sometimes it is claimed that people from certain ethnic backgrounds are particularly likely to be so. We would have liked to explore these issues, but a sample of 2,000 cases does not permit making the many ethnic distinctions that would be necessary.[12] However, it was possible to distinguish between second-generation Americans and those who are third

[10] Anti-Semitism seems to be more salient for immigrants than for the native-born. Even when they are uneducated, immigrants tend to have opinions about Jews. Among persons with only a grade school education, 72 per cent of the immigrants had no more than one don't know on the Index, compared to half of the native-born.

[11] For example, in the oldest age category 58 per cent of the native-born and 62 per cent of the foreign-born score as anti-Semitic. Among those with a grade school education, 67 per cent of the native-born and 62 per cent of the foreign-born score as anti-Semitic.

[12] As a mundane methodological note, it was an error even to attempt to measure specific ethnic background. Our sample yielded only 51 respondents' fathers born in Germany, 48 in Italy, 35 in Poland, 19 in Russia. Once education was controlled, these were too few cases to allow for meaningful comparisons. Where comparisons were possible, ethnicity had no marked effect. However, a recent study reports that "the Irish are lowest on the anti-Semitism index; . . . the Poles are the highest" (Andrew M. Greeley, "Ethnicity as an Influence on Behavior," p. 9, unpublished paper, 1968).

generation or more. No significant difference was found: 38 per cent of those with foreign-born parents and 41 per cent of those with native-born parents scored as anti-Semitic.

Evaluation of the Findings

If present trends continue, there should be a steady decline of anti-Semitism in the future. Not only do older people contribute disproportionately to the national pool of anti-Semitism, they appear to have acquired their anti-Semitism early in their lives and not with increasing age. Therefore the level of anti-Semitism in the country is bound to decline as the young replace the more anti-Semitic generation of their elders. Yet the decline is likely to be slow. Even among those under 35 years of age, 20 per cent say Jews have too much power in the business world, 23 per cent that Jews are more loyal to Israel than to America, 36 per cent that Jews are more willing than others to use shady practices, and 46 per cent that Jews stick together too much; 29 per cent scored at least 5 on the Index of Anti-Semitic Belief. These figures hardly suggest that the United States has reached a turning point in the elimination of anti-Semitic prejudice.

The findings with respect to age are consistent with those of the trend analysis in Chapter 1. There we saw that the belief in excessive Jewish power in the United States has declined sharply in recent decades; we now find that it is held by only 5 per cent of the youngest age group in the sample. This is further evidence that a preoccupation with Jewish power is dropping out of contemporary anti-Semitism. On the other hand, beliefs concerning Jewish clannishness and unethical business practices have undergone only a modest decline since the 1950s; as this chapter shows, these beliefs are held often enough by the young to assure their persistence in the future.

There is one reason more for not overestimating the prospective decline of anti-Semitism. Not only do anti-Semitic beliefs continue at fairly high levels among the relatively young in the adult sample, a concurrent study in this series reveals that anti-Semitic beliefs are widely accepted by adolescents.[13] Several items included in the adolescent study are similar enough to permit comparisons with young adults—persons under 35 years of age—in the national sample. Whereas 21 per cent of young adults agreed that "Jews don't care what happens to anyone but their own kind,"

---

[13] Jane Allyn Hardyck and M. Brewster Smith, *Friendship and Prejudice in Adolescence: Attitudes Towards Jews and Negroes in Three High Schools* (forthcoming publication in this series). The sample is of tenth- and twelfth-grade students in three high schools in the East.

48 per cent of the adolescent sample agreed "Jews are likely to be selfish, concerned only for themselves or their own group"; 23 per cent of young adults agreed "Jews are more loyal to Israel than to America," 42 per cent of the adolescents agreed that "Jews tend to be more loyal to their own group than to the United States"; 24 per cent of the young adults denied that "Jews are just as honest as other businessmen," 37 per cent of the adolescents agreed that "Jews are likely to be somewhat dishonest in their dealings with others."

Perhaps not too much importance should be attached to the fact that acceptance is greater among this group of adolescents than among young adults in the national sample. The adolescent sample was drawn from three high schools and is not representative of adolescents in the general population. One would not want to conclude that all adolescents of like age and educational level are as anti-Semitic as those sampled or that these adolescents will continue to be as anti-Semitic as they are now. There is every reason to believe that the next generation will be less anti-Semitic than the present one, just as the present generation is less anti-Semitic than the preceding one.

A question raised in this chapter was whether this decline is a product of broad social change encompassing the society as a whole or of a single change—the rising level of education. If broad social change were operating, the disparity in anti-Semitism between the young and the old should go beyond what can be explained by the disparity in their education. But the greater education of the young stands out as the primary factor in their lower anti-Semitism. If the increasing climate of tolerance has had an effect, it has been mainly through the educational institutions.

7 : Religion, Region, and Race

Unlike many of the variables considered in previous chapters, religion, region, and race tend to form unique historical configurations. The South is heavily rural, Protestant, and fundamentalist. Catholics are predominantly white, urban, and non-Southern. Compared to whites, more Negroes live in the rural South; outside the South most Negroes are urban. Because of these historical configurations, certain categories of people, such as Episcopalians in the South or rural Negroes outside the South, are virtually unrepresented in a sample of 2,000. It thus becomes difficult and sometimes impossible to factor out the separate and independent effects of the three variables—religion, region, and race—on anti-Semitism.

Even when simultaneous controls are possible, one cannot always determine the independent effect of these variables. This is because religion, region, and race have interacted over time, each shaping the other. For example, the fundamentalist religion of the South has been of major importance in shaping the regional culture. However, once a fundamentalist perspective is embodied in the larger cultural milieu, it may affect persons who do not identify with fundamentalist churches. In this way the original effect of religion becomes submerged and manifests itself as a regional difference between the South and other sections of the country. To take another example: most Catholics live in urban areas outside the South, and this could be a factor in leading the Church to take a stand against racial discrimination. Once the Church takes a stand, attitudes of Catholics in the South might also undergo change. Thus, what was originally the effect of northern and urban residence on Catholic attitudes would be manifested in the South as an apparent religious difference between Catholics and Protestants.

Partly out of these concerns, partly because the anti-Semitism of Negroes is in some ways different from that of whites, Negroes are omitted from the sections on religion and region. Negro-white differences in anti-Semitism are examined separately at the end of the chapter.[1]

Religious Affiliation

Virtually all Americans identify with some religious group, whether or not they actually belong to a church or accept the precepts of their faith. It is further evidence of the representativeness of our sample that its religious distribution is almost identical to that of the country, as determined by a 1957 Census Bureau survey based on a sample of 25,000 cases. According to Census Bureau figures, 66 per cent of the population are Protestant, compared to 68 per cent of our sample. Both sets of figures show Catholics to be 26 per cent and Jews 3 per cent of the population.

Compared to Protestants, Catholics appear to be somewhat less anti-Semitic, though not greatly so. Among whites who go to church at least once a month, 36 per cent of Protestants and 32 per cent of Catholics score high on anti-Semitism. A somewhat larger proportion of Protestants are opinionless, and when this is taken into account the rate of anti-Semitism is 43 per cent for Protestants and 35 per cent for Catholics.

When Protestant denominations are viewed individually, a slightly different picture emerges. Three Protestant denominations—the Unitarian, Congregationalist, and Episcopalian—stand out as lower on anti-Semitism than Catholics: the composite rate for these three denominations is 24 per cent (Table 34, bottom row). Numerically, these three denominations constitute a very small proportion of Protestants; of white Protestants in the sample, only 11 per cent belong to one of these three denominations. The other and more theologically conservative denominations vary somewhat among themselves, but in every case their rates of anti-Semitism exceed that of Catholics. Thus the data order themselves into three groups: "liberal" Protestant denominations low on anti-Semitism (24 per cent); Catholics (35 per cent); and "conservative" Protestant denominations (46 per cent).[2]

---

[1] Negroes were not omitted from previous chapters since they were too few to seriously affect the results. For example, the relation between education and anti-Semitic belief is the same whether Negroes are omitted or not; in either case, it ranges from 66 per cent to 16 per cent. However, since Negroes constitute a large proportion of respondents in the South, it now becomes necessary to analyze Negroes and whites separately.

[2] The category of conservative Protestants consists of Presbyterians, Methodists, Baptists, Lutherans, Evangelical and Reformed, Disciples of Christ, and sects. Mormons and persons belonging to small Protestant denominations such as Jehovah's Witnesses and German Reformed are excluded. For data on the theological orientations of the various denominations, see Charles Y. Glock and Rodney Stark, *Christian Beliefs and Anti-Semitism* (New York: Harper & Row, 1966), Chapters 1 and 2.

Table 34.   ANTI-SEMITIC BELIEF BY RELIGIOUS AFFILIATION

(white churchgoers only[a])

	Liberal Protestant[b]		Catholic		Conservative Protestant[c]	
Anti-Semitic	23%		32%		38%	
Extreme		5%		14%		17%
High		18		18		21
Non-anti-Semitic	77		68		62	
Unconvinced		5		9		18
Convinced		72		59		44
100% (N) =	(78)		(411)		(604)	
Per cent convinced among non-anti-Semites	93%		87%		72%	
100% (N) =	(60)		(281)		(373)	
Per cent anti-Semitic excluding the unconvinced	24%		35%		46%	
100% (N) =	(74)		(375)		(499)	

[a]A churchgoer is one who attends church at least once a month.

[b]Unitarians, Congregationalists, Episcopalians.

[c]Presbyterians, Methodists, Baptists, Lutherans, Evangelican and Reform, Disciples of Christ, sects.

A striking characteristic of the liberal Protestant denominations is their extraordinarily high level of education: 62 per cent have attended college in contrast to 21 and 23 per cent among Catholics and conservative Protestants. Table 35 shows that, when compared to their educational peers in the liberal Protestant denominations, Catholics no longer exhibit higher rates of anti-Semitism. If Catholics were as educated as Unitarians, Congregationalists, and Episcopalians, their over-all rate of anti-Semitism would be the same. This cannot be said of those in conservative Protestant denominations. Even when education is held constant, they continue to exhibit higher rates of anti-Semitism than either liberal Protestants or Catholics. There is one exception: college graduates are low on anti-Semitism no matter what their religious affiliation.

A number of studies have shown Catholics to be less anti-Semitic than Protestants. Ironically, opinion among Jews tends to hold the reverse— that Catholics are more anti-Semitic than Protestants.[3] It is not difficult

---

[3] Jewish respondents in a national sample were asked whether they thought Protestant and Catholic employers would discriminate against them because of their religion. Twenty-six per cent named Protestants, 37 per cent named Catholics (*Catholic Digest,*

to imagine how such a misapprehension could arise. Historically Catholics and Jews have lived in the same urban centers with the result that the anti-Semitism Jews encountered was apt to come from Catholics. Another factor is the tendency to infer the contemporary sources from the historic sources of anti-Semitism, and to assume that the authoritarian structure and theological dogmas of the Catholic Church must necessarily engender prejudice and bigotry. However, American Catholics are actually less likely than Protestants to hold some of the religious beliefs associated with secular anti-Semitism.[4]

Table 35.   ANTI-SEMITIC BELIEF BY RELIGIOUS AFFILIATION AND EDUCATION[a]

(per cent anti-Semitic among white churchgoers only)

	Liberal Protestant	Catholic	Conservative Protestant
Grade school	b (3)	59% (86)	69% (130)
High school	31 (26)	32 (204)	44 (240)
Some college	20 (15)	15 (41)	36 (70)
College graduate	13 (30)	18 (44)	17 (59)
Total	24% (74)	35% (375)	46% (499)

[a]See notes to Table 34 for definition of "churchgoer" and denominations included in each religious category.

[b]Too few cases to compute percentage.

August 1967, pp. 113–116). In another 1966 national survey, Jewish respondents were asked: "Do you think most (Protestants, Catholics) look down on people of your beliefs or not?" Forty-four per cent of Jews agreed for Catholics, only 16 per cent for Protestants. Another question asked: "Do you think that (Protestants, Catholics) as a group try to interfere in any way with your religious beliefs or personal liberties, or not?" Nineteen per cent of Jews said Catholics try to interfere, while 9 per cent said this of Protestants (*Catholic Digest*, November 1966, p. 59).

[4] In the national sample 49 per cent of Catholics but 64 per cent of Protestants said that belief in Jesus is necessary for salvation; 21 per cent of Catholics but 35 per cent of Protestants said that Christians are God's Chosen People today; 15 per cent of Catholics but 23 per cent of Protestants agreed with the statement that "the reason that Jews have so much trouble is because God is punishing them for rejecting Jesus."

It should also be noted that Catholics who have attended parochial schools, even for five or more years, exhibited no higher rates of anti-Semitism than their coreligionists who attended public schools. Another recent study also found no difference in anti-Semitism between Catholics who attended parochial schools and those who received a public education. [Andrew M. Greely and Peter H. Rossi, *The Education of Catholic Americans* (Chicago: Adeline Publishing Co., 1966), pp. 122–123.]

Despite differences in anti-Semitism among liberal Protestants, Catholics, and conservative Protestants, within each group education is strongly related to anti-Semitism (Table 35). Among those in conservative Protestant denominations, there is a 52-percentage-point spread between grade schoolers and college graduates, almost exactly as occurs in the sample as a whole. Compared to· education, the impact of religious affiliation is not great. Nor for that matter is church attendance: within each religious category churchgoers and nonchurchgoers exhibit virtually the same rates of anti-Semitism.[5] The important factor in religion, as *Christian Beliefs and Anti-Semitism* showed, is not nominal religious affiliation but acceptance of certain tenets of religious ideology.

In the present study three questions were combined to form a measure of Religious Predisposition to Secular Anti-Semitism. Respondents were scored one point for denying that a person can be saved "who doesn't accept Jesus," for naming Jews as the group "most responsible for killing Christ," and for believing that Christians "are God's Chosen People today." Among those accepting two or three of these beliefs 50 per cent scored as anti-Semitic in contrast to 26 per cent of those who accepted none (Table 36, Total column). This relation continues at every level of education. While the uneducated are higher on the Index of Religious Predis-

Table 36. ANTI-SEMITIC BELIEF BY RELIGIOUS PREDISPOSITION

AND EDUCATION

(per cent anti-Semitic among white churchgoers)

Predisposition[a]	Grade School	High School	Some College	College Graduate	Total
High (2–3)	70%	45%	40%	24%	50%
	(122)	(183)	(50)	(25)	(380)
Medium (1)	64	38	24	24	40
	(77)	(192)	(53)	(55)	(377)
Low (0)	53	29	12	6	26
	(34)	(123)	(34)	(46)	(237)
Total	66%	39%	27%	16%	
	(234)	(503)	(141)	(131)	

[a]Comprises three beliefs: that a person who doesn't accept Jesus cannot be saved; that Jews are the group most responsible for killing Christ; and that Christians are God's Chosen People today.

[5] No systematic relation between frequency of church attendance and anti-Semitism was found among either Protestants or Catholics. There was one exception: of the 12 Catholics who said they never or almost never attend church, 9 scored as anti-Semitic. Such a small number could not be analyzed.

position to Secular Anti-Semitism than are the educated, this does not explain the relation between religious and secular anti-Semitism. Similarly, whether people are high or low on Religious Predisposition, the relation of education to anti-Semitic prejudice continues strong. In other words, both have independent effect. Since religious ideology is independently related to anti-Semitism, changes in religious dogma and practice could play a role in reducing anti-Semitism. Our data were collected soon after the Vatican Council issued its schema on the Jews. In response to a question about the Crucifixion, one Catholic respondent said, "I used to believe that the Jews killed Christ, but they're changing the law in Rome."

Discriminatory Attitudes

Just as Catholics are slightly less likely than Protestants to accept anti-Semitic beliefs, so they are slightly more likely to oppose discrimination. Although Catholics defend social club discrimination as often as Protestants, comparatively more of them (40 per cent versus 25 per cent) are militant opponents. Catholics compare favorably even to liberal Protestants, of whom 31 per cent are militant opponents. That liberal Protestants "fall down" on this issue can be understood in terms of their relatively high social status. As Chapter 5 established, a college education, especially when combined with high income, is strongly associated with support of social club discrimination.

Religious differences are larger on the presidential issue. Only 16 per cent of Catholics say they would be very much or somewhat disturbed if their party nominated a Jewish presidential candidate. This proportion is lower than that for liberal Protestants (24 per cent), and very much lower than that for conservative Protestants (42 per cent). Among Catholics who score as extreme anti-Semites 34 per cent expressed disapproval, but the comparable figure for conservative Protestants is 69 per cent.[6] Catholics may well be responding to their own experiences as an excluded minority, and to the election in 1960 of the first Catholic President.

However, Catholics show no disproportionate tendency to resist political anti-Semitism, as defined in this study. Being a little less prejudiced, they are a little more likely to oppose an anti-Semitic candidate and an anti-Jewish immigration law. But on both issues less than 10 percentage points separate Catholics from Protestants.

---

[6] No comparison is possible for liberal Protestants since only four scored as extreme anti-Semites.

Region

At first glance regional differences in anti-Semitism appear to be small (Table 37). In the South and the Midwest 39 and 37 per cent score as anti-Semitic. Rates for the Northwest and Northeast are only slightly lower—33 and 31 per cent. The similarity of these figures is somewhat misleading however. Respondents in the South and Midwest are more

Table 37. ANTI-SEMITIC BELIEF BY REGION[a]

(whites only)

	South	Midwest	Northwest	Northeast
Anti-Semitic	39%	37%	33%	31%
Extreme	17%	15%	16%	14%
High	22	22	17	17
Non-anti-Semitic	61	63	67	69
Unconvinced	19	15	10	9
Convinced	42	48	57	60
100% (N) =	(456)	(522)	(274)	(403)
Per cent convinced among non-anti-Semites	69%	76%	85%	87%
100% (N) =	(276)	(327)	(184)	(281)
Per cent anti-Semitic excluding the unconvinced	48%	44%	36%	33%
100% (N) =	(371)	(444)	(247)	(366)

[a]Census classification of regions is used.

often opinionless, and when this is taken into account region has a greater impact on anti-Semitism than first appeared. In the South and Midwest, less than half are convinced non-anti-Semites (42 and 48 per cent), whereas in the Northwest and Northeast, a majority are convinced non-anti-Semites (57 and 60 per cent). The difference between the South and the Northeast is now 18 percentage points, about twice that first reported.

But further analysis gives us pause. In urban areas there is no relation between region and anti-Semitism: about a third are anti-Semitic regardless of region (Table 38). Furthermore, in the Northwest and Northeast, rural areas are no more apt to be anti-Semitic than urban areas; again about a third are anti-Semitic. Only in the Midwest and the South does rural residence increase anti-Semitism: in the rural Midwest the rate is 52 per cent; in the rural South it is 60 per cent. Thus the higher rates of

Table 38.   ANTI-SEMITIC BELIEF BY REGION AND RURAL-URBAN RESIDENCE
(per cent anti-Semitic among whites only)

Rural-Urban Residence[a]	South	Midwest	Northwest	Northeast
Rural	60%	52%	33%	35%
	(176)	(179)	(61)	(85)
Urban	38%	38%	36%	33%
	(194)	(263)	(171)	(273)
Total	48%	44%	36%	33%
	(371)	(444)	(247)	(366)

[a]The 1960 Census classification of urban and rural is used. "Urban" includes small communities that are within a standard metropolitan statistical area. "Rural" refers to counties outside metropolitan areas.

anti-Semitism in the South and Midwest are attributable solely to the higher rates of anti-Semitism in their rural areas. Otherwise, rates of anti-Semitism are fairly uniform throughout the country, regardless of either region or rural-urban residence.

It is frequently contended that anti-Semitism is peculiarly associated with rural life.[7] Our findings do not contradict this view but suggest the need to distinguish between rural residence in regions that are basically rural, like the Midwest and the South, and rural residence in regions that are predominantly urban in character. The South has a higher proportion of rural residents than the Midwest, and both have higher proportions of rural residents than either the Northeast or Northwest. The ranking of the proportion anti-Semitic among rural residents is precisely the same.

The higher anti-Semitism of the rural South and Midwest does not by itself prove that distinctively rural influences are involved. Rural Southerners and Midwesterners are generally less educated and more fundamentalist in their religion than people in other parts of the country. However, even when these factors are controlled, rates of anti-Semitism continue to be highest in the rural South and Midwest.[8] There is one important exception to this pattern. The relatively few college graduates living in the rural South and Midwest are no more likely to be anti-Semitic than college graduates living in other areas of the country.[9]

[7] For example, Arnold Rose, "Anti-Semitism's Root in City-Hatred," *Commentary*, October 1948, pp. 374–378.

[8] As we saw in Chapter 5, however, equal amounts of schooling do not always signify equal intellectual sophistication. When the writers test is examined by region, those in the rural Northeast and Northwest are just as likely as urbanites to know nationally prominent writers, as well as politicians, entertainers, and sports figures. Only the rural South and Midwest stand out as comparatively low on knowledge.

[9] While few Catholics live in the rural South and Midwest, their rate of anti-Semitism is closer to that of Protestants in these areas than of Catholics in the rest of the country. In the rural South and Midwest combined, the rate of anti-Semitism

One further word should be said concerning anti-Semitism in the South. In addition to being anti-Catholic and anti-Negro, the Ku Klux Klan has historically been anti-Semitic as well. In remarks volunteered to interviewers, several southern respondents implied that Jews are responsible for recent judicial decisions and federal action against segregation. As one Birmingham, Alabama, resident said: "Remove some of them from the White House. They have too much power as federal judges. . . . We have too many Jews in our federal department now. I think some of them should be removed."

There is no evidence that such sentiments are widespread in the South. Respondents were asked which group they thought was most in favor of racial integration—Protestants, Catholics, or Jews. Of the whites in the sample, over half (54 per cent) had no opinion or said there was no difference; 22 per cent said "Catholics," 15 per cent said "Protestants," just 9 per cent said "Jews."[10] Whether rural or urban, Southern whites were no more likely than other whites to name Jews as most in favor of racial integration.

However, white Protestants in the South were more likely than white Protestants elsewhere to single out Catholics (26 per cent versus 12 per

---

(among whites with opinions) is 59 per cent for conservative Protestants and 49 per cent for Catholics. In the rest of the country, the figure is 39 per cent for conservative Protestants, 36 per cent for Catholics. Only eleven liberal Protestants in the sample lived in the rural South or Midwest, five of whom (38 per cent) scored as anti-Semitic. For liberal Protestants in the rest of the country, the figure is 19 per cent.

[10] The responses of Negroes were as follows: 20 per cent named Protestants, 39 per cent Catholics; 9 per cent Jews; 32 per cent said "no difference" or answered "don't know." This response pattern closely resembles that of whites except that Negroes mentioned Catholics even more frequently than did whites. The similarity of response with respect to Jews is somewhat deceptive, however. Sixty-one per cent of Negroes live in the South, and only 5 per cent of them named Jews as the group most in favor of civil rights. In the North 14 per cent did so.

The special study of Negroes reported in Gary T. Marx, *Protest and Prejudice* (New York: Harper & Row, 1967), asked a similar question: "On the whole, do you think that Jews are more in favor of civil rights for Negroes than other white people are, less in favor, or is there no difference?" To this question, 45 per cent said "more in favor," 3 per cent said "less," and 52 per cent said "no difference" or "don't know" (p. 152). The disparity in responses to the two questions has several sources. First, the special sample contains proportionately more Northern Negroes. Second, the question posed to the national sample specifically mentioned Catholics who, as it turns out, are the group most often named by both Negroes and whites. Together the two questions suggest that many Negroes rank Jews higher than whites generally but, as among whites, lower than other *religious* groups, especially Catholics. It should be noted that in 1964 Catholics were actively integrating parochial schools and were conspicuous in civil rights demonstrations by virtue of their religious attire. When Jews participate in the struggle for civil rights, they typically do so in a secular rather than a religious role. To frame the question in religious terms is to minimize the number who will name Jews and maximize the number who will name Catholics.

Jewish respondents were also asked which religious group was most in favor of racial integration. Over half (56 per cent) named their own group, 5 per cent named Protestants or Catholics, the remainder said "no difference" or "don't know."

cent).[11] In part this might reflect the high visibility of Catholic nuns and priests in Southern civil rights demonstrations and the integration of parochial schools in parts of the South. There is evidence, however, that anti-Catholic prejudice is involved. Respondents were asked to agree or disagree with the statement "Catholics are getting too much power in the United States." Urban Southerners were again no more likely than urban dwellers elsewhere to express prejudice. However, in the rural South 39 per cent of white Protestants said Catholics have too much power, compared to 23 per cent for the rest of the country. In the rural South, as elsewhere, persons who said Catholics have too much power in the country were also more apt to name them as most in favor of racial integration.[12] Despite the high level of anti-Semitic prejudice in the rural South, Jews were rarely singled out as especially in favor of integration. This mixed blessing was more frequently conferred on Catholics.

Discriminatory Attitudes

Historically, in the South discrimination against Negroes was not left to individual discretion or the operation of private and informal sanctions but incorporated into law and legally enforced. It is therefore not surprising that a disproportionate number of Southerners defend social clubs' right to exclude Jews. About 4 out of 10 do so compared to 27 per cent outside the South. The greater tendency of Southerners to defend social club discrimination cannot be traced solely to their greater anti-Semitic prejudice. At every level of anti-Semitic belief, Southerners disproportionately defend social club discrimination. This is obviously linked to their long history of legally sanctioned discrimination against Negroes. Where discrimination is regarded as a legitimate prerogative of the prejudiced, it can be defended in one case as well as the next.

Since anti-Semitism and opinionlessness are both highest in the rural South and Midwest, these areas show the greatest susceptibility to political anti-Semitism. Opposition to the anti-Semitic candidate is at lower levels in the rural South (47 per cent) and rural Midwest (50 per cent) than in the rest of the country (62 per cent).[13]

---

[11] Catholic respondents were more likely than Protestants to name their own group as most in favor of racial integration and are excluded from the above comparison.

[12] Among white Protestants in the sample, 23 per cent of those who said Catholics have too much power in the United States also named Catholics as most in favor of racial integration; the comparable figure for those who denied that Catholics have too much power is 14 per cent. However, when opinion on Catholic power is held constant, Southerners, especially those in rural areas, continue to name Catholics as most in favor of racial integration.

[13] With respect to the anti-Jewish immigration law, only the rural South stands out as particularly in favor of it (36 per cent). In the rest of the country support ranges from 16 per cent in the urban Northeast to 24 per cent in the rural Midwest.

One other issue is of interest. The proportion of whites who would be very much or somewhat disturbed if their party nominated a Jew for the Presidency varies widely by region: it is 41 per cent in the South, 31 per cent in the Midwest, 26 per cent in the Northwest, and 19 per cent in the Northeast. Again disapproval is highest in the rural South and Midwest (45 and 38 per cent).[14]

Not only the extent, but also the flavor of anti-Semitism undoubtedly varies from one region to another. This much is suggested by the Oklahoma farmer who, when asked whether Jews have more money than others, said: "Put one of them in a silo, and he'll come up with five thousand dollars."

Race

As early as 1937 Richard Wright wrote: "To hold an attitude of antagonism or distrust toward Jews was bred in us from childhood; it was not merely racial prejudice, it was part of our cultural heritage."[15] In 1948 James Baldwin wrote:

Jews in Harlem are small tradesmen, rent collectors, real estate agents, and pawnbrokers; they operate in accordance with the American business tradition of exploiting Negroes, and they are therefore identified with oppression and are hated for it. I remember meeting no Negro in the years of my growing up, in my family or out of it, who would really ever trust a Jew, and few who did not, indeed, exhibit for them the blackest contempt.[16]

It was not until the summer riots of 1964—a short time before interviews were conducted for this study—that the issue of "Negro anti-Semitism" came to the attention of the general public. At that time the press reported that rioters seemed bent on damaging stores owned by Jews and that cries of "Let's get the Jews" were heard. While such reports have not accompanied subsequent riots, since 1964 there have been sporadic instances in which black militants have resorted to the language of anti-Semitism.[17] In 1967 James Baldwin resigned from a Negro magazine after it had published a series of anti-Semitic articles. He then wrote an article

---

[14] This is not an artifact of there being fewer Catholics in the rural South and Midwest; the relation is the same when only Protestants are examined. It should be emphasized that these figures are for whites only. If Negroes were included, opposition to a Jewish President would be lowered, especially in the South.

[15] Quoted in Pettigrew, *A Profile of the Negro American* (Princeton: D. Van Nostrand Company, 1964), p. 44.

[16] James Baldwin, "The Harlem Ghetto: Winter, 1948," *Commentary*, February 1948, p. 169.

[17] For example, *Newsweek*, August 28, 1967; *New York Times*, October 23, 1968, pp. 1 and 32.

in the *New York Times Magazine* entitled "Negroes Are Anti-Semitic Because They Are Anti-White."[18] In it he said:

He [the Jew] is singled out by Negroes not because he acts differently from other white men, but because he doesn't. His major distinction is given him by that history of Christendom, which has so succesfully victimized both Negro and Jew. He is playing in Harlem the role assigned him by Christians long ago: he is doing their dirty work.

Like other writers Baldwin argued that anti-Semitism has long been widespread among Negroes and is rooted in the special economic relations between Jewish businessmen and impoverished Negroes.

It should come as no surprise that anti-Semitism exists among Negroes. It would be illusory to think that, because they are an oppressed minority, Negroes reject anti-Semitic stereotypes which, to some degree, characterize every segment of American society. The issue is not whether anti-Semitism is present among Negroes, but the extent to which it exists. A few articles and press reports—even virulent anti-Semitism in extremist groups—tell us little or nothing about the general prevalence of anti-Semitism in the Negro population. Three questions direct this analysis: (1) Are Negroes in fact more anti-Semitic than whites, as is often implied? (2) Does anti-Semitism among Negroes differ in content or kind from that found among whites? (3) Is the quality of Negro-Jewish contacts a factor in Negro anti-Semitism?[19]

In order to determine whether Negro and white anti-Semitism differ in content, each of the eleven beliefs in the Index of Anti-Semitic Belief is examined by race (Table 39). The Ratio of Negro Acceptance (last column) shows the extent to which Negroes over- or underaccepted each belief relative to whites. For example, for every 100 whites who said that Jews use shady practices, 145 Negroes gave this response. For every 100 whites who denied that Jews are as honest as other businessmen, 129 Negroes did so. On eight of the eleven beliefs the ratio is greater than 100, indicating overacceptance of these beliefs by Negroes. However, the extent of overacceptance depends on the content of the belief. Of the five beliefs most overaccepted by Negroes, four are clearly economic in content, and the other—that "Jews don't care what happens to anyone but their own kind"—is consistent with the image of Jews as economically exploitative.[20] However, on the remaining six beliefs in the Index, Negro-

[18] *New York Times Magazine*, April 9, 1967, p. 137.

[19] Other issues regarding Negro anti-Semitism are dealt with in an earlier volume in this series based on special samples of urban Negroes. See Marx, *op. cit.*, Chapters 6 and 7. Our analysis is limited to a comparison between Negroes and whites in the national sample.

[20] Two economic beliefs, not explicitly anti-Semitic and not included in the Index, were also overaccepted by Negroes. The proportion saying Jews have more money

white differences are small or reversed. The data, in other words, allow no blanket comparison between whites and Negroes. In the economic area, Negroes are more anti-Semitic than whites. In the noneconomic area, no consistent differences exist.

This finding contrasts with those for education and age. Earlier we reported that the uneducated and the elderly are more anti-Semitic on

Table 39. ACCEPTANCE OF INDIVIDUAL ANTI-SEMITIC BELIEFS BY RACE

	Whites	Negroes	Ratio of Negro Acceptance (white rate = 100)[a]
Care only about own kind	24%	43%	180
Use shady practices to get ahead	40	58	145
Control international banking	28	40	143
Shrewd and tricky in business	34	46	135
Not as honest as other businessmen	27	35	129
Always like to head things	53	60	113
Have a lot of irritating faults	40	44	110
More loyal to Israel than to America	30	32	107
Stick together too much	53	48	90
Too much power in U.S.	11	9	82
Too much power in business world	31	19	61

[a]Determined by dividing the rate for Negroes by the rate for whites.

every anti-Semitic belief in the Index, and it could be stated unambiguously that they are more anti-Semitic than the educated and the young. No such statement can be made about Negroes who are more anti-Semitic with respect to certain beliefs only. This has methodological as well as substantive implications. It means that no index can combine economic and noneconomic items without obscuring the relation between race and

than others is 66 per cent for Negroes and 60 per cent for whites; the proportion saying that Jews go out of their way to hire other Jews is 59 per cent for Negroes and 48 per cent for whites. These differences are noteworthy only in the context of Negro-white differences on other economic beliefs whose anti-Semitic content is beyond question.

However, Negroes underaccepted both statements concerning excessive Jewish power. In view of the recent emergence of the Black Power movement and the demand for ghetto autonomy, these beliefs—especially the belief that Jews have too much power in business—may now be more widespread than they were in 1964. It is interesting to note that young Negroes were as likely as young whites to say that Jews have too much power in the business world. It was only elderly Negroes who greatly underselected this belief: only 11 per cent accepted it.

anti-Semitism.[21] For this reason the Index of Anti-Semitic Belief is divided into an Index of Economic Anti-Semitism, comprising the five economic items overaccepted by Negroes, and an Index of Noneconomic Anti-Semitism, which consists of the remaining six items.

These indexes confirm what was previously observed for individual beliefs. On the Index of Noneconomic Anti-Semitism there is essentially no difference between whites and Negroes; 29 per cent of whites and 26 per cent of Negroes have high scores.[22] Despite their lower level of education, Negroes are if anything less likely than whites to hold noneconomic stereotypes. However, a sharp difference appears on the Index of Economic Anti-Semitism (Table 40). Here 54 per cent of Negroes have high scores in contrast to 32 per cent of whites.[23] Among whites the proportion scoring high on both indexes is roughly the same, but among Negroes

Table 40.   ECONOMIC AND NONECONOMIC ANTI-SEMITISM BY RACE

	Whites	Negroes	Percentage Difference[a]
High on economic anti-Semitism	32% (1,322)	54% (182)	+22
High on noneconomic anti-Semitism	29% (1,282)	26% (168)	−3

[a]Between Negroes and whites.

twice as many score High on Economic as on Noneconomic Anti-Semitism. Table 40 leaves no doubt that economic beliefs have special appeal for Negroes.

Among Negroes, as among whites, greater education is associated with

[21] This helps to explain discrepant findings in the literature on the relation between race and anti-Semitism. A measure of anti-Semitism heavily weighted with economic items and a measure heavily weighted with noneconomic items will produce different results. For example, using an index combining both economic and noneconomic items, Marx found no consistent difference in anti-Semitism between Negroes and whites (op. cit., p. 146). However, Marx also notes that when items were examined individually, "Negroes were more likely to accept negative economic stereotypes about Jews than were whites" (p. 147).

[22] These figures exclude respondents who had three or more don't-know responses on the six-item Index of Noneconomic Anti-Semitism. When the opinionless are included, the rate of noneconomic anti-Semitism is 26 per cent for whites and 20 per cent for Negroes.

[23] This 22-percentage-point difference is greater than the difference that would have been found had the over-all Index of Anti-Semitic Beliefs been used. On that index 41 per cent of whites and 56 per cent of Negroes score as anti-Semitic when the opinionless are excluded; when they are included, the figures are 35 and 47 per cent.

The rates of economic anti-Semitism reported in the text exclude respondents who had two or more don't-know responses on the five-item index. When the opinionless are included, the rate of anti-Semitism is 28 per cent for whites and 45 per cent for Negroes.

lower rates of anti-Semitism (Table 41). Nevertheless, Negroes continue to be higher on economic anti-Semitism even when compared to whites at the same educational level. Though Negroes have had much less education than whites, this does little to explain their greater economic anti-Semitism. If Negroes were as educated as whites, their over-all rate of

Table 41. ECONOMIC AND NONECONOMIC ANTI-SEMITISM BY RACE AND EDUCATION

	Whites	Negroes	Percentage Difference
Per Cent High on Economic Anti-Semitism			
Grade school	55% (307)	65% (66)	+10
Some high school	38% (235)	60% (50)	+22
High school graduate	27% (436)	45% (38)	+18
Some college	20% (179)	41% (17)	+21
College graduate	10% (164)	18% (11)	+8
Total	32% (1,321)	54% (182)	+22
Per Cent High on Noneconomic Anti-Semitism			
Grade school	50% (307)	30% (53)	−20
Some high school	30% (230)	34% (50)	+4
High school graduate	26% (409)	19% (37)	−7
Some college	15% (172)	18% (17)	+3
College graduate	11% (163)	0 (11)	−11
Total	29% (1,281)	26% (168)	−3

economic anti-Semitism would be slightly reduced, from 54 per cent to 48 per cent.[24] It must be recognized, however, that Negroes and whites with the same amount of education have not generally received education of equal quality, and some of the remaining educational differences in

[24] For a description of the standardization procedure, see Chapter 6, footnote 4.

economic anti-Semitism may reflect this fact.[25] However, educational differences would not explain why Negroes overselect economic rather than noneconomic stereotypes. Moreover, there is additional evidence that factors peculiar to their situation in American society serve to increase economic anti-Semitism among Negroes.

In Chapter 6 it was reported that younger people are less anti-Semitic than the elderly. While true for whites, this is not true for Negroes. One of the more striking findings with regard to Negroes—and one that is consistent with the view that Negro anti-Semitism is rising—is that acceptance of anti-Semitic beliefs is disproportionately high in the youngest as well as the oldest age group. Whereas only 17 per cent of whites under 35 scored as anti-Semitic, among Negroes the figure is 49 per cent. This is higher than the rate of anti-Semitism for middle-aged Negroes (34 per cent), and almost as high as the rate for Negroes in the oldest age group (53 per cent).[26] Though young Negroes are more educated than older Negroes, they are no less anti-Semitic.[27]

On the Noneconomic Index the younger segments of the Negro community scored no higher than do young whites.[28] It is only with respect to economic beliefs that younger Negroes score comparatively high. Indeed if Negroes as a group score so much higher than whites on economic anti-Semitism, this is largely, though not entirely, due to the high level of economic anti-Semitism in the younger segments of the Negro population.

Because of the small size of the Negro sample (244 cases), and the skewed composition of the Negro population, it is impossible to examine age and education simultaneously. Analysis of other background factors is similarly hampered. The overwhelming majority of Negroes are Protes-

---

[25] At every level of education, Negroes have less knowledge of writers and contemporary politicians and score lower on other measures of cultural and intellectual sophistication.

[26] Because it is descriptively interesting to know how many at each age level are anti-Semitic, the figures reported above include the opinionless. If only those with no more than one don't-know response on the Index of Economic Anti-Semitism are considered, the results are essentially the same. The proportions anti-Semitic for young, middle-aged, and older whites are 20, 29, and 50 per cent. The corresponding figures for Negroes are 53, 44, and 70 per cent.

There is a considerable discrepancy in the rate of anti-Semitism among elderly Negroes depending on whether the opinionless are excluded or included. It is 53 per cent when they are included, 70 per cent when only those with one or no don't knows are considered. This discrepancy occurs because a sizable minority of the elderly were opinionless. In contrast, few young Negroes in the youngest age group were opinionless, and therefore the proportion scoring high on economic anti-Semitism is hardly changed when the opinionless are excluded.

[27] Young Negroes are also more antiwhite than older Negroes (Marx, op. cit., p. 185).

[28] About 20 per cent of Negroes score high on the Noneconomic Index regardless of age. Among whites the figures at the three age levels are: 16, 23, and 37 per cent.

tant and belong to conservative denominations. While Negro Catholics resemble white Catholics in being relatively low in anti-Semitism, only 18 Negroes in the sample are Catholic, too small a number to permit a firm conclusion. The same difficulty arises in considering region and urban-rural residence. The number of Negro respondents in each region is so small (there are none in rural areas outside the South) that generalization is precarious at best. The data indicate that Negroes in the South and North-east are higher in economic anti-Semitism than those in the Midwest and Northwest, and in each region the rate of economic anti-Semitism is higher for Negroes than for whites.[29]

Two basic findings have emerged from the analysis so far: first, that Negroes are more anti-Semitic than whites, but only with respect to economic beliefs; second, that their greater economic anti-Semitism goes beyond what can be explained by their generally lower level of educa-tion. Both findings are consonant with the view that Negro anti-Semitism is rooted in the special economic relations of Negroes with Jews.

Respondents were asked eight questions concerning different kinds of contact with Jews. Replies to such questions are always suspect and must be treated with caution since, as past research has shown, some respondents overreport their actual contacts. Another study in this series provides a convenient example of the kinds of problems that arise.[30] Respondents in that study were asked whether they had entertained a Jew in their homes during the past year. It was found that those low on anti-Semitism more often said they had entertained a Jew than did those high on anti-Semitism. Taken at face value, this finding suggests either that being free of prejudice encourages friendly contact with Jews, or conversely, that friendly contact with Jews reduces anti-Semitism. However, there was good reason to suspect that unprejudiced respondents were exaggerating their contacts. In the city studied, as well as in many surrounding communities, Jews comprised no more than 1 per cent of the total population. But 26 per cent of the sample reported that they had entertained a Jew in their home during the previous year. Either Jews in that city spent an extraordinary amount of time visiting with non-Jews or, as was apparently the case, a disproportionate number of unprejudiced respondents were

[29] The proportion of whites and Negroes in each region high on economic anti-Semitism is as follows: urban South, 26 per cent versus 48 per cent; rural South, 40 vs. 47; urban Northeast, 23 vs. 47; urban Midwest, 26 vs. 37; and urban North-west, 27 vs. 33. Thus the largest Negro-white differences occur in the urban Northeast (24 percentage points separate Negroes and whites) and the urban South (a percentage point difference of 22). These results are basically unchanged when the opinionless are excluded, though, to repeat, all figures are based on small numbers of cases.

[30] Charles Y. Glock, Gertrude J. Selznick, and Joe L. Spaeth, *The Apathetic Majority* (New York: Harper & Row, 1966), p. 192.

overreporting such contacts. Overreporting among the unprejudiced undoubtedly arises from a desire on their part to show that they are willing to entertain Jews, or from a tendency to interpret even casual encounters with Jews as actual visits. Whatever the reason, lack of prejudice can and does lead to overreporting.

It is also possible that prejudiced respondents overreport their contacts with Jews. A respondent who believes that Jews cheat in business may wish to justify his belief by claiming that it is rooted in actual experience with Jewish businessmen. Or when he encounters dishonest businessmen he may assume that they are Jewish even when they are not. Consequently, a finding that economic contact is associated with anti-Semitism may be false in its implication. Far from showing that contact with Jewish businessmen increases anti-Semitism, it might only reflect a possible tendency of anti-Semites to overreport nonexistent contacts with Jews. To avoid these difficulties, one would need more reliable data than can be obtained from surveys. The ideal method would be to observe interaction between Jews and non-Jews in concrete situations, and to measure its impact on anti-Semitism. While survey data fall far short of this ideal, they may nevertheless shed some light on the role that contact plays in the relation between race and anti-Semitism.

About the same proportion of whites and Negroes (44 per cent and 48 per cent) report contact with Jews in work or business.[31] This small quantitative difference between Negro and white contacts with Jews obviously masks a very large qualitative difference. Since Negroes are generally employed at lower occupational levels than are whites, work contact for Negroes often means working for Jews as domestics or in some other menial and poorly paid capacity. Whites on the other hand are reporting contacts in which they meet with Jews as peers or near-peers and in which no invidious social or economic distinctions are implied.

Table 42 shows how work contact relates to anti-Semitism for whites and Negroes. Among whites there is an inverse relation: those with contact are less likely to score as anti-Semitic on both economic and non-

---

[31] This figure appears highly inflated. However, the kinds of people who report having contact with Jews are the kinds who, given the geographical distribution of Jews, have the greatest opportunity of encountering Jews in their lives. In the rural South and Midwest, where there are few Jews, the proportion reporting contact with Jews in their work or businesses is at its lowest, roughly a quarter. In the urban Northwest and Northeast, where Jews are most concentrated, the proportions reporting work contact are at their highest: 52 and 63 per cent. It also happens that reported work contact steadily rises with greater education, from 28 per cent among grade schoolers to a high of 67 per cent among college graduates. This is as it should be since Jews tend to be of above-average education. That the data conform to expectations does not rule out all difficulties but does increase confidence in their relative validity.

Table 42.   ECONOMIC AND NONECONOMIC ANTI-SEMITISM BY RACE
AND WORK CONTACT WITH JEWS

Work Contact	Whites	Negroes
	Per Cent High on Economic Anti-Semitism	
Yes	26%	61%
	(621)	(95)
No	38	47
	(701)	(87)
Total	32%	54%
	(1,322)	(182)
	Per Cent High on Noneconomic Anti-Semitism	
Yes	23%	22%
	(613)	(93)
No	34	31
	(669)	(75)
Total	29%	26%
	(1,282)	(168)

economic anti-Semitism.[32] The same holds for Negroes on noneconomic
anti-Semitism. On the Economic Index, however, work contact among
Negroes is associated with greater anti-Semitism. For those without work
contact, the rate of economic anti-Semitism is 47 per cent; for those with
work contact it is 61 per cent.[33] This relation stands up when education
is controlled. Regardless of education, Negroes with work contact are higher
on economic anti-Semitism than Negroes without such contact.[34]

[32] Analysis shows that among whites the inverse relation of work contact to anti-
Semitism is explained by education; it is the more educated whites who are apt to
have contacts with Jews.
[33] Marx also reports that among Negroes impersonal contacts with Jews is associated
with greater anti-Semitism (op. cit., p. 158).
[34] The figures are as follows: grade school Negroes, 73 per cent versus 68 per cent;
high schoolers, 62 vs. 44; college educated, 33 vs. 20.
Earlier we questioned the validity of reports of economic contacts with Jews. The
reversal in Table 42, whereby work contact is associated with greater anti-Semitism
only among Negroes makes it doubtful that the relations are being seriously affected
by overreporting.
An early study found that, among Negroes, females are much higher on anti-
Semitism than males, and went on to speculate that Negro domestics working in
Jewish homes were contributing disproportionately to anti-Semitism. (Richard Simp-
son, "Negro-Jewish Prejudice: Authoritarianism and Some Social Variables as Correlates," Social Problems, Fall 1959, pp. 138–146.) In contrast, our data show
anti-Semitism, both economic and noneconomic, to be more prevalent among Negro
males than among females. For economic anti-Semitism, the figures are 62 per cent
for males, 47 per cent for females. However, among Negroes who have work con-

Essentially the same findings emerge when shopping at a Jewish-owned store is examined. Suspiciously large numbers of both whites and Negroes—65 and 84 per cent—report that they shop at a Jewish store. Nonetheless, whites who report shopping at Jewish stores are less anti-Semitic than those who do not; the same is true of Negroes when it comes to non-economic anti-Semitism. But unlike whites, Negroes who report shopping at Jewish stores are higher on economic anti-Semitism than those who do not.[35]

One conclusion that *cannot* be drawn from the findings is that Negroes have worse experiences with Jews than with whites in general. Not only would this be an incorrect inference from the data, logically it could not explain why Negroes are higher on economic anti-Semitism *than are whites*. The opposite contention, that Negroes actually have better relations with Jews than with other whites, also misses the point. In fact, it is irrelevant whether Negroes have better or worse experiences with Jews than with other whites.[36] What is relevant is whether Negroes have worse experiences with Jews than whites have. That Negro contacts with Jews are worse than white contacts with Jews hardly needs documentation. Exploitation and humiliation are built into the situation of most Negroes, and the experiences of Negroes with Jewish employers and shopkeepers are obviously worse than the corresponding experiences of whites. This would remain true even if it could be demonstrated that Negroes are less exploited by Jews than by non-Jewish whites.

Whites and Negroes also come into contact with different kinds of Jews. The Jews with whom Negroes come into contact undoubtedly tend to be older and less educated. Just as these factors contribute to anti-Semitism among non-Jewish whites, they contribute to anti-Negro prejudice among Jews.[37] Furthermore, Negroes and ghetto merchants tend to meet in direct,

---

tacts with Jews, the proportion high on economic anti-Semitism is about as great for women (59 per cent) as for men (62 per cent).

[35] Because so high a proportion of Negroes report shopping at Jewish stores, the analysis has focused on work contact. Insofar as it was possible to analyze the effect of shopping, the findings are similar to those for work contact.

[36] This fact *would* be relevant were we trying to understand why Negroes are more anti-Semitic than antiwhite. But we have no evidence that anti-Semitism exceeds anti-white feeling. In any event, our main preoccupation is with understanding why economic anti-Semitism is greater among Negroes than among whites.

[37] On every question concerning Negroes, Jews with less than a college education were more likely to give anti-Negro responses than were the college educated. Some examples are as follows: "To be frank, I would not want my child to go to school with a lot of Negroes": "Agree," 29 per cent versus 15 per cent. "Do you think there should be laws against marriage between Negroes and whites?": "Yes," 26 per cent versus 11 per cent. "These days you hear too much about the rights of minorities and too little about the rights of the majority": "Agree," 38 per cent versus 15 per cent.

face-to-face contact that easily engenders personal antagonism. As is frequently argued, while intergroup relations are often improved when contact
occurs between peers, prejudices are reinforced when one of the parties
in the interaction is defined as inferior. When the merchants are Jewish,
personal antagonism is apt to find expression in anti-Semitic stereotypes.

Negroes have heard the anti-Semitic beliefs current in the larger society
and, *more than whites*, find them confirmed in their own experience with
Jews. Numerous caveats can be appended to this statement: Jews are
probably no worse than other merchants in the ghetto; the behavior of
Jewish merchants has little or nothing to do with their Jewishness, but is
characteristic of marginal businessmen generally; the economic realities of
the ghetto, not the personal attributes of ghetto merchants, are responsible
for the kinds of business practices that prevail.[38] However valid, these are
theoretical niceties that have little relevance to the average Negro in the
ghetto, who is relatively uneducated as well as materially deprived. He has
heard that Jews are unethical, untrustworthy, and indifferent to the fate of
others, and his experience seems to confirm these images. If there were a
historic image of Christians as being exploitative and dishonest, Negroes
would find abundant grounds in their experience for being anti-Christian.
The growth of the Black Muslim movement is testimony to the fact that
some Negroes are responding to their experiences by becoming anti-Christian as well as antiwhite. The matter boils down to this: the kinds of anti-
Semitic beliefs that are current in the larger society provide a meaningful
and ready-made framework into which Negroes can place their personal
experience with Jews.

The presence of anti-Semitism in our society makes "being Jewish" a
salient characteristic of the "bad" Jewish employer, shopkeeper, landlord.
But there is no ideology that makes "being Christian" a salient characteristic of the "bad" Christian. Prejudice and superstition resemble each other
in many ways. Take, for example, the superstition that if a black cat crosses
one's path, some misfortune will certainly occur. The consequence of such
a superstition is to make black cats, *but only black cats*, highly visible.
Nonblack cats are hardly noticed, since the superstition implies that they
pose no danger. The very logic of a superstitious belief discourages its
disconfirmation. That ill fortune sometimes occurs when a nonblack cat
crosses one's path goes unobserved; but when a black cat crosses one's
path, it is a simple matter to find some instance of misfortune, no matter
how slight or delayed in time. Moreover, so long as superstitious beliefs are
not ruled out in principle, hearsay evidence concerning the conjunction of
black cats and misfortune tends to be credited and accepted. For both

---

[38] See David Caplovitz, *The Poor Pay More* (New York: Free Press of Glencoe,
1967) for an analysis of the economic and social realities of the ghetto economy.

superstitions and prejudiced beliefs, rejection seems to depend on a fairly high level of education and intellectual sophistication.

In accepting anti-Semitic beliefs, whether or not supported by contacts with Jews, Negroes are making the same unwarranted generalizations and exhibiting the same gullibility as do whites when they accept anti-Semitic beliefs (or anti-Negro beliefs for that matter). It is hardly relevant that the same beliefs describe non-Jewish whites as well; who can doubt that, from the Negro's perspective, whites in general tend to be shrewd and tricky, shady, and not very honest in business, that they control banking and are careless of the welfare of others.[39] And, indeed, many Negroes have developed hostility toward whites *qua* whites. It would be astonishing were it otherwise.

Since other groups do not do so, Negroes can hardly be expected to reject pejorative statements about Jews on the sophisticated ground that such pejorative statements hold of shopkeepers or employers in general, rather than of Jews in particular. Jews themselves are not the "cause" of the disproportionate amount of economic anti-Semitism to be found among Negroes. Rather Negro anti-Semitism is traceable to two factors: the historic presence of economic anti-Semitism in our society and the deprivation and exploitation inherent in the situation of the American Negro. The presence of Jews in the ghetto economy—regardless of how they compare to other whites—is enough to bring these factors together, resulting in greater economic anti-Semitism among Negroes.

We do not wish to exaggerate the role of economic contact in Negro anti-Semitism. Many Negroes who have economic encounters with Jews do not subscribe to economic anti-Semitism, and economic anti-Semitism frequently exists among Negroes who have no contacts. Some Negroes exhibit economic anti-Semitism simply because they are Americans and live in a society in which such beliefs remain current. Yet if Negroes had no economic contact with Jews, or if Negroes had the same kind of economic contact with Jews that whites have, Negro-white differences in economic anti-Semitism would be smaller. Negro economic anti-Semitism has an existential element in it that appears to be absent among whites. Among whites, anti-Semitism tends to be largely a hearsay phenomenon, with little or no relation to actual Jews known; it thus tends to be a cogni-

---

[39] There has been little research on Negro images of whites. However, Pettigrew reports several old studies indicating that Negro images of whites closely correspond to traditional anti-Semitic stereotypes (*op. cit.*, p. 42). And as Marx notes: ". . . where Jews do not predominate in the ghetto, the particular ethnic group that does is likely to be the recipient of economically inspired hostility. . . . Drake and Cayton [*Black Metropolis*, p. 432] note that in New Orleans, where Italians are predominant in Negro areas, they are targets of attack, and in the past, when Negroes had disproportionate contact with the Irish, considerable hostility was felt toward them [B. Berry, *Race and Ethnic Relations*, p. 448]" (*op. cit.*, p. 167).

tive phenomenon with education strongly determining the likelihood that an individual will accept or reject the anti-Semitic beliefs he becomes acquainted with. Among Negroes, most anti-Semitism, whether economic or noneconomic, is also a hearsay phenomenon, basically cognitive in nature and dependent on education. However, for Negroes, economic anti-Semitism is also an existential phenomenon involving experience as well as hearsay. This reality element, we have been at pains to reiterate, does not consist in worse treatment of Negroes by Jews than by whites in general. It consists rather in the fact that the traditional beliefs of economic anti-Semitism describe Negro experiences with whites in general, and therefore their experiences with Jews in particular.

Discriminatory Attitudes

On the questions concerning the anti-Semitic candidate and the anti-Jewish immigration law, the response of Negroes was not markedly different from that of whites. In other respects, despite their greater economic anti-Semitism, Negroes are a good deal less likely than whites to hold discriminatory attitudes. Almost all Negroes—91 per cent—said that the members of a club do not have a right to exclude Jews; the figure for whites was 69 per cent. Moreover, while only a third of whites (31 per cent) indicated a willingness to combat social club discrimination in practice as well as in principle, twice as many Negroes (68 per cent) did so. More Negroes than whites (68 per cent versus 51 per cent) said they would not be disturbed at all if their party nominated a Jew as President. Even when Negroes scored as extreme anti-Semites, 89 per cent said that employers should hire the best man, whether he is Jewish or not. The corresponding figure for whites is 70 per cent.

The finding that Negroes are comparatively low on support of discrimination is analogous to the earlier finding that Southerners are especially high on social discrimination against Jews. Just as discriminatory feeling against Negroes leads Southerners to a disproportionately greater defense of discrimination against Jews, so Negroes respond to their own circumstances as an oppressed minority by a disproportionately greater rejection of discrimination against Jews.

Evaluation of the Findings

Given the nature of anti-Semitism and the conditions of economic hardship that persist in the ghetto, it is hardly surprising that economic anti-Semitism has special appeal for Negroes. As an ideology anti-Semitism blames Jews for social and economic ills. In a society where anti-Semitic beliefs are indigenous and in which Jews are a prominent part of the ghetto economy, it would be nothing short of miraculous to find Negroes immune to economic anti-Semitism. As among whites, however, the extent of immunity is largely a function of education. It takes intellectual sophistication to resist blaming the economic ills of the ghetto on the immediate agents of exploitation, whether Jewish or not, and to see these ills as products of impersonal social and economic forces that transcend the responsibility of particular individuals.

Does this mean that the Jew is becoming a scapegoat for Negro frustrations and dissatisfactions? According to the scapegoat theory, anti-Semitism is a displacement or ¬edirection of hostility away from groups too powerful or legitimate to attack, and toward a powerless and already maligned group such as the Jews. Anti-Semitism is thus viewed as a secondary hostility stemming from a more basic and primary hostility whose expression is blocked. Two versions of the scapegoat theory can be distinguished, depending on whether the primary object of hostility is seen as too legitimate or too powerful. If it is seen as legitimate, the psychological response is typically guilt; hostility is repressed and passes into the unconscious. There it joins forces with the primitive and sadistic Id, thus accounting for the excessive hatred and violence that has historically been directed against Jews. On the other hand, when the primary object of hostility is seen as too powerful, hostility is blocked out of a realistic fear of retribution, and need not entail an active act of repression. This weaker version of the scapegoat theory would explain the excessive hatred and violence often directed against Jews as an expression of the intense feelings of frustration and powerlessness experienced by submerged groups.

It seems clear that Negroes are not using Jews as a scapegoat in either of these ways. Another study in this series found it rare for Negroes to be anti-Semitic without being antiwhite as well,[40] and, in recent disturbances Negroes have taken action against whites as such, without singling out Jews for special treatment. If Jews are sometimes targets of Negro aggression, they appear to be targets simply in their status as whites. To put the matter another way, being white, they would be targets even if they were not Jewish.

In economic anti-Semitism Negroes find a language for describing their experiences and expressing their resentments. Moreover, as Allport cautions: "What seems like displacement, may, in some instances, be an aggression directed against the true source of frustration."[41] Many Negroes have in mind not the mythical Jew, but Jewish businessmen who are implicated in an economic system that exploits them. So long as this is

[40] Marx, *op. cit.*, Chapter 7.
[41] Allport, *The Nature of Prejudice* (New York: Anchor, 1958), p. 332.

the case, Negroes and Jews are engaged, in part, not in mutual prejudice, but in a genuine conflict of interests. Such conflict can, and does, spill over into the realm of prejudice. This is true when Jewish businessmen are singled out for blame, when the behavior of Jewish businessmen is seen as somehow derived from their Jewishness, or when resentment against Jewish businessmen is directed against Jews generally. Ironically, in accepting anti-Semitic beliefs Negroes bear witness to their participation in Western culture and its symbols.

PART III EXPLANATION

Since the publication of The Authoritarian Personality *in 1950, there has been heavy emphasis in the literature on the role of psychological factors in prejudice. This emphasis is thrown into question by the massive relation between education and anti-Semitism. Among those with a grade school education, 66 per cent score as anti-Semitic; among college graduates only 16 per cent do so. Part III now asks: What is it about lack of education that accounts for its strong association with anti-Semitic prejudice?*

8 : Education and Anti-Semitism

The literature on anti-Semitism is especially rich in theory and speculation. The many aspects of anti-Semitism, and the many different questions that can be asked about it, are bound to generate a diversity of theories, each partial and limited in scope. Few writers, however, specify the precise aspect of anti-Semitism they are trying to explain. Limited theories are presented as general theories, explanations of one aspect as explanations of the whole. Even when special theories are presented as such, they are often generalized by other writers beyond their proper domain. For these reasons the literature on anti-Semitism gives the impression of far greater theoretical contradiction than actually exists.

In the interests both of accurate description and theoretical clarity, a number of distinctions are necessary. Routine anti-Semitism cannot be equated with virulent anti-Semitism, conventional anti-Semitism with political anti-Semitism. Acceptance of anti-Semitic beliefs must be distinguished from their expression, discriminatory attitudes from discriminatory behavior. Other divisions are necessary—between the historic and the contemporary sources of anti-Semitism and between the origins and the functions of anti-Semitic beliefs. The reasons people accept such beliefs and the reasons they cling to them are also different. No single theory can possibly encompass all these facets of anti-Semitism, and a diversity of theories necessarily results. Implicitly or explicitly, different writers have different aspects of anti-Semitism in mind, and their theories vary accordingly.

In the following analysis only one aspect of anti-Semitism is considered —the greater acceptance of anti-Semitic beliefs by the less educated. However, knowing why people accept anti-Semitic beliefs is a first step toward understanding why they support or engage in discrimination.

Two Explanatory Models

All anti-Semitic beliefs have both a cognitive and an emotive component. Emphasis in the past has been on the emotive or expressive aspects of anti-Semitism. Largely ignored has been the sheerly cognitive dimension. Viewed in their cognitive aspect, anti-Semitic beliefs are intellectually unenlightened. They are generalizations about an entire group, usually accepted uncritically and on the basis of hearsay. When not patently false, they typically involve false inferences about Jewish motives and purposes. Viewed in this way, anti-Semitic beliefs are a small subset of a very large class of unsophisticated and cognitively primitive beliefs. Among their closest relatives are superstitious and magical beliefs, characteristic of almost any preliterate or semiliterate group.

Anti-Semitic beliefs also have a distinctively emotive component: they are pejorative, derogatory, often hostile. Those who accept anti-Semitic stereotypes accept them as fact just as the superstitious accept their beliefs as fact. But facts have normative implications: the superstitious avoid black cats; anti-Semites avoid Jews. They do so because anti-Semitic beliefs, in addition to being statements of alleged fact, are reasons for disliking Jews. In learning anti-Semitic beliefs, the individual learns what is allegedly true about Jews and simultaneously what is allegedly wrong with them.

Not all anti-Semitic beliefs are equally unenlightened and equally pejorative. That Jews stick together too much is a belief neither markedly divorced from reality nor necessarily evocative of hostility. But people who believe that Jews are so shrewd and tricky that others don't have a fair chance in competition, or that Jews have too much power in the business world, not only exhibit lack of cognitive sophistication but also accept a hostile characterization. Cognitive and emotive factors are closely intertwined in many socially relevant beliefs. Anti-Semitic beliefs, in common with other prejudiced beliefs, are examples par excellence of this fact.

While the cognitive and the emotive content of anti-Semitic beliefs can be conceptually distinguished, in real life they are inseparable. Both are "contained" in the same belief. One individual may accept an anti-Semitic belief because he is positively attracted to its pejorative emotive content, but in doing so, he becomes involved in a cognitive distortion. Another may accept an anti-Semitic belief because he lacks the intellectual sophistication to reject it, but in doing so, he accepts a derogatory and hostile stereotype. Both individuals accept anti-Semitic beliefs, but it is impossible to say, without further investigation, how each came to his anti-Semitism.

That anti-Semitic beliefs have an emotive dimension does not necessarily mean they are accepted out of emotional need. Nevertheless, most theories of anti-Semitism have been committed to the primacy of the emotive factor:

They automatically assume that, when an individual accepts an anti-Semitic belief, he does so for emotive rather than for cognitive reasons. Emotive theories characteristically ground the anti-Semitism of the individual either in some form of personal psychopathology or in existential deprivations and frustrations.[1] Instead of anti-Semitic beliefs being seen as engendering hostility toward Jews, they are seen as satisfying some antecedent "need" to be hostile. The capacity of anti-Semitic beliefs to "satisfy" or "objectify" this presumed need is then offered as the explanation of why individuals adopt them.

Many emotive theories are based on the "frustration-aggression" model: individuals in frustrating situations, usually of an economic or social nature, experience feelings of aggression, and these feelings are expressed in acceptance of anti-Semitic beliefs and in action against minorities. Other emotive theories invoke more subtle psychodynamic processes. In psychodynamic theory emotional conflict—and efforts to "resolve" such conflict through projection, displacement, reaction-formation—is regarded as more basic to anti-Semitic prejudice than the stresses of material deprivation. Nevertheless some psychological need to be hostile is always posited in the emotive approach, whether this is a direct response to existential frustration or a more indirect outcome of inner psychic conflict.

Emotive theories do not ignore the fact that anti-Semitic beliefs are intellectually and morally benighted. On the contrary, they regard anti-Semitic beliefs as the best evidence that some form of pressing psychological need is involved in their acceptance: only a person driven by inner conflict, or the pressures of existential frustration, could accept the fantasies and untruths embodied in anti-Semitic ideology. It would be incorrect to say that the cognitive and moral distortions implicit in anti-Semitic prejudice have gone unrecognized in the literature. But they are customarily regarded as secondary and epiphenomenal, derivatives of a more primary emotive factor—the role that prejudiced beliefs play in the psychic economy of the individual.

It is also possible to view anti-Semitic beliefs as a species of unenlightened belief, accepted in much the same way as other unenlightened beliefs and for much the same reasons of ignorance, cognitive incompetence, and lack of intellectual sophistication.[2] To emphasize the benighted nature of anti-

[1] T. W. Adorno et al., *The Authoritarian Personality* (New York: John Wiley and Sons, 1964) is the most outstanding example of the emphasis on personality needs. An example emphasizing the role of existential deprivation and frustration is Bruno Bettelheim and Morris Janowitz, *Social Change and Prejudice* (New York: Free Press of Glencoe, 1964).

[2] ". . . prejudices against minority groups are learned. They may reflect deep, irrational personality processes, but they need not. . . . There is the real possibility that . . . prejudices may be learned in the same way that we learn that the world is round (or flat, or held up on the back of a giant turtle)" [Robin M. Williams, Jr., *Strangers Next Door* (Englewood Cliffs, N.J.: Prentice-Hall, 1964), p. 90].

Semitic beliefs is not to deny they are hostile beliefs which, *once accepted*, can serve social and psychological functions. The cognitive approach does suggest, however, that lack of intellectual sophistication is sufficient reason for accepting anti-Semitic stereotypes, especially when they are promulgated by authoritative persons in the individual's environment. On this view, the uneducated accept many unenlightened beliefs, including anti-Semitic beliefs, primarily because they lack cognitive criteria for rejecting them.

The cognitive approach looks for positive reasons why people reject anti-Semitic beliefs. These it finds in the cognitive criteria which education provides. Among these are the rules of evidence and inference. As descriptions of whole groups, most prejudiced beliefs are either untrue or overgeneralized. Cognitive criteria may also be found in intellectual appreciation of the nature and social implications of a democratic order. In addition to being false and inaccurate, most prejudiced beliefs are incongruent with democratic ideals. While science and democracy are abstract values, they are not empty; they contain criteria for evaluating socially relevant beliefs and for deciding on the appropriateness of many feelings and actions. The ultimate test of the viability of these values is whether they are strong enough to act as a countervailing influence, not only to the incidental social pressures to which individuals are exposed, but to the primitive psychological impulses which, if Freud and history are to be believed, are the common heritage of man in society. On the cognitive approach, the unsophisticated become anti-Semitic largely by default; they accept anti-Semitic beliefs, not out of some antecedent psychological need, but for want of intellectual and moral reasons for rejecting them.

The massive relation between education and anti-Semitism is itself strong evidence for the cognitive model. Insofar as scientific and democratic values represent one avenue to the rejection of anti-Semitic beliefs, one would expect anti-Semitism to decline with greater education. Ideally, the educational institutions of our society are committed to the promulgation of these values, and the relatively low level of prejudice found at higher levels of education is a measure of their success. Conversely, the finding in Chapter 5 that the anti-Semitism of the uneducated is not explained by their low incomes or their occupational status casts doubt on the emotive theory of anti-Semitism. If people accepted anti-Semitic beliefs as an outlet for feelings of frustration, then one would expect the less educated to be high on anti-Semitism largely because they are relatively deprived. But one of the striking findings of Part II is that the uneducated are comparatively high on anti-Semitism no matter what other characteristics describe them. This is only indirect evidence for the cognitive model, however. For more direct evidence we turn to an examination of some of the ways in which the more and less educated differ in cognitive style, in knowledge, and in their commitment to democratic values.

Simplism

Respondents were asked to agree or disagree with the following nine statements:

1. People can be divided into two distinct classes—the weak and the strong.
2. No weakness or difficulty can hold us back if we have enough will power.
3. Reading the stars can tell us a great deal about the future.
4. Much of our lives are controlled by plots hatched in secret places.
5. Sex crimes, such as rape and attacks on children, deserve more than mere imprisonment; such criminals ought to be publicly whipped or worse.
6. Getting to the top is more a matter of luck than ability.
7. A little practical experience is worth more than all the books put together.
8. The answers to this country's problems are much simpler than the experts would have us think.
9. I don't like to hear a lot of arguments I disagree with.

Agreement with these statements is strongly related to education (Table 43). The proportion agreeing that people can be divided into two classes, the weak and the strong, declines from 68 per cent among grade schoolers to 50, 28, and finally 20 per cent among college graduates. Belief in astrology similarly declines from 26 to 5 per cent. For each of the nine items the impact of education is consistent and strong.

The first five items in Table 43 are taken directly or in revised form from the well-known F scale developed in *The Authoritarian Personality* as a covert measure of anti-Semitism. In the original study, F beliefs were regarded as symptomatic expressions of deep-lying personality trends laid down in early childhood and characterized as authoritarian or fascist (hence the designation of the scale as the fascism or F scale). This psychological interpretation of the origin of F beliefs found apparent support in the failure of *The Authoritarian Personality*, using small *ad hoc* samples, to find strong educational differences.[3] Subsequent research based on more representative samples has found scores on F to be highly dependent on education.[4] In the present study, 59 per cent of grade schoolers, 36 per cent of high schoolers, and 20 per cent of college graduates scored high on F.[5]

[3] Nowhere in the original volume was the relation of education and F reported. Data are presented only for the relation between education and ethnocentrism (Adorno *et al.*, *op. cit.*, p. 287).

[4] For example, Herbert H. Hyman and Paul B. Sheatsley, "'The Authoritarian Personality'—A Methodological Critique," in Richard Christie and Marie Jahoda (eds.), *Studies in the Scope and Method of "The Authoritarian Personality"* (New York: Free Press of Glencoe, 1954), pp. 50–122.

[5] The first five items in Table 43 were combined into an index and scores of 3 or more are designated as High on F.

Table 43.   ACCEPTANCE OF INDIVIDUAL SIMPLISTIC BELIEFS BY EDUCATION

	Grade School	High School	Some College	College Graduate	Total
1. No weakness or difficulty can hold us back if we have enough will power.	80%	80%	70%	66%	78%
2. Sex crimes, such as rape and attacks on children, deserve more than mere imprisonment; such criminals ought to be publicly whipped, or worse.	70	58	42	38	57
3. People can be divided into two distinct classes—the weak and the strong.	68	50	28	20	50
4. Much of our lives is controlled by plots hatched in secret places.	33	24	20	15	25
5. Reading the stars can tell us a great deal about the future.	26	16	5	5	16
6. I don't like to hear a lot of arguments I disagree with.	76	64	53	40	64
7. A little practical experience is worth more than all the books put together.	74	58	42	29	58
8. The answers to this country's problems are much simpler than the experts would have us think.	37	27	19	16	28
9. Getting to the top is more a matter of luck than ability.	33	11	9	7	17
100% (N) =	(536)	(957)	(226)	(193)	(1,913)

The strong association between lack of education and score on F led two of the earliest critics of *The Authoritarian Personality* to suggest that F beliefs resemble other beliefs characteristic of the less educated, that they are primarily indicators of lack of cognitive sophistication and do not deserve to be singled out as having unique relevance to prejudice.[6] On their face value alone it is evident that—whatever else they may or may not represent—F beliefs are unenlightened beliefs and embody a primitive cognitive style. Moreover, statistical analysis shows that all nine items in Table 43 are so highly intercorrelated that any combination of them could serve as a summary measure of cognitive sophistication. From the nine statements above, items 1, 2, 7, 8, and 9 were chosen. Because each statement represents an intellectually simplistic belief or attitude the index is

[6] Hyman and Sheatsley, *op. cit.*

called the Index of Simplism. By "simplism" is meant first of all an intellectual failure to comprehend complexity and to accept ambiguity, indeterminancy, and open-mindedness in the realm of belief and cognitive judgment. The Index is more specifically focused than this, however. It also measures a failure to comprehend and appreciate the complexities of social reality. Implicit in these intellectually primitive beliefs is an equally primitive ethic; apparent are impatience with social problems, intolerance of dissent, attitudes of blame, and indifference to the suffering of others. Those familiar with *The Authoritarian Personality* will recognize the many respects in which we agree with the original interpretation of the manifest content of F beliefs.[7] What is at issue is not the face meaning of F beliefs but the reasons they are accepted. Does acceptance of F beliefs have psychological sources and intellectual consequences, as the original study claimed? Or does acceptance of F beliefs have intellectual sources and psychological consequences, as their relation to education strongly suggests?

Table 44.   SIMPLISM BY EDUCATION

Simplism[a]	Grade School	High School	Some College	College Graduate	Total
Low (0–1)	9%	18%	34%	49%	20%
Medium (2–3)	40	48	51	42	46
High (4–5)	51	34	15	9	34
100% (N) =	(528)	(949)	(222)	(192)	(1,893)

[a]Index consists of Items 1, 3, 6, 7, and 9 in Table 43.

The relation between education and simplism is hardly different from that between education and F (Table 44). As education increases, simplism systematically decreases. A striking feature of Table 44 is that the scores of grade schoolers and college graduates are mirror images of each other: Grade schoolers are as apt to hold simplistic beliefs as college graduates are to reject them. Only 9 per cent of grade schoolers are low on simplism; only 9 per cent of college graduates are high. Conversely, half the grade schoolers (51 per cent) score High, half the college graduates (49 per cent) score Low. These comparisons dramatically illustrate the implications of education for a person's intellectual sophistication and social attitudes.

[7] We should like to emphasize that undue importance should not be given to the precise content of the items that make up the Index of Simplism. Both the original F scale and the Index of Simplism are samples from a very large universe of beliefs and attitudes that indicate lack of intellectual sophistication. One would expect education to correlate strongly with any such measure, regardless of the content of its component items.

It is hardly surprising to find lack of education associated with lack of intellectual sophistication. Far more significant is the implicit relation between lack of education and lack of moral sensibility. On certain issues where their economic self-interests are involved, as in the case of social welfare measures, the uneducated are more likely than the educated to favor liberal and progressive policy.[8] But as their scores on simplism, F, and prejudice demonstrate, the uneducated do not generally exhibit compassion for the underdog or sympathetic understanding of the plight of others. On the contrary, their lack of cognitive sophistication leads them to accept beliefs whose implications are antihumanitarian, blaming, and socially divisive.

Because of the relation between lack of education and simplism, we stress the primitive intellectual content of simplism and similar measures. However, we do not deny that the Index of Simplism measures a general emotional or psychological capacity to tolerate differences. On the contrary, we argue that unenlightened beliefs, even when they are accepted largely because individuals lack intellectual and moral criteria for rejecting them, have profound consequences for attitudes, personality, and behavior. It would be misleading to stress the cognitive sources of F without also stressing their adverse psychological and moral consequences.

Holding simplistic beliefs is highly associated with anti-Semitic prejudice (Table 45). As simplism goes from low to medium to high, the proportion anti-Semitic rises from 17 to 39 to 64 per cent. The overall impact of simplism (47 percentage points) is almost as great as that of education (50 percentage points). While somewhat reduced when education is controlled, the relation of simplism to anti-Semitic prejudice continues strong at every level of education.

The association between F (or simplism) and anti-Semitic prejudice has been used to argue that acceptance and rejection of anti-Semitism is determined by basic personality. Such an interpretation is far too strong and unwarranted by the data. As we have argued, anti-Semitic beliefs are a small subset of a much larger number of unenlightened beliefs that people accept, especially when they are uneducated. That anti-Semitic beliefs are highly associated with other unenlightened beliefs hardly requires a recondite explanation. The less educated the individual, the less likely he is to

---

[8] Using data from the present study, we analyzed the social class and ideological sources of support for Goldwater and Johnson in the 1964 election. The data showed that workers were disproportionately in favor of Medicare and that this (or some related) factor helped to explain the large working class vote. However, many of the same workers agreed with Goldwater's stand on noneconomic issues. In short, the pocketbook voting of workers cannot be taken as a sign of a liberal political philosophy, as subsequent elections have made evident. "Social Class, Ideology, and Voting Preference," in Celia Heller (ed.), *Structured Social Inequality: A Reader in Comparative Social Stratification* (New York: Macmillan, 1969), pp. 216–226.

Table 45.   ANTI-SEMITIC BELIEF BY EDUCATION AND SIMPLISM
(per cent anti-Semitic)

Simplism	Grade School	High School	Some College	College Graduate	Total
High (4–5)	74%	59%	42%	38%	64%
	(228)	(282)	(31)	(16)	(557)
Medium (2–3)	60	38	26	21	39
	(159)	(396)	(102)	(76)	(733)
Low (0–1)	46	14	21	8	17
	(32)	(138)	(72)	(92)	(336)
Total	66%	41%	26%	16%	
	(423)	(822)	(209)	(185)	

possess the requisite cognitive and ethical criteria for rejecting all such beliefs, whatever their content. As Table 45 indicates, one reason the uneducated accept anti-Semitic beliefs is that they *generally* accept unenlightened beliefs.[9]

However, even at equal levels of simplism, the more educated continue to exhibit lower rates of anti-Semitism. A few college graduates scored high on simplism, and are more anti-Semitic than college graduates who scored low. But they are still less likely to be anti-Semitic than high scorers at lower levels of education. It is evident that other factors besides a simplistic belief system are involved in the tendency of the uneducated to accept anti-Semitic beliefs.

Knowledge and Support of Democratic Norms

According to the original conception of the F scale, high scorers have antidemocratic or authoritarian personalities formed in early life. Such an interpretation has roots, not only in psychoanalytic theory, but in a long-standing philosophic tradition that conceives moral attitudes to be little more than emotive preferences. Sometimes these have been traced to personality make-up, sometimes to the exigencies of social-class position or life situation. However, democratic principles are abstract and complex, and their apprehension requires cognitive sophistication. For this reason alone one would expect the uneducated to be less committed to them. Modern education would have to be judged a failure were the uneducated as prepared as the educated to comprehend the ideals and purposes, the objective conditions and social implications, of a democratic order.

[9] When degree of simplism is controlled, the educational difference in anti-Semitism is reduced from 50 to an average of 38 percentage points.

That cognitive support for democratic practices is weak among the uneducated is evident in their relative lack of knowledge of civil libertarian norms. We already know from their scores on simplism and anti-Semitism that fewer of the uneducated are committed to norms of tolerance. The data now show that more of the uneducated are ignorant of the democratic provisions of the Constitution; in other words many are unaware of at least one sense in which they "should" be tolerant of diversity and dissent.

Respondents were asked two questions about the United States Constitution. The first posed a hypothetical situation: "Suppose Congress wanted to pass a law saying that groups who disagree with our form of government could not hold public meetings or make speeches. As far as you know, would Congress have a right under the Constitution to pass such a law?" While a majority (65 per cent) of the sample correctly answered "no," the proportion greatly varied with education. Among college graduates, knowledge was at virtually maximum levels; nearly 9 out of 10 (87 per cent) said the law would be unconstitutional. Among high schoolers the figure dropped to 67; among grade schoolers, to 48 per cent.

The second question asked whether Congress has a right under the Constitution to pass a law requiring that the President believe in God. To this question only half the sample correctly answered "no." But again, knowledge was strongly correlated with education. Only 33 per cent of grade schoolers said the law would be unconstitutional compared to 53 per cent of high schoolers and 72 per cent of college graduates.

Respondents were then asked whether they favored the restrictive laws.[10] Even among college graduates, 1 out of 5 (19 per cent) favored the restrictive speech law, but this figure increases to 28 per cent among high schoolers and 39 per cent among grade schoolers. As many as 46 per cent of college graduates favored religious restrictions on the President but again this figure rises to 76 per cent among grade schoolers. Comparatively, the less educated neither know nor favor the official civil libertarian norms of our society.

On both questions the relation between knowledge of the Constitution and civil libertarianism is very strong (Table 46). Those who knew the norms generally supported them. Those who did not know the norms tended to oppose them. The relation is not perfect, however. Some people—especially at lower levels of education—knew but disagreed with the provisions of the Constitution. Among those who knew that the restrictive speech law was unconstitutional, 26 per cent of grade schoolers and 20 per cent of high schoolers favored it, compared to 10 per cent of college graduates. Thus the less educated are more often in conscious disagreement with the

---

[10] For respondents who correctly said that the restrictive laws were unconstitutional, the question was prefaced with: "Supposing it were Constitutional. . . ."

Table 46.   SUPPORT OF THE CONSTITUTION BY KNOWLEDGE
OF THE CONSTITUTION

Reply to: "Suppose Congress wanted to pass a law saying that groups who disagree with our form of government could not hold public meetings or make speeches. As far as you know, would Congress have the right under the Constitution to pass such a law? Would you be in favor of a law saying that groups who disagree with our form of government could not hold public meetings or make speeches, or opposed to it?"[a]

| | Knowledge of the Constitution | | |
Support of the Constitution	Knowledgeable	Not Knowledgeable	Total
Yes	83%	40%	77%
No	15	53	19
Don't know	2	7	4
Total	65%	35%	
	(1,239)	(669)	

Reply to: "How would you feel about a law saying that the President must be a man who believes in God? As far as you know, could Congress have the right under the Constitution to pass such a law? Would you be in favor of a law saying that the President must be a man who believes in God, or opposed to it?"[a]

| | Knowledge of the Constitution | | |
Support of the Constitution	Knowledgeable	Not Knowledgeable	Total
Yes	61%	9%	52%
No	36	88	44
Don't know	3	3	3
Total	50%	50%	
	(953)	(951)	

[a]Respondents who thought the law was unconstitutional were asked the same question with the introduction: "Suppose it were Constitutional?"

Constitution in the sense that they know the norms but disagree with them.[11] Nevertheless, at every level of education, most who knew the constitutional norms supported them.[12]

The strong association between knowledge and support of the Constitu-

[11] Much the same happens on the President question. Among those who knew that religious restrictions on the President are unconstitutional, 43 per cent of grade schoolers, 39 per cent of high schoolers, and 19 per cent of college graduates still favored them.

[12] Knowledge of the Constitution reduces the relation between education and support of the Constitution to about half its original strength. In other words, one reason that the uneducated tend to be less civil libertarian than the educated is that they tend to be less informed of democratic norms.

tion is as much a case of attitudes influencing knowledge as the other way around. Evidently those who were uninformed about the Constitution responded according to their attitudes toward civil liberties, allowing their preferences to color their cognitive judgments. Nor can it be assumed that all who opposed the restrictive laws did so with specific knowledge of the Constitution. More plausible is that, especially at higher levels of education, people are aware that the Constitution is generally designed to protect diversity of belief and to uphold a secular government, and were able to infer the unconstitutionality of the two laws on which they were queried. While some guessing undoubtedly occurred at all educational levels, the fact remains that the educated tended to guess right, the uneducated wrong. One may wish to question the depth of knowledge of the educated, but it was enough to allow them to draw the proper inferences.

On the other hand, lack of knowledge of the Constitution creates an intellectual and moral vacuum in which narrow perspectives can operate. Those uninformed of official norms experience no intellectual obstacle in opposing civil liberties, and if they tend to be intolerant can be so with a good conscience. An absence of knowledge means an absence of constraint; it leaves the individual free to assimilate whatever prejudices exist in his environment.

Knowledge of the Constitution is inversely associated with anti-Semitism: as knowledge decreases from both norms to one to neither, anti-Semitism increases from 28 to 48 to 59 per cent. Since low knowledge is associated both with lack of education and with simplism, Table 47 examines the simultaneous relation of all three factors to anti-Semitism. Three observations are important.

1. Among people who knew neither Constitutional norm, there is relatively little difference in anti-Semitism by education (third row). Among the two college-educated groups over 40 per cent are anti-Semitic. This is almost as many as among high schoolers (54 per cent) and grade schoolers (68 per cent).[13] Thus among those ignorant of the Constitution the original educational difference of 50 percentage points is now reduced to 22. However, only 7 per cent of college graduates knew neither norm. Theoretically, if college graduates were as uninformed as the less educated they would be almost as anti-Semitic. In actuality, college graduates are far more knowledgeable of official norms, and this is one reason for their comparatively low rate of anti-Semitism.

2. By itself knowledge of the Constitution has little effect on anti-

---

[13] We have found two "pure" knowledge factors affecting anti-Semitism among college graduates: not knowing all four writers (Chapter 5) and being uninformed on the Constitution. The two kinds of knowledge are of course highly related.

Table 47.   ANTI-SEMITIC BELIEF BY EDUCATION, SIMPLISM, AND KNOWLEDGE
OF THE CONSTITUTION

(per cent anti-Semitic)

Knowledge of the Constitution[a]	Simplism[b]	Grade School	High School	Some College	College Graduate
Knew neither norm	High	72% (104)	60% (127)	47% (15)	c (8)
	Low	53 (32)	31 (32)	38 (13)	c (5)
Total		68% (137)	54% (160)	43% (28)	46% (13)
Knew one norm	High	71% (138)	56% (200)	38% (26)	31% (16)
	Low	61 (33)	23 (105)	30 (33)	26 (27)
Total		69% (171)	44% (305)	34% (59)	28% (43)
Knew both norms	High	67% (79)	43% (178)	18% (40)	19% (26)
	Low	32 (22)	22 (163)	18 (77)	6 (101)
Total		59% (102)	33% (344)	18% (118)	9% (127)

[a]See Table 46.
[b]High Simplism = 3–5; Low Simplism = 0–2.
[c]Too few cases to compute percentage.

Semitism among grade schoolers (Grade School column, Table 47). Those who knew both norms were almost as apt to be anti-Semitic as those who knew one or neither. What does have an effect is the combination of knowing both Constitutional norms and being low on simplism. In this group of knowledgeable and relatively sophisticated grade schoolers, only 32 per cent scored as anti-Semitic. The inference from this is that if grade schoolers were as knowledgeable of democratic norms and as free of simplistic beliefs as the educated, their rate of anti-Semitism would approach that of the more educated. However, only 22 of 535 grade schoolers met this double criterion.

3. Knowledge of the Constitution and level of simplism appear to have independent effects on acceptance of anti-Semitic beliefs. As we saw

earlier, knowledge of the Constitution predicts but does not guarantee support of civil libertarian practices. Similarly, knowledge of the Constitution predicts but does not guarantee rejection of prejudiced beliefs; it is most effective when simplism is low. Knowing democratic norms is not enough; also necessary is the capacity to understand and interpret them. It requires intellectual sophistication to draw out the social implications of the Constitution, to understand that while prejudice may not violate the letter it does violate the spirit of a democratic order.

Exposure to Mass Media

The evidence presented so far suggests that the significance of education for prejudice is that it brings people into contact with the official norms and values of our society. It is important to ask whether there are other sources of exposure to norms of tolerance. The mass media are one bridge between official society and the general population. They not only report the opinions of leaders and the formal acts of government but have become spokesmen for tolerance in their own right. Particularly for the less educated the mass media constitute a potential source of exposure to norms of tolerance and an opportunity to learn in adult life what was not learned in school.

This potential can be realized only if the uneducated are actually reached by the media. Along with many past studies, our data show that contact with the mass media is highly influenced by education (Table 48, Part A). Virtually all college graduates—91 per cent—said they read a newspaper almost every day, in contrast to 74 per cent of high schoolers and 57 per cent of grade schoolers. Magazine reading shows the same systematic relation to education. Respondents were asked whether they read any of the following: *Life, Look, Newsweek, The New Yorker, Reader's Digest, Saturday Evening Post, Time,* or *U.S. News and World Report.* The proportion reading none of these magazines sharply decreases with greater education, from 65 per cent among grade schoolers to 11 per cent among college graduates. With magazines as with newspapers, the less educated are less often exposed to sources of information.

Merely reading a newspaper or magazine says little about what is singled out for attention or how much the individual profits from it. Included in the interview was a names test, referred to earlier, in which respondents were read a list of prominent Americans and asked to identify each as a writer, a politician, an entertainer, or a sports figure. The four politicians were Hubert Humphrey, William E. Miller, Dean Rusk, and Douglas Dillon. Like knowledge of writers, knowledge of politicians is largely a function of education (Table 48, Part B). Whereas

Table 48.   MEDIA EXPOSURE BY EDUCATION

Media Exposure	Grade School	High School	Some College	College Graduate
Part A				
Read a newspaper almost every day	57%	74%	81%	91%
	(534)	(952)	(225)	(193)
Read no "serious" magazines[a]	65	40	21	11
	(536)	(957)	(226)	(193)
Part B				
Identified at least 3 of 4 politicians[b]	46%	74%	86%	95%
	(536)	(957)	(226)	(193)
Among newspaper readers	59%	79%	86%	95%
	(304)	(693)	(182)	(175)
Among nonreaders	29%	56%	86%	94%
	(230)	(259)	(43)	(18)
Part C				
Serious readers[c]	34%	58%	70%	87%
Nonserious readers[c]	23	15	11	5
Knowledgeable nonreaders[c]	12	15	16	8
Unknowledgeable nonreaders[c]	31	12	3	0
Total	100%	100%	100%	100%
	(534)	(952)	(225)	(193)
Part D				
Identified at least 2 of 3 sports figures[d]	40%	76%	80%	87%
	(536)	(957)	(226)	(193)
Identified at least 3 of 4 entertainers[e]	33%	72%	75%	75%
	(536)	(957)	(226)	(193)

[a]*Life, Look, Newsweek, The New Yorker, Reader's Digest, Saturday Evening Post, Time, U.S. News and World Report.*

[b]Hubert Humphrey (1964 Democratic Vice Presidential candidate), William E. Miller (1964 Republican Vice Presidential candidate), Dean Rusk (Secretary of State, Douglas Dillon (Secretary of the Treasury).

[c]Serious reader = reads a newspaper every day and identified at least three of four politicians; nonserious reader = reads a newspaper every day but identified fewer than three politicians; knowledgeable nonreader = reads a newspaper less often than every day but identified at least three politicians; unknowledgeable nonreader = reads a newspaper less often than every day and identified fewer than three politicians.

[d]Roger Maris (baseball), Y. A. Tittle (football), Arnold Palmer (golf).

[e]William Holden (movies), Paul Newman (movies), Frank Fontaine (television),Vince Edwards (television).

95 per cent of college graduates knew at least three of the four politicians, 74 per cent of high schoolers and only 46 per cent of grade schoolers did so. Moreover, even when they regularly read newspapers, the less educated are far less likely to be knowledgeable. Among grade schoolers who said they read a newspaper almost every day, 59 per cent knew three of the four politicians as compared to 79 per cent of high schoolers and 95 per cent of college graduates. Not only are the less educated less likely to read newspapers regularly, but even when they do, are less likely to be informed. The educated, in contrast, are likely to be informed whether they regularly read a newspaper or not.

Let us define a "serious newspaper reader" as one who reads a newspaper almost every day and correctly identified at least three of the four politicians. The proportion at each level of education who met this minimal standard of a serious newspaper reader was as follows: college graduates, 87 per cent; some college, 70 per cent; high schoolers, 58 per cent; grade schoolers, 34 per cent (Table 48, Part C). If newspapers are a vehicle for transmitting enlightened ideas, their success in reaching the individual largely depends on his education.

The criticism is frequently made that sociologists improperly evaluate the working class by middle-class standards. Workers, it is said, have their own cultural interests and concerns, as unfamiliar to the upper classes as politicians are to workers. We therefore included some well-known entertainers and sports figures in our names test. Education is almost as strongly related to knowledge of entertainers or sports figures as to writers or politicians (Table 48, Part D). Only 40 per cent of grade schoolers correctly identified at least two of the following three as sports figures: Roger Maris (baseball), Y. A. Tittle (football), and Arnold Palmer (golf). In contrast, 76 per cent of high schoolers and 87 per cent of college graduates did so.[14] The four entertainers in the names test were William Holden, Paul Newman, Vince Edwards, and Frank Fontaine, the former two being movie actors, the latter two television performers. On entertainers, high schoolers scored as well as the college educated; in each case about three-quarters knew at least three of the four names. But once again only a small minority of grade schoolers—33 per cent—

---

[14] We intended the sports test to include a fourth name—that of Cleveland Williams, a well-known boxer, but mistakenly used the name Clarence Williams. It is noteworthy that 81 per cent did not guess what he was but answered "don't know." Some of the remaining 19 per cent may have been familiar with one of the several Clarence Williamses in public life. Interviewers for the study, intrigued to learn the identity of the mysterious Clarence Williams, investigated the matter and discovered that there was indeed a boxer as well as a football player and a jazz musician, all named Clarence Williams but all rather obscure. In any case, the sports test consists of only three names.

correctly identified three of the four entertainers.[15] Even when entertainers
and sports figures were considered individually, the least educated were
in every instance the least knowledgeable. Thus, compared to the more
educated, and regardless of their reported newspaper reading, the uneducated tend to be less integrated into the larger society, including popular
culture.

Television viewing was also examined. Unlike newspaper or magazine
reading, number of hours spent viewing television hardly varies by education. However, even when they reported frequent television viewing, the
less educated recognized entertainment and sports figures less often than
did the college educated. There is little point in further documenting the
basic finding: even with equal exposure, the less educated come away with
less information.[16]

Lack of education is clearly a double handicap. First, it leaves people
with few intellectual resources and little knowledge. But the uneducated
also end up in disprivileged positions and have little reason in adult life
to identify with the larger society and acquire information about it. In
this way lack of education makes for the cumulative isolation of the
individual from the official norms.

This may explain why newspaper reading has little relation to anti-
Semitism (Table 49). Among regular newspaper readers 40 per cent score

Table 49.   ANTI-SEMITIC BELIEF BY EDUCATION AND NEWSPAPER READING

(per cent anti-Semitic)

Newspaper Reading[a]	Grade School	High School	Some College	College Graduate	Total
Nonreaders	71%	46%	24%	18%	52%
	(165)	(214)	(38)	(17)	(435)
Readers	64	40	27	16	40
	(258)	(607)	(171)	(168)	(1,205)
Percentage difference	+7	+6	−3	+2	+12

[a]Readers = read a newspaper every day; nonreaders = read a newspaper less often than
every day.

[15] Education and age are independently related to knowledge on all four names
tests. But the effect of education is more powerful on knowledge of writers and politicians, the effect of age more powerful on knowledge of entertainers and sports figures.

[16] This is not to say that the less educated always perceive less in the real world
than do the more educated. The very norms that guide the conduct of the educated
may inhibit many of their perceptions just as, according to Freud, the sexual norms
of our society prevent the educated from recognizing childhood sexuality when they
see it.

as anti-Semitic; among those who infrequently read newspapers the rate is slightly higher—52 per cent. But regular newspaper readers are more educated, and when this is taken into account, the 12-percentage-point difference is reduced or reversed. In other words, it is because they are more educated that regular newspaper readers exhibit a lower rate of anti-Semitism. This is not to say that the mass media are ineffective, especially in creating a climate of tolerance in the society as a whole.[17] But so far as the individual is concerned the media apparently do not overcome the handicaps imposed by lack of education.

Intolerance of Cultural Diversity

Earlier we found that the more education a person has, the more apt he is to be familiar with the provisions of the Constitution. Knowledge of the Constitution was in turn associated with tolerance of political and religious nonconformity. This section continues to examine the attitudes of the educated and uneducated toward social and cultural diversity.

However nominal their religious affiliation, most Americans have a firm belief in God. When offered six statements distinguishing various degrees of belief in God, 79 per cent of the national sample chose the statement: "I know God really exists and I have no doubts about it." Only 5 per cent admitted to no belief in God. In view of this almost universal belief in God, a good indicator of general tolerance is whether people are willing to accept atheists in positions of influence.

Respondents were asked the following question: "Suppose a man admitted in public that he did not believe in God. Do you think he should be allowed to teach in a public high school? Should he be allowed to hold public office? Do you think a book he wrote should be removed from the library?" The greatest amount of intolerance was expressed on the first question (Table 50, Part A); 60 per cent of the sample indicated they did not think an atheist should be allowed to teach in a public high school. Almost the same proportion (54 per cent) said he should not be allowed to hold public office. Finally, 34 per cent said a book written by a confessed atheist should be removed from public libraries.[18] On each of the three questions the uneducated were far less willing to tolerate atheists than the educated. For example, 38 per cent of college graduates but 78 per cent of grade schoolers said that atheists should not be allowed to teach in a public high school. While comparatively small, the figure of 38

---

[17] This question is discussed in another volume in this series: Charles Y. Glock, Gertrude J. Selznick, and Joe L. Spaeth, *The Apathetic Majority* (New York: Harper & Row, 1966), Chapter 7.

[18] In contrast to the first two items, the intolerant response to this one was "yes." This may account in part for the drop in intolerant responses.

Table 50.   MEASURES OF INTOLERANCE OF CULTURAL DIVERSITY
BY EDUCATION

(per cent giving intolerant response as indicated in parentheses after each item)

Intolerance of Cultural Diversity	Grade School	High School	Some College	College Graduate	Total
Part A					
Suppose a man admitted in public that he did not believe in God:					
1. Should he be allowed to teach in a public high school? (no)	78%	58%	46%	38%	60%
2. Should he be allowed to hold public office? (no)	70	54	42	30	54
3. Do you think a book he wrote should be removed from a public library? (yes)	55	30	20	12	34
Part B					
4. America owes a great deal to the immigrants who came here. (disagree)	30	26	16	12	24
5. It bothers me to see immigrants succeeding more than Americans who were born here. (agree)	28	18	9	6	18
6. Foreigners who come to live in America should give up their foreign ways and learn to be like other Americans. (agree)	86	66	56	39	67
7. Nothing in other countries can beat the American way of life. (agree)	86	71	54	41	70
Part C					
8. Persons who insist on wearing beards should not be allowed to teach in public schools. (agree)	39	23	16	12	25
Part D					
Per cent high on Index of Intolerance of Cultural Diversity[a]	70	46	34	19	49
100% (N) =	(531)	(945)	(223)	(193)	(1,892)

[a]Index consists of five items· the two in Table 46 that measure support of the Constitution and 1, 6, and 8 in the above table; scores of 3 or more are designated as High.

per cent for college graduates is not insignificant. About the same proportion of college graduates expressed support of a law requiring that the President believe in God; a majority also favored Christmas celebrations and prayers in the public schools. Together these findings show that even at higher levels of education many people subordinate democratic principles to religious values. Thus many more of the college-educated waver in their tolerance of atheists than waver in their tolerance of political nonconformists. But this is only to say that the educated are more tolerant on some issues than on others, that they place limits on their tolerance. On every measure examined in this chapter the educated are as a group more tolerant than the uneducated.

At first glance, there appears to be more tolerance of immigrants than of atheists. Seventy per cent agreed that "America owes a great deal to the immigrants who came here"; 79 per cent denied that "it bothers me to see immigrants succeeding more than Americans who were born here." However, it is one thing to value cultural pluralism, it is another to accept immigrants on the condition that they give up their ethnic identities. When respondents were presented with the statement "Foreigners who come to live in America should give up their foreign ways and learn to be like other Americans," two out of three (67 per cent) agreed.[19] Roughly the same proportion (70 per cent) accepted the statement "Nothing in other countries can beat the American way of life." On each of the four questions, the less educated are more likely to express provincial attitudes (Table 50, Part B).

Diversity does not always imply broad social or political difference but may refer to individual eccentricity. Respondents were asked whether they agreed that "persons who insist on wearing beards should not be allowed to teach in public schools" (Table 50, Part C). Though the data were collected at a time when newspapers carried reports of teacher dismissals on these grounds, only one-fourth of the national sample agreed that bearded teachers should not be permitted in the public schools. Nonetheless, agreement is correlated with other forms of intolerance and decreases with greater education, from 39 per cent among grade schoolers to 12 per cent among college graduates.

Due to the methodologist's own difficulties in coping with diversity, it is necessary to construct an Index of Intolerance of Cultural Diversity. The following five items were selected for this purpose:

Would you be in favor of a law saying that groups who disagree with our form of government could not hold public meetings or make speeches, or opposed to it? (favor)

[19] At each level of education the foreign-born were just as likely as native Americans to agree.

Would you be in favor of a law saying that the President must be a man who believes in God, or opposed to it? (favor)

Suppose a man admitted in public that he did not believe in God. Should he be allowed to hold public office? (no)

Foreigners who come to live in America should give up their foreign ways and learn to be like other Americans. (agree)

Persons who insist on wearing beards should not be allowed to teach in public schools. (agree)

That this Index is a sensitive measure of intolerance of diversity is nicely demonstrated in the following way: As scores on the Index increase from 0 to 5, so do the proportions who say "I'm suspicious of people who try to be different from everybody else." The figures are 22, 32, 39, 48, 62, and 71 per cènt.

Education correlates more strongly with the Index than with its component items (Table 50, Part D). Among grade schoolers, a substantial majority (70 per cent) are high on intolerance of cultural diversity. This proportion declines with greater education to 46 per cent among high schoolers and just 19 per cent among college graduates. This difference of 51 percentage points equals the educational difference on the Index of Anti-Semitic Belief. It is becoming increasingly evident that the uneducated are intolerant not only of Jews but of other people as well.

Table 51 brings anti-Semitism into the picture. As scores on the Index of Intolerance of Cultural Diversity increase from Low to Medium to High, the proportions anti-Semitic increase from 20 to 45 to 69 per cent. Furthermore, when degree of intolerance is taken into account, the

Table 51.   ANTI-SEMITIC BELIEF BY EDUCATION AND
INTOLERANCE OF CULTURAL DIVERSITY

(per cent anti-Semitic)

Intolerance of Cultural Diversity[a]	Grade School	High School	Some College	College Graduate	Total
High (4–5)	81%	64%	38%	42%	69%
	(166)	(176)	(26)	(12)	(380)
Medium (2–3)	59	42	32	29	45
	(207)	(391)	(88)	(59)	(746)
Low (0–1)	47	23	16	6	20
	(45)	(247)	(92)	(114)	(499)
Total	66%	41%	26%	16%	
	(423)	(822)	(209)	(185)	

[a]See footnote to Table 50 for composition of index.

original educational difference in anti-Semitism is reduced. The implication of Table 51 is that the uneducated are intolerant of Jews partly because they tend to be intolerant of *all* social and cultural differences.

We have seen that simplism and intolerance of cultural diversity are both related to anti-Semitic prejudice and each helps to explain the greater anti-Semitism of the less educated. These two Indexes are of course related to each other. As score on the Simplism Index rises from Low to Medium to High, the proportion High on the Index of Intolerance of Cultural Diversity rises from 27 to 45 to 67 per cent. The authors of *The Authoritarian Personality* similarly found F to be highly correlated with ethnocentrism. However, they interpreted this relation as causal: they assumed that F measures basic personality, as formed in early childhood, and that basic personality determines ethnocentrism (as well as other ideologies, including anti-Semitism).[20] In our view it is an error to regard the relation between F and ethnocentrism (or between the Indexes of Simplism and Intolerance of Cultural Diversity) as in any sense causal. If anything, the relation has a formal or logical character. The major difference between Simplism and Intolerance of Cultural Diversity is degree of generality. Both measure intolerance of complexity and diversity, but the former is more abstract and general, the latter more specific and concrete. Similarly, the major difference between the Indexes of Intolerance of Cultural Diversity and of Anti-Semitic Belief is that the latter concerns Jews only. What is involved is not a causal chain but, as *The Authoritarian Personality* more correctly calls it, a syndrome. This syndrome encompasses a primitive cognitive style, ignorance of democratic norms, a blaming and apocalyptic orientation toward social reality, rejection of civil libertarian principles, intolerance of cultural diversity, and anti-Semitic prejudice. All these are highly interrelated; all are most often found among the least educated segments of the population.

The Question of F

How is this syndrome to be explained? According to *The Authoritarian Personality* repressive child-rearing practices create authoritarian personalities who are forced by inner psychological need to seek out authoritarian beliefs and to reject enlightened beliefs even when exposed to them.[21] In

[20] "Since . . . opinions, attitudes, and values depend upon human needs, and since personality is essentially an organization of needs, then personality may be regarded as a *determinant* [authors' emphasis] of ideological preferences. . . . The major influences upon personality development arise in the course of child training as carried forward in a setting of family life" (Adorno *et al., op. cit.*, pp. 5–6).

[21] ". . . ideologies have for different individuals, different degrees of appeal, a matter that depends upon the individual's needs and the degree to which these needs are being satisfied or frustrated" (*ibid.*, p. 2).

view of the relation between lack of education and the "syndrome of un-enlightenment," a simpler explanation is in order: The uneducated are cognitively and morally unenlightened because they have never been in-doctrinated into the enlightened values of the larger society and in this sense are alienated from it.

For analytic purposes, we can distinguish in the United States between the official, or ideal culture and the unofficial, or common culture. The official culture contains the ideal norms that characterize our society in its public and secular spheres. These norms are derived from scientific and democratic values and represent the cognitive and moral commitments of a society whose political order is a democracy and whose economy is based on technology. Scientific and democratic values provide ample grounds for rejecting prejudice and discrimination. Intellectually and morally, the official culture is enlightened and unprejudiced.

Alongside the official culture is an unofficial or common culture which not only differs from the ideal culture but is at odds with it. Historically more archaic, the common culture is not only prescientific and predemo-cratic but antiscientific and antidemocratic. Nevertheless, it is the culture that is normally taken on by Americans unless they acquire criteria for rejecting it.

It is important to emphasize that the distinction between the ideal culture and the common culture is analytic. By definition, an ideal culture is never fully realized in social reality. But, like any culture, it is embodied in institutions that provide for its transmission. In our society the transmis-sion and elaboration of the official culture have been largely delegated to a particular social institution—the formal educational system. As in-dividuals move from grade school to high school, to college and the university, they are brought into progressively closer contact with ideal values and increasingly acquire criteria for the rejection of the common culture. The result is a tendency in our society for the more and the less educated to participate in different and antithetical cultures, and for the less educated to be untouched by the cognitive and social ideals of the larger society.

An important difference between the present study and *The Au-thoritarian Personality* concerns the relation of culture to personality. The authors of *The Authoritarian Personality* correctly described F and similar beliefs as socially generated and as available in the culture. They also took for granted the presence of more than one ideology—more than one cul-tural strain—in Western society. They assumed, however, that democratic and antidemocratic ideologies are equally available to all, and sought for some special factor in the individual that could account for his acceptance of one belief system rather than another. This they located in psychological need: allegedly faced with an array of beliefs in the society, the authoritarian personality chooses those that satisfy his quasi-pathological inner needs.[22] On this view, "deep-lying personality trends" created in the earliest years of life determine whether the individual will participate in the unenlightened, antidemocratic culture or the enlightened, democratic culture. It was not the argument of *The Authoritarian Personality* that children born into the unenlightened, antidemocratic culture may be ill-prepared, cognitively, psychologically, and socially, for full participation in the formal educational system, or that the primary significance of the family of origin is that it can effectively isolate the child from the enlightened culture. Rather it was assumed that all individuals have equal access to the official values and only some form of personal psychopathology can explain why some individuals reject them. As one later study put it: "The group's culture provides the developing individual with some choice of attitudes, ranging from more prejudiced to more tolerant, so that he may select the attitude most congenial to his personality needs."[23]

It is difficult to accept the implication that our heterodox culture is presented, cafeteria-style, to be rejected or accepted according to the individual's personality needs. The significance of lack of education is that it is a form of social isolation from the ideal culture. It is not so much that the uneducated actively reject enlightened values—though they do that too. More to the point is that they have never been effectively brought into contact with them, and remain within the traditional culture. The dominant strain in Western society has long been authoritarian; governments, social institutions, societies have more often than not been antihumanitarian, punitive, and intolerant of dissent and diversity. Commitment to scientific, democratic, humanitarian, and legal values is historically recent and largely confined to an elite minority. Insofar as the ideal culture fails to reach the individual, the society can be expected to produce individuals with antidemocratic orientations, and to do so in a routine way. No special psychological explanation need be invoked; among those who remain unintegrated into enlightened social institutions, the authoritarian strains in the culture are "normally" taken on.[24] Once ac-

---

[22] "In modern society . . . it is rare for a person to be subjected to only one pattern of ideas, after he is old enough for ideas to mean something to him. Some selection is usually made, according, it may be supposed, to the needs of his personality" (*ibid.*, p. 9).

[23] Jerome Himelhoch, "Tolerance and Personality Needs," *American Sociological Review*, February 1950, p. 80.

[24] "When ethnic distinctions have been built into the cultural definitions and the norms of routine behavior in a social system, prejudiced attitudes and discriminatory behavior will be characteristic of normal personalities in that system. The manifestation of prejudice is not necessarily a symptom of unusual psychological needs or of neurotic or psychotic tendencies" (Williams, *op. cit.*, p. 24).

cepted, F and similar beliefs enter into, in fact help to constitute, the "surface" or "social" personality of the individual. Authoritarian personalities do not choose the unenlightened culture; rather the unenlightened culture creates authoritarian personalities.

Since the publication of *The Authoritarian Personality* a great deal of research has been done on the F scale and a number of interpretations offered.[25] As with prejudice in general, the F scale can be given either a cognitive or an emotive interpretation. The emotive focuses on the psychological content of individual beliefs, and traces acceptance of F and similar beliefs to some peculiar psychological affinity between the beliefs and the individuals who accept them. In other words, people are said to accept authoritarian beliefs because they have authoritarian personalities. This is the emphasis that has dominated the literature since the publication of *The Authoritarian Personality* in 1950. In contrast, the cognitive approach looks for an *intellectual* affinity between F beliefs and those who accept them. In short, the beliefs are cognitively unsophisticated and so are the people who accept them. Empirically this reveals itself in the strong relation between lack of education and acceptance of F beliefs. To be sure, in accepting F beliefs for want of cognitive criteria for rejecting them, individuals acquire precisely those psychological orientations that constitute "the authoritarian personality" in the surface sense. The authoritarian personality neither antedates nor "determines" acceptance of F beliefs; rather F beliefs are constitutive of the authoritarian personality. It is true that F beliefs can be integrated into the individual's underlying psychodynamic personality structure and utilized to serve the perverse emotional functions for which their manifest content so obviously suits them. However, whatever psychological and social functions F beliefs may subsequently serve, these must be distinguished from the lack of cognitive sophistication that enters into their initial acceptance.[26]

In *The Authoritarian Personality* acceptance rather than rejection of F beliefs was assumed to be the more "abnormal" procedure. This departs from the orthodox Freudian view that projection, displacement, and reaction-formation—so prominent in many unenlightened beliefs—are the "normal" defense mechanisms of man in his natural state of cognitive innocence. These defense mechanisms are pathological in the sense that they result in distortions of reality. But according to Freud such pathologies are inherent in man; in the absence of strong countervailing influences, they are routine

[25] For a judicious review of this research, see Roger Brown, *Social Psychology* (New York: Free Press of Glencoe, 1965), Chapter 10.

[26] "The association of both prejudice and personality items with formal education forces us to take seriously the possibility that widespread indoctrination, relatively independent of individual psychological needs, may account for at least a considerable part of the correlation of authoritarianism and prejudice" (Williams, *op. cit.*, p. 90).

responses of the ego to the restrictions placed on the id by man's life in society. It is part of man's nature to externalize and project, and this accounts for the emergence of projective and paranoid belief systems in whole cultures. But once such beliefs are incorporated into culture, the individual does not have to be personally paranoid or even under psychic stress to accept them. Freud is frequently misunderstood on this point. While he characterized certain religious practices, for example, as resembling the obsessive practices of certain neurotics, he never contended that everyone who engages in such practices is clinically classifiable as an obsessive. He saw religion as a social neurosis, not as an individual neurosis;[27] the same can be said of anti-Semitism. Freud's view was that only a high level of cognitive sophistication—as embodied in science with its relentless pursuit of the reality principle—can counteract the natural tendency of man to resort to primitive modes of coping with his id, including his impulses to aggression.[28] The role of education as a countervailing factor to prejudice is thus far from inconsistent with the Freudian view of man.

The authors of *The Authoritarian Personality* implied that the child is virtually intractable to extrafamilial influences, that having been raised in a certain manner the child is destined to hold certain beliefs—concerning astrology, sex criminals, and Jews—regardless of how much education he subsequently receives. But *The Authoritarian Personality* measured adult responses to F beliefs, and the premise that the psychological basis of F is laid down in early childhood was, for the most part, unsupported by direct evidence. Since our data are also derived from an adult sample, we are unable to test the extent to which an authoritarian orientation develops early in life. Nevertheless there is evidence to suggest that it is not a person's family background but the extent of his education that determines the probability that, as an adult, he will accept F beliefs.

We have seen that there is a systematic relation between amount of education and respondent's F: as education increases, the proportion scoring high on F decreases. When parents' education is also examined, the data seem to confirm the thesis of *The Authoritarian Personality*: respondents from less educated and presumably more authoritarian back-

---

[27] ". . . their acceptance of the universal neurosis spares them the task of constructing a personal one" [Sigmund Freud, *The Future of an Illusion* (Garden City, N.Y.: Anchor, 1964), p. 72].

[28] *The Authoritarian Personality* also saw the rejection of prejudice as an attribute of the mature ego. ". . . the personality variables which have most to do with determining the objectivity and rationality of an ideology are those which belong to the ego, that part of the personality which appreciates reality, integrates the other parts, and operates with the most conscious awareness" (Adorno *et al.*, *op. cit.*, p. 11). What is surprising is the failure of *The Authoritarian Personality* to connect the development of the rational ego with the educational process.

grounds are disproportionately high on F (Table 52, Total column). Among respondents from a grade school background, 47 per cent score high on F compared to 31 and 27 per cent of those from high school and college backgrounds. However, when respondent's own education is taken into account, it becomes evident that whether a person scores high

Table 52. F SCALE BY RESPONDENT'S EDUCATION AND PARENT'S EDUCATION

(per cent High on F scale[a])

| | Respondent's Education | | | |
Parent's Education[b]	Grade School	High School	College	Total
Grade school	62% (267)	43% (383)	21% (87)	47% (737)
High school	42% (43)	34% (303)	22% (148)	31% (494)
College	47% (15)	40% (83)	18% (147)	27% (245)
Total	59% (325)	36% (769)	20% (382)	
Percentage difference[c]	15	3	3	20

[a]F scale consists of the first five items listed in Table 43; scores of 3 or more are designated as High.

[b]Education of parent with greater amount of education is used. The 430 respondents who did not know or report either parent's education are excluded.

[c]Between those with grade-school parents and those with college-educated parents.

on F is determined by the amount of education he himself has had, not by the education of his parents. There is one exception: grade schoolers from grade school backgrounds are especially high on F. However, when respondents from grade school backgrounds attended either high school or college they are no more likely to be high on F than their educational counterparts from more educated backgrounds. Similarly when respondents from college backgrounds have less education than their parents, they resemble their educational counterparts from less educated backgrounds.[29]

[29] It is possible that respondents whose education exceeds that of their parents had parents who were relatively low on F, and that respondents who had less education than their parents came from parents relatively high on F. Without longitudinal data it is never possible to discount such a possibility, though it is implausible for a number of reasons. For one thing, the upgrading of education is part of an historical trend and the role of parents' F in this historical trend is obviously limited. Secondly, the data leave no doubt as to the powerful effect of education on F, and it is not surprising to find that people who are educated overcome their family environment.

In short, the reason that less educated parents have children high on F is that less educated parents tend to have less educated children.[30]

The Question of A

There is a second widely used scale—the Anomie or A scale—that past research has shown to be related to anti-Semitism.[31] Three items from the original five-item scale were included in the present study:

Most people in government are not really interested in the problems of the average man.[32]

You sometimes can't help wondering whether anything is worthwhile anymore.[33]

Nowadays a person has to live pretty much for today and let tomorrow take care of itself.

Like the F scale, anomie is strongly related to lack of education. The proportion high on anomie (score of 2 or 3 on the Index) declines with greater education, from 57 per cent among grade schoolers to 40 per cent among high schoolers, 29 per cent among those with some college, and finally 18 per cent among college graduates. Table 53 shows that, while somewhat reduced, the relation of anomie to anti-Semitism is strong at every level of education and partly interprets the relation between lack of education and anti-Semitic prejudice. The combined effect of education and anomie is such that among grade schoolers high on anomie 76 per cent are anti-Semitic compared to 5 per cent among college graduates low on anomie. Anomie is also associated with lack of knowledge of the Constitution, with high scores on the Index of Intolerance of Cultural Diversity, and as past studies have shown with simplism (or F).

From a statistical point of view there is little reason to treat anomie as a unique or isolated set of beliefs. From every indication anomie is another facet of the "syndrome of unenlightenment" found among the less educated. However, anomic beliefs seem to express feelings of despair and meaning-

---

[30] The findings of Table 52 are repeated when anti-Semitic belief is the dependent variable. Parent's education makes for a 20-percentage-point difference in the anti-Semitism of respondents. But when respondent's education is controlled, this difference is either reduced or reversed in each of the partials; the average remaining difference is just 1 percentage point.

[31] Leo Srole, "Social Integration and Certain Corollaries: An Exploratory Study," *American Sociological Review,* December 1956, pp. 709–716. In this article Srole uses the Greek "anomia" rather than the French "anomie."

[32] The original item read: "There's little use writing to public officials because they aren't really interested in the problems of the average man."

[33] The original item read: "It's hardly fair to bring children into the world with the way things look for the future."

Table 53.   ANTI-SEMITIC BELIEF BY EDUCATION AND ANOMIE

(per cent anti-Semitic)

Anomie[a]	Grade School	High School	Some College	College Graduate	Total
High (2–3)	76%	58%	46%	42%	63%
	(251)	(327)	(41)	(33)	(652)
Medium (1)	60	38	27	18	39
	(112)	(248)	(78)	(55)	(494)
Low (0)	40	22	17	5	20
	(60)	(244)	(89)	(95)	(489)
Total	66%	41%	26%	16%	
	(423)	(822)	(209)	(185)	

[a]Index consists of three items adapted from Srole's five-item A scale. See p. 162 for details.

lessness absent from other beliefs examined in this study. On their face, simplism and intolerance of cultural diversity reflect the extent to which individuals reject certain ideal norms. But anomie appears to reflect the extent to which they reject norms per se. It is one thing to reject this or that norm; it is another to question the efficacy and viability of norms in general. While in previous pages we stressed the lack of intellectual sophistication inherent in simplism, it seems less appropriate to do so in the case of anomic beliefs. There is some indication that anomie has a psychological component absent in simplism: when we examined psychic "distress" or "inadequacy" by level of education, we found it to be related to anomie but not to simplism.[34] This suggested that the anomie—and the prejudices —of the uneducated may be at least partly rooted in existential factors. For this reason a good deal of attention was given to possible existential sources of frustration in the life situations of high scorers. Since amount of education is doubtless the major determinant of life situation, the crucial question is whether, at each educational level, the more and the less deprived, the more and the less satisfied, differ in the extent to which they exhibit anomic attitudes.

[34] The Index of Psychic Inadequacy was composed of five items: "I am [not] very happy"; "I worry a lot"; "I often feel quite lonely"; "I tend to go to pieces in a crisis"; "When problems come up I'm generally [not] able to solve them." Only 30 per cent of the sample had scores of 2 or more, but less education was consistently related to greater psychic inadequacy. When those with scores of 2 to 5 are designated as High, 42 per cent of grade schoolers scored High on the Index of Psychic Inadequacy, compared to 28, 14, and 12 per cent at higher levels of education. The Index of Psychic Inadequacy is related to anti-Semitic prejudice: among those Low, Medium, and High, anti-Semitic prejudice ranges from 39 to 47 to 62 per cent. However, when education is controlled, this difference is almost entirely wiped out.

One familiar interpretation is that anomie is a response to a distinctive kind of deprivation: the failure of the individual to be integrated into social groups. Respondents were asked a series of questions concerning the frequency with which they visited relatives, neighbors, and friends outside the neighborhood. Both the quantity and the quality of social relationships varied by education. First of all, the less educated were more likely to be social isolates: 14 per cent of grade schoolers versus 6 per cent of college graduates rarely visited either relatives, neighbors, or friends outside the neighborhood. Second, the social contacts of the less educated tended to be of a parochial kind: 40 per cent of grade schoolers versus 20 per cent of college graduates visited relatives at least once a week. On the other hand, visiting friends outside the neighborhood increased with education, from 48 per cent among grade schoolers and 51 per cent among high schoolers to 72 per cent among college graduates.

Theoretically, social isolates should be high on anomie, while kinship ties should provide protection from anomic feelings. However, when education is controlled, social isolates show no disproportionate tendency to express anomic attitudes, while people who frequently visit relatives are no less anomic than those who have friendship ties instead. In short, neither the quantity nor the quality of primary contacts was found to be a factor in anomie. Attempts were also made to measure secondary participation in the larger society—by number of club memberships, church attendance, voting, and reading newspapers. None of these was more than incidentally related to anomie once education was controlled.

Anomic attitudes have also been attributed to frustration of life goals, resulting in a general rejection of the efficacy of norms.[35] Questions were asked concerning satisfaction with income, job, neighborhood, and relative success in life, but there was little or no tendency for those who expressed dissatisfaction to score higher on anomie than the satisfied.

One reason that the various measures of satisfaction and frustration are not correlated with anomie is that they are not correlated with education. The less educated are no more likely than the educated to express dissatisfaction with either their job or their neighborhood. The uneducated are more dissatisfied with their incomes—34 per cent of grade schoolers versus 23 per cent of college graduates—but this is only an 11-percentage-point difference, and could not possibly explain their greater anomie. Moreover, at the two highest income levels, the relation is reversed: it is the more educated who are more dissatisfied with their incomes. Just as the less educated are satisfied with less income, so they adjust their job aspirations. Fewer of the less educated expect a promotion, but fewer say they want one. There are evidently two roads to job satisfaction. One is neither to

[35] Dorothy L. Meier and Wendell Bell, "Anomia and Differential Access to the Achievement of Life Goals," *American Sociological Review*, April 1959, pp. 189–202.

want nor to expect a promotion, and almost half the grade schoolers (44 per cent) gave this response compared to 21 per cent of college graduates. The other is to want and also expect a promotion: 54 per cent of college graduates were in this category compared to 14 per cent of grade schoolers. The result is that job satisfaction does not vary by education: Among the less educated, job satisfaction comes from the tailoring down of aspirations; among the more educated it comes from the congruence of high aspiration and high expectation. There was nevertheless a sizable minority of grade schoolers who wanted but did not expect a promotion (32 per cent versus 16 per cent for college graduates). However, being in this presumably frustrating job situation did not increase anomie. From the evidence, the uneducated do not have to be in more deprived and frustrated circumstances than their educational counterparts before they express anomic attitudes. Lack of education appears to be a sufficient condition.[36]

One clue to the relation between lack of education and anomie is that both are related to simplism, lack of knowledge of the Constitution, and intolerance of cultural diversity. By every criterion, the less educated have less knowledge of and are less committed to modern values than are the more educated. It is hardly surprising to find among those who accept prescientific and predemocratic values a strong tendency to interpret contemporary society as lacking in values. One who accepts the belief that sex criminals should be publicly whipped, or who is ignorant of the Constitution, is bound to be bewildered by many of the official society's practices. Far from seeing due process as the application of moral and cognitive norms, such a person will see it as an instance of their abdication.[37] Insofar as simplism implies an either-or categorization of reality, it may also lead people to confuse norms imperfectly applied with an absence of norms. Unable

[36] The only exception was the twenty-four grade schoolers earning $10,000 or more; they were comparatively low on anomie. As we had occasion to mention in Chapter 5, this group is also relatively high in cultural and intellectual sophistication. Otherwise, degree of deprivation and frustration had no impact on anomie, at least not when education was controlled.

In a study of Swedish workers, Melvin Seeman similarly found that, once education was held constant, there was no relation between work alienation, on the one hand, and anomie and prejudice on the other ("On the Personal Consequences of Alienation in Work," *American Sociological Review*, April 1967, pp. 273–285).

[37] "Those whose intellectual or cognitive equipment lacks power and efficiency find it difficult to organize and understand the events and ideas they encounter, and this difficulty apparently produces, not security and confidence, but bewilderment and anxiety" (Herbert McClosky and John H. Schaar, "Psychological Dimensions of Anomy," *American Sociological Review*, February 1965, p. 21).

The above remarks also apply to the elderly, who at every level of education are comparatively high on anomie. The old, having been reared in a less libertarian era, are less committed to modern values, and compared to the young, test high on simplism, regardless of their education. The striking effect of youth combined with greater education is seen in the fact that among white college graduates under 35 a mere 3 per cent scored high on anomie.

to come to terms with the ambiguities of political reality, they easily conclude that "Most people in government are not really interested in the
problems of the average man." Nor would it be surprising to find that persons who score High on the Index of Intolerance of Cultural Diversity
interpret dissent and disagreement, not to mention cultural pluralism, as
evidence of normative disintegration. More is involved in normlessness than
not having been educated into specific norms. Also involved is the intellectual incapacity to understand and appreciate complex, subtle, higher-order
norms.

Thus it appears that intellectual disabilities and a failure to accept the
ideal norms of the official order are one source of the greater anomie of
the less educated. However, we argued earlier that a low level of education
is a double disability: besides leaving the individual intellectually unpre-
pared to participate in the larger society, it also places him at the periphery
of society. Even if the uneducated were intellectually prepared to comprehend the norms, they are not in a position to observe them in operation.
This is a further source of normlessness:

Persons who do not share in the life of the articulate and active community
are prone to confusion about the norms. . . . This . . . impairs their ability to
learn the norms of the larger community which, in turn, gives rise to feelings
of normlessness.[38]

Furthermore, the uneducated are not beneficiaries of the normative
order. Hard work may reward the educated, but the payoff for the uneducated is slim. From the perspective of those who profit little from adhering
to norms, it is a short step to concluding that norms are nonexistent and
illusory. Thus for three reasons—lack of cognitive sophistication, existential
isolation, and paucity of rewards—the uneducated have little reason to
understand or identify with the norms of the larger society.

The same three factors apply with even greater force to Negroes, who
at every level of education are higher on anomie than are whites.[39] First,
the education of Negroes has generally been inferior in quality to that of
whites, and for this reason alone one would expect Negroes to score higher
on anomie (just as they score higher on simplism, ignorance of the Constitution, and intolerance of cultural diversity). Secondly, being confined to a
black ghetto is an extreme form of isolation; and third, compared to their
educational counterparts among whites, Negroes share still less in the system of rewards. Finally, it is characteristic of the disprivileged, and especially of ghettoized Negroes, that their immediate social environment tends
to be marked by social disorganization and violation of conventional norms.

[38] *Ibid.*, pp. 19–20.
[39] The combined effect of education and race is such that among grade school
Negroes 74 per cent scored high on anomie while among college-educated whites
16 per cent did so.

In such environments the only conclusions that could possibly be based on personal experience are the beliefs of the A scale: Government is indifferent; postponing gratification is futile; life is chaotic, precarious, and without meaning. For some, normlessness may be a distorted vision of reality; for others it *is* reality.

It does not necessarily follow that *individuals* who are socially isolated or dissatisfied with their life situation are especially likely to hold anomic attitudes. As we reported earlier, the uneducated varied little in their tendency to express anomie; the more socially integrated and the more satisfied among them were just as likely to do so as the socially isolated and the dissatisfied. The reason for this is that the *culture* of the uneducated— as of Negroes—tends to be anomic. When a whole class of individuals is excluded from society and is unable to form a separate community, an ideology of normlessness—a culture of despair and alienation—is almost bound to emerge. It then becomes an environment of belief for all members of the group, and tends to be routinely accepted regardless of the particular life circumstances of the individuals involved. In expressing anomic attitudes, the uneducated and Negroes are responding to their status as disprivileged groups in the society rather than to the particular vicissitudes of their personal lives.

It is also not surprising that an anomic ideology should be associated with anti-Semitism, since prejudice itself generally contains anomic elements. Many prejudiced beliefs impute normlessness—a lack of ethics—to minority groups. To hold that Jews are dishonest in business or that they conspire to gain control over non-Jews is in effect to accuse Jews of suspending norms in their dealings with others. Other examples are the charge that Negroes are naturally promiscuous or that confession leaves Catholics free to sin with impunity. Prejudiced beliefs are anomic in still another sense: they prepare the way for the suspension of norms in dealing with minorities. Indeed the image of minority groups as violators of basic human values has often provided the justification for the worst crimes against them. From a psychoanalytic perspective, the imputation of normlessness to others is an example of projection and a rationalization for primitive and unrestrained aggression. But as we have argued, the projection is built into the ideology; individuals are not necessarily or even typically engaging in personal acts of projection when they accept anomic or prejudiced beliefs.

Evaluation of the Findings

Much speculation in the past focused on anti-Semitism as an irrationality peculiar to Western culture. This has sometimes led to the unspoken assumption that anti-Semitism is a unique, isolated, and peculiar irrationality on the part of the individual. Anti-Semitism is seen as a baffling and irritating puzzle: Why should large numbers of people be anti-Semitic when —it is tacitly assumed—they are in other respects tolerant, committed to democracy, respectful of evidence, refined in their moral sensibilities, and devoted to a just legal order?

As *The Authoritarian Personality* first showed, and as this study confirms, anti-Semitism is but one element in a syndrome of unenlightened beliefs and values. There are individuals whose anti-Semitism is an island in an otherwise placid sea, and such instances need to be understood. On the whole, however, most anti-Semitic prejudice is firmly embedded in a network of beliefs and values not dissimilar to prejudice itself. Anti-Semitism may represent a peculiar irrationality of Western society, but it does not usually represent a peculiar irrationality on the part of the individual.

While we are indebted to the findings of *The Authoritarian Personality* we have departed from its interpretations. *The Authoritarian Personality* located the unity of the "syndrome of unenlightenment" in the psychic unity of the authoritarian personality.[40] In contrast we have identified its internal consistency with the internal consistency of the unenlightened culture. The values of this culture are archaic and premodern—they are prescientific, predemocratic, prehumanitarian—but they are still current and commonplace. Anti-Semitic prejudice is as integral a part of this culture—as ancient and historic an aspect of it—as the F beliefs used to measure the authoritarian personality.

This is not to deny the existence of the so-called authoritarian personality. On the contrary, we have emphasized the psychological consequences of acceptance of F beliefs and the role of education in shaping the surface personality and the expressions of "depth" personality. Nor do we wish to deny that the "true" authoritarian is a pathological personality in the sense that he has an emotional investment in rigid, punitive, and "paranoid" beliefs. Undoubtedly some people seek out such beliefs and score high on F (and similar measures) for reasons of personal psychopathology. But the evidence suggests that most people score high on F for lack of intellectual sophistication. There is no reason to believe that the basic psychological needs and basic psychodynamics of the uneducated differ from those of the educated. Rather the common culture and the enlightened culture differ in their psychodynamic import, the unenlightened culture giving freer reign to the more primitive psychic mechanisms. As both Freud and Durkheim

---

[40] ". . . the political, economic, and social convictions of an individual form a broad and coherent pattern, as if bound together by a 'mentality' or 'spirit' and . . . this pattern is an expression of deep-lying trends in his personality" (Adorno *et al.*, *op. cit.*, p. 1).

recognized, the enlightened culture is an inhibiting culture; it is designed to restrain and discipline the more primitive impulses of man.

In common with many other studies, *The Authoritarian Personality* was led astray by asking: Why do people *accept* anti-Semitic beliefs? In a culture that embodies anti-Semitism, no recondite or elaborate theory is required: individuals acquire anti-Semitism through the normal processes of socialization. The more pertinent question is why in such a society some people *reject* anti-Semitic beliefs. Once the question is posed in this way, instead of looking for inner pressures that impel people toward prejudice, one looks for countervailing forces that lead people to renounce it. Countervailing forces are also to be found in American culture, especially in its official and ideal values. But these are transmitted mainly through the educational system. It is precisely the mission of the educational institutions to develop and transmit general criteria for evaluating the beliefs and attitudes of the common culture. Thus not only do the educated tend to reject anti-Semitic beliefs, they tend to reject many other equally unenlightened aspects of the common culture—its anti-intellectual and antidemocratic attitudes, its superstitions and rigidities, its provincialism and particularistic orientations. In effect there are at least two antithetical cultural traditions in Western society. The implicit assumption of *The Authoritarian Personality* was that individuals were "free" to choose either one depending on their latent personality dispositions. However, the two traditions are not uniformly distributed in society nor equally available to all. The enlightened culture is an overlay on the common culture. Generally speaking, one participates in it only to the extent that one ascends the educational ladder.

9 : Anti-Semitism and Anti-Negro Prejudice

The purpose of this chapter is partly descriptive—to assess the extent of anti-Negro prejudice; partly methodological—to test our basic findings using data on anti-Negro prejudice; and partly analytic—to compare and contrast the two kinds of prejudice.

The Prevalence of Anti-Negro Prejudice

Table 54 reports responses of whites to eleven questions asked in the interview concerning Negroes. These questions are grouped somewhat arbitrarily into three categories. The first consists of two traditional stereotypes of Negroes—as less intelligent than whites and as lazy and unambitious. These items are analogous to the anti-Jewish stereotypes in the Index of Anti-Semitic Belief. The next five questions bear more directly on discrimination, the last four on sympathy with the Negro plight.

Stereotypes

Of the eleven questions, the one concerning Negro intelligence drew the smallest anti-Negro response; 19 per cent denied that Negroes "can learn things just as well as whites if they are given the same education and training." The figure for the North is 12 per cent; for the South, 37 per cent. A virtually identical question has been asked in past polls. Between 1942 and 1964 the proportion of Southerners saying that Negroes are as intelligent as whites increased from 21 to 58 per cent. Northerners showed a similar increase—from 50 to 85 per cent.[1]

About a third (34 per cent) in the North and about half (55 per cent) in the South accept the stereotype that "Negroes are lazy and don't

[1] Herbert H. Hyman and Paul B. Sheatsley, "Attitudes Toward Desegregation," *Scientific American*, July 1964, p. 16.

Table 54.   WHITE ATTITUDES TOWARD NEGROES BY REGION

(per cent giving response shown in parentheses after each belief item)

	North	South	Total
1. In general, do you think that Negroes are as intelligent as white people—that is, can they learn things just as well if they are given the same education and training? (no)	12%	37%	19%
2. Generally speaking, Negroes are lazy and don't like to work hard. (agree)	34	55	40
3. Do you think white children and Negro children should go to the same schools or to separate but equal schools? (separate but equal schools)	26	72	38
4. To be frank, I would not like my child to go to school with a lot of Negroes. (agree)	47	76	54
5. Do you think there should be laws against marriages between Negroes and whites? (yes)	53	79	60
6. A restaurant owner should not have to serve Negroes if he doesn't want to. (agree)	47	82	56
7. An owner of property should not have to sell to Negroes if he doesn't want to. (agree)	89	96	91
8. Negroes who want to work hard can get ahead just as easily as anyone else. (agree)	66	70	67
9. Before Negroes are given equal rights, they have to show that they deserve them. (agree)	58	74	62
10. As you see it, are Negroes today demanding more than they have a right to? (yes)	43	58	47
11. I'd like to ask you to compare your feelings about Negroes now with your feelings a year or so ago. Would you say that you are much less sympathetic to Negroes now, somewhat less sympathetic, somewhat more sympathetic, or much more sympathetic?			
Somewhat or much less sympathetic	35	42	37
Somewhat or much more sympathetic	17	10	15
Feel about the same	48	48	48

like to work hard." The proportion for the over-all sample is 40 per cent, a figure comparable to that for many anti-Semitic stereotypes. For example, 34 per cent of whites agreed that Jews are shrewd and tricky in business, 40 per cent that Jews use shady practices. At least with respect to these stereotypes, anti-Semitic and anti-Negro prejudice are about equally prevalent. The major differences between the two are to be found in the realm of behavior rather than the realm of belief.[2]

[2] Admittedly, the two prejudices, being unique in content, are incommensurable. But it is possible to compare the relative prevalence of traditional stereotypes and discriminatory attitudes in each.

Discrimination

Previous chapters showed that support of discrimination against Jews is generally less prevalent than acceptance of anti-Semitic beliefs. The opposite appears to be true of anti-Negro prejudice: support of discrimination far exceeds acceptance of traditional stereotypes. Nineteen per cent see Negroes as intellectually inferior; 40 per cent accept the stereotype of Negroes as lazy. But on discrimination, the figures start with the 38 per cent who favor segregated schools; climb to 60 per cent, the proportion favoring antimiscegenation laws; and reach a peak of 91 per cent in the proportion who defend a property owner's "right" not to sell to Negroes (Table 54).[3]

How can support for discrimination exceed stereotyping? This is one of the paradoxes of prejudice discussed in Chapter 3: many who reject anti-Semitism on the level of belief are willing to defend or acquiesce in some of its institutional expressions, notably the restricted social club. Similarly, many who reject traditional stereotypes of Negroes defend or acquiesce in residential segregation. There are a number of reasons for this. An aura of social undesirability can continue to hang over a minority group even while traditional stereotypes are being abandoned. The mere existence of prejudice in a society makes associating with minorities a form of status degradation. Besides, social barriers tend to be respected just because they exist. Persons who support discrimination frequently resent the charge that they are prejudiced. In one sense, they are right: some do reject the grosser stereotypes of Negroes and Jews. However, they are implicated in prejudice in that they participate in and defend some of the historic institutions of prejudice. When Negroes accuse whites of being racist, they do not necessarily mean that all whites have racist attitudes. More to the point is that the institutions of white society are racist, in the sense that exclusion of Negroes occurs independently of the motivations and attitudes of individuals.

On the other hand, supporters of discrimination may not be as free of prejudiced beliefs as they appear in our data. Prejudice changes and new rationalizations replace older ones. For example, it is now frequently argued that Negro children, while not biologically inferior, are culturally inferior, and this claim is often used to justify school segregation.[4] However, not all stereotypes are equally damaging, and the new argument is a retreat from the hard-line position of innate differences. It is a weaker

---

[3] For a trend analysis of the questions on school segregation and miscegenation laws, see Hyman and Sheatsley, *op. cit.* and Paul B. Sheatsley, "White Attitudes Toward the Negro," *Daedalus*, Winter 1966, pp. 217–238. These papers document the steady decline in anti-Negro prejudice since the 1940s.

[4] See Kenneth B. Clark, *Dark Ghetto* (New York: Harper & Row, 1965), pp. 129–148.

defense of discrimination if only because the assumed cultural inferiority of Negroes is as much an argument for school integration as it is an argument against it.

While Southerners are consistently more likely than Northerners to support discrimination, the magnitude of the difference depends on the item examined. On the belief that "an owner of property should not have to sell to Negroes if he doesn't want to" (Item 7 in Table 54) the difference between North and South is small (89 per cent versus 96 per cent). However, on the belief that "a restaurant owner should not have to serve Negroes if he doesn't want to" (Item 6), the North-South difference is large (47 per cent versus 82 per cent). Most Southerners who defended the property owner also defended the restaurant owner. But many Northerners make a distinction between the two; whereas 89 per cent defended the property owner, half as many—47 per cent—defended the restaurant owner.[5]

Items 3 and 4 in Table 54 present a similar contrast. Early in the interview respondents were asked whether they thought Negro and white children should go to the same or to separate but equal schools. Later they were asked to agree or disagree with the statement "To be frank, I would not want my child to go to school with a lot of Negroes." Among Southerners, roughly three-quarters gave an anti-Negro response in each instance. In other words, Southerners are willing to translate their personal preferences into legal sanctions; this obviously reflects their history of legal discrimination. Outside the South there is a large discrepancy in responses to the two questions: 47 per cent said they would not like their child to go to school with a lot of Negroes but far fewer (26 per cent) favored segregated schools.[6] This discrepancy undoubtedly reflects in part the absence of *de jure* segregation in the North; but it also makes it easier to understand the prevalence of *de facto* segregation. While only one-quarter of parents in the North actually advocated separate schools, nearly twice as many expressed reluctance to send their children to schools with many Negroes.

As with school segregation, Southerners are more likely than Northerners to invoke legal sanctions against racial intermarriage. In the South 79 per cent favor miscegenation laws, but even in the North 53 per cent do so. Since these data were collected, the Supreme Court has declared such laws to be unconstitutional. In the past civil rights legislation and court decisions

---

[5] Among Southerners who defended the property owner, 83 per cent also defended the restaurant owner. The comparable figure for Northerners was 51 per cent.

[6] Among Southerners who said they would not like their child to go to school with a lot of Negroes, 86 per cent advocated separate but equal schools. For Northerners the figure is 48 per cent.

have usually been followed by a gradual reduction in popular support for the officially repudiated practice, and a survey might now find less support for antimiscegenation laws.

Sympathy

The final four questions in Table 54 measure understanding of and sympathy with the plight of Negroes. This is not so clearly the case with the first two questions: "Negroes who want to work hard can get ahead just as easily as anyone else" and "Before Negroes are given equal rights they have to show they deserve them." These beliefs were accepted by roughly two out of three Northerners and three out of four Southerners. Their popularity cannot be attributed solely to a lack of sympathy. Indeed, half the Negroes in the sample accepted the belief that Negroes can get ahead as easily as others, and a third said that Negroes must show that they deserve equal rights. It must be remembered that such beliefs are part of the American ethic—no matter how badly off, everyone can improve his lot in life and "God helps those who help themselves." On the other hand, such beliefs often are interpreted so as to absolve the oppressors and place responsibility on the oppressed. To believe that Negroes can get ahead as easily as others or that Negroes must show themselves deserving of equal treatment clearly involves both cognitive and moral insensitivity. But it is not so clear that such clichés are accepted only by those who are personally insensitive. Rather they are the kinds of conventional platitudes that *produce* insensitivity in individuals. The beliefs themselves are insensitive and need not reflect a peculiar insensitivity on the part of those who accept them.

"As you see it, are Negroes today demanding more than they have a right to?" is a less ambiguous measure of sympathy (Table 54, Item 10). This much is suggested by the Negro response: only 4 per cent answered in the affirmative. In contrast, 43 per cent of whites in the North and 58 per cent of those in the South said Negroes are demanding too much. Finally, respondents were asked to compare their present feelings about Negroes with how they felt a year earlier. A small proportion of whites in the sample—15 per cent—said they were more sympathetic. Another 50 per cent said their feelings had not changed. This group obviously contains persons who have been consistently sympathetic as well as those who have been consistently unsympathetic. Finally, 37 per cent said the past year had made them less sympathetic. As on the other "sympathy" questions, the North-South difference is small (35 per cent versus 42 per cent). It is also small on the belief "These days you hear too much about the rights of minorities and too little about the rights of the majority"; in the

North 62 per cent of whites agreed, in the South 67 per cent did so.[7] These data were collected in 1964, a period of heightened Negro protest but prior to the major disturbances in the ghettos. Though a white backlash did not materialize in the 1964 election, it is evident that the ingredients were present: a high degree of anti-Negro prejudice and growing disaffection with the Negro protest movement.

Sources of Anti-Negro Prejudice

In order to examine the social sources of anti-Negro prejudice, a five-item Index of Anti-Negro Prejudice was constructed (combining Items 2, 3, 5, 9, and 10 in Table 54). The Index systematically predicts anti-Negro responses on other items. For example, the proportion saying that in the past year their feelings had become less sympathetic toward the Negro steadily increases—from 15 per cent among those with a score of zero to 63 per cent among those with a maximum score of 5. The average score on the Index is 2.6; those above this average (scores of 3 or more) are classi-fied as High. On this criterion, 40 per cent of whites in the North and 72 per cent of whites in the South score high on anti-Negro prejudice.

Education and Social Class

As with anti-Semitism, the relation between education and anti-Negro prejudice is powerful and systematic (Table 55, Part A). In the North 58 per cent of grade schoolers score as anti-Negro, and this declines to 41 per cent for high schoolers, 25 per cent for those with some college, and 16 per cent among college graduates. The impact of education is just as great in the South. The proportions begin at 86 per cent for grade schoolers and declines to 77 for high schoolers, 50 for those with some college, and 43 per cent among college graduates. Though Southerners are on the whole less educated than Northerners, the regional effect is strong at every level of education. Anti-Negro prejudice, as measured in this study, is as high among college graduates in the South as among high schoolers in the North. The combined effect of education and region is even more dramatic than the figures in Table 55 indicate. Not a single grade schooler in the South scored zero on the Index of Anti-Negro Prejudice, not one college graduate in the North had a maximum score of 5.

The evidence is again strong that prejudice is not a distinctively social-class phenomenon but is mainly a function of lack of education. As with anti-Semitism, the statistical associations of income and occupation to anti-

[7] While only 4 per cent of Negro respondents said that Negroes are demanding more than they have a right to, 34 per cent agreed to this item.

Table 55.   ANTI-NEGRO PREJUDICE BY REGION AND EDUCATION, SEX, AGE, AND RURAL-URBAN RESIDENCE[a]

(per cent anti-Negro among whites only)

	North	South	Total
A. **Education**			
Grade school	58%	86%	68%
	(279)	(147)	(426)
High school	41	77	49
	(624)	(189)	(813)
Some college	25	50	32
	(142)	(58)	(200)
College graduate	16	43	23
	(127)	(49)	(176)
B. **Sex**			
Males	40	76	50
	(564)	(213)	(777)
Females	41	69	48
	(609)	(231)	(840)
C. **Age**			
Less than 35	29	63	39
	(231)	(129)	(460)
35–54	37	71	46
	(481)	(161)	(642)
55 or older	55	81	63
	(361)	(154)	(515)
D. **Rural-urban**			
Urban	41	64	46
	(766)	(218)	(984)
Rural	40	81	55
	(378)	(225)	(603)
Total	40%	72%	49%
	(1,173)	(444)	(1,617)

[a]Index consists of Items 2, 3, 5, 9, and 10 in Table 54. Scores of 3 or more are designated as anti-Negro.

Negro prejudice are largely explained by education. But again prejudice increases at the highest income level ($15,000 or more).[8] That the affluent tend to be prejudiced against Negroes as well as Jews casts further doubt on the idea that anti-Semitism results from being in special competition

[8] The rate of anti-Negro prejudice declines from 58 per cent among those earning less than $5,000 to 44 per cent among the $5000–$9,999 group, to 41 per cent

with Jews for money and status. As suggested in Chapter 5, the prejudice of affluent college graduates is largely explained by the fact that many of them have had specialized educations and are unsophisticated relative to their educational peers.[9]

Chapter 5 found as many of the uneducated opposed to a Jewish presidential candidate as to intermarriage. This was in contrast to the educated, who were far less opposed to the candidate than to intermarriage. From this we inferred that lack of education is associated with a failure to distinguish between public and private forms of discrimination. The same pattern emerges with respect to discrimination against Negroes (Table 56; to simplify matters we discuss figures only for the North). In the North almost as many grade schoolers advocated separate schools for Negroes as said, "To be frank, I would not want my child to go to school with a lot of Negroes" (40 per cent versus 53 per cent). College graduates, in contrast, tended to distinguish between their private sentiments and their stand on public policy. While many (34 per cent) said they would not want their child to go to school with a lot of Negroes, relatively few (8 per cent) advocated school segregation.

It might be argued that the children of college educated middle-class parents would not be apt to go to school "with a lot of Negroes" and that this accounts for their opposition to segregated schools. However, there is

---

among the $10,000–$14,999 group. This 17-percentage-point difference is reduced to an average of 1 when education is controlled. At the $15,000-or-more level, the rate of prejudice increases to 46 per cent; this increase holds up at the high school and some-college levels, but vanishes among college graduates.

The effect of occupation is also largely explained by education. The original difference between blue- and white-collar workers is 17 percentage points, but this is reversed in one of the partials and reduced to 6 percentage points in the remaining three.

[9] As with anti-Semitic prejudice, higher income among college graduates is associated with greater anti-Negro prejudice only among the relatively unsophisticated— those with less than perfect scores on the writers test. Among the sophisticated, greater income is if anything associated with less anti-Negro prejudice. The figures are as follows:

Score on Writers Test	Annual Income	Anti-Negro	
		Per Cent	Number
4	Less than $10,000	21	(48)
4	$10,000 or more	13	(53)
Less than 4	Less than $10,000	21	(38)
Less than 4	$10,000 or more	45	(31)

Incidentally, the zero-order relation shows almost no relation between income and anti-Negro prejudice among college graduates: among those with incomes of less than $10,000, 21 per cent are anti-Negro; among those with incomes of $10,000 or more, 25 per cent are anti-Negro. This occurs because within categories of cultural sophistication, income has opposite effects.

Table 56.   SUPPORT FOR DISCRIMINATION AGAINST NEGROES
BY EDUCATION AND REGION
(whites only)

	Grade School	High School	Some College	College Graduate	Total
North					
Favor separate but equal schools[a]	40%	26%	12%	8%	26%
Would not like their child to go to school with a lot of Negroes[b]	53	49	36	34	47
100% (N) =	(295)	(638)	(145)	(128)	(1,197)
South					
Favor separate but equal schools[a]	83%	75%	56%	42%	72%
Would not like their child to go to school with a lot of Negroes[b]	84	75	59	66	76
100% (N) =	(149)	(195)	(59)	(50)	(454)
North					
Favor miscegenation law[c]	68%	57%	30%	20%	53%
Defend restaurant owner[d]	44	50	43	41	47
South					
Favor miscegenation law[c]	94%	85%	59%	42%	79%
Defend restaurant owner[d]	86	79	78	80	82

[a]Item 3, Table 54.   [b]Item 4, Table 54.   [c]Item 5, Table 54.   [d]Item 6, Table 54.

other evidence of their opposition to public forms of discrimination. Among grade schoolers and high schoolers in the North more favor miscegenation laws than defend the right of a restaurant owner not to serve Negroes (68 per cent versus 44 per cent and 57 per cent versus 50 per cent). The opposite holds at the two college levels: fewer favor miscegenation laws than defend the restaurant owner (30 per cent versus 43 per cent and 20 per cent versus 41 per cent). Once again we see the *relative* reluctance of the college educated to support public forms of discrimination that clearly violate civil rights.

Notwithstanding their greater rejection of anti-Negro prejudice and their greater support of civil rights, the educated were as likely as the uneducated to come to the defense of property rights. This was true for the restaurant owner as well as for the property owner. However, the attitudes of the uneducated toward Negroes and toward property rights are congruent and mutually reinforcing. In contrast, more of the educated are ambivalent; they defend both the civil rights of Negroes and what they perceive to be the rights of individual property owners. We encountered a similar pattern before: college graduates tend to oppose political anti-Semitism but to defend the right of a social club to exclude Jews.

Sex

As with anti-Semitism, sex bears little relation to anti-Negro prejudice (Table 55, Part B). In the South males are slightly more likely than females to score high on anti-Negro prejudice; in the North there is no difference whatsoever.

Age

In both the North and the South, the young exhibit a lower rate of anti-Negro prejudice than the old (Table 55, Part C). However, region continues to have a strong impact. Among whites under 35 years of age, 29 per cent in the North score as anti-Negro compared to 63 per cent in the South. Young people in the South are more prejudiced than old people in the North, while Southerners in the oldest age group are the most prejudiced of all.

In the South the age difference is mostly explained by education. This suggests that traditional beliefs about Negroes continue to be effectively transmitted: the young are just as prejudiced as the old unless they have had more education. In the North the story is different. Age is independently related to prejudice, and in the North young college graduates are of all groups the least prejudiced (8 per cent). The educated young have stood out as low on every measure of intolerance examined: only 8 per cent scored High on the Index of Anti-Semitic Belief, 3 per cent on the Index of Simplism, 5 per cent on the Index of Intolerance of Cultural Diversity. If there is a nucleus of principled opposition to prejudice, it is to be found among the college-educated young.

Rural-Urban Differences

In the North the geographical distribution of anti-Negro prejudice is rather uniform. There are no urban-rural differences (Table 55, Part D), and sectional differences are small: in the Midwest the rate is 44 per cent; in the Northeast , 40 per cent; in the Northwest, 34 per cent. In the South, however, rural areas exhibit a higher rate of prejudice than do urban areas (81 per cent versus 64 per cent). This difference is partly a function of the comparatively low educational level of whites in the rural South.[10] But part appears to be a genuine cultural effect. Even when education is controlled, the rural South is consistently more prejudiced, whether against Negroes, Jews, or Catholics.

Anti-Semitism and Anti-Negro Prejudice

For all their differences—in history, in content, and in degree—anti-Negro and anti-Jewish prejudice are basically alike in social location. Both are concentrated in the same social strata, especially the uneducated and the elderly. That they tend to be found in the same individuals is shown in Tables 57 and 58. Among those high and low on anti-Semitism 74 and 35

Table 57.   ANTI-NEGRO PREJUDICE BY EDUCATION AND ANTI-SEMITIC BELIEF
(per cent anti-Negro among whites)

Anti-Semitism[a]	Grade School	High School	Some College	College Graduates	Total
High	81%	73%	60%	59%	74%
	(223)	(277)	(48)	(27)	(576)
Low	53	37	23	17	35
	(203)	(536)	(152)	(149)	(1,041)
Total	68%	49%	32%	23%	
	(426)	(813)	(200)	(176)	

[a]Includes unconvinced non-anti-Semites; see Table 19 for details.

per cent score as anti-Negro. Among those high and low on anti-Negro prejudice, 54 and 18 per cent score high on anti-Semitism. The two are empirical cousins: if a person is prejudiced in one way, the chances are that he is prejudiced in the other.

Tables 57 and 58 also show that educational differences in one kind of prejudice are reduced when the other prejudice is controlled. The educational difference in anti-Semitism among whites is reduced from 38 percentage points to 24 and 23 among those low and high on anti-Negro prejudice. The educational difference in anti-Negro prejudice is reduced from 45 percentage points to 22 and 36 among those low and high in anti-Semitism. As we cautioned earlier, these relations are not causal. The

[10] Among rural Southern whites in the sample, 45 per cent do not have more than a grade school education compared to 21 per cent of whites in the urban South. If rural Southerners were as educated as urban Southerners, their rate of prejudice would be lowered from 81 to 75 per cent, a figure closer to the 64 per cent for urban Southerners.

Table 58. ANTI-SEMITIC BELIEF BY EDUCATION AND
ANTI-NEGRO PREJUDICE

(per cent anti-Semitic[a] among whites)

Anti-Negro Prejudice	Grade School	High School	Some College	College Graduates	Total
High	63% (288)	50% (402)	45% (64)	39% (41)	54% (796)
Low	31 (138)	18 (411)	14 (136)	8 (135)	18 (821)
Total	53% (434)	34% (836)	24% (204)	15% (179)	

[a]Includes unconvinced non-anti-Semites; see Table 19 for details.

uneducated are not more prejudiced against Jews *because* they are more prejudiced against Negroes, or vice versa. Rather the implication is that the uneducated tend to be intolerant not of any one group but of social and cultural diversity in general.[11]

Table 59 arranges the data in a different way. Respondents are classified into four groups. The single largest group are the 45 per cent who are low on both anti-Semitism and anti-Negro prejudice. Twenty-six per cent are high on both; 20 per cent are high only on anti-Negro prejudice; 9 per cent are high only on anti-Semitism. These figures should not be taken as descriptively precise since different definitions of prejudice would produce different estimates. But they serve to show, once again, that people tend to be either consistently prejudiced or consistently unprejudiced; 71 per cent of the sample are either high or low on both forms of prejudice. Table 59 also shows that anti-Negro prejudice outruns anti-Semitism in the sense that when people are prejudiced against only one group, they tend to be prejudiced against Negroes. This is especially true in the South where 35 per cent score as prejudiced against Negroes but not against Jews.

Anti-Catholic Prejudice

Respondents were asked to agree or disagree with the statement "Catholics have too much power in the United States." Of the non-Catholics in the

[11] When the Indexes of Simplism and Intolerance of Cultural Diversity are combined into a single Index of General Intolerance, the educational difference in anti-Negro prejudice largely disappears. For example, in the North among those scoring Low on the Index of General Intolerance, 25 per cent of grade schoolers, 22 per cent of high schoolers, and 10 per cent of college graduates score as anti-Negro. This 15-percentage-point difference compares to an original difference of 42.

Table 59.   ANTI-NEGRO PREJUDICE AND ANTI-SEMITIC BELIEF BY REGION
(whites only)

	North	South	Total
Neither anti-Negro nor anti-Semitic	48%	25%	45%
Anti-Negro only	18	35	20
Anti-Semitic only	12	3	9
Both anti-Negro and anti-Semitic	22	37	26
100% (N) =	(1,173)	(444)	(1,617)

sample, 24 per cent agreed.[12] Again there is a tendency for persons prejudiced in one way to be prejudiced in another. Among white Protestants low
on both anti-Negro and anti-Semitic prejudice, only 10 per cent said that
Catholics have too much power. This figure rises to 21 per cent among
those prejudiced against only one group and to 46 per cent among those
prejudiced against both groups. Anti-Negro, anti-Jewish, and anti-Catholic
prejudice are all highly interrelated and form an empirical syndrome. It is
the rare respondent who is anti-Semitic only.

Evaluation of the Findings

Earlier we noted that the historical and the contemporary sources of
prejudice may bear little resemblance to each other. Nowhere is this more
apparent than in anti-Semitism and anti-Negro prejudice, one a vestige
inherited from medieval Europe, the other an indigenous outgrowth of
American slavery. Their differing historical origins are reflected in the
greater prevalence of anti-Negro prejudice in the South, as well as the
greater prevalence of discriminatory attitudes toward Negroes as compared
with Jews. Otherwise, however, the two phenomena are very much alike. In
both cases acceptance of traditional stereotypes is more frequent among
the uneducated than among the educated, as is support of public forms of
discrimination. Again, a distinction must be drawn between public and
private forms of discrimination. With respect to Negroes, the educated
tend to be opposed to obvious violations of civil rights, such as a segregated
school system or antimiscegenation laws. But they are just as ready as
the uneducated to defend the property rights of those who wish to discriminate against Negroes. It cannot be assumed that everyone who
defended the property owner approves of residential segregation, would

[12] Twenty per cent of the Jews in the sample agreed that Catholics have too much
power. Among those with less than a college education, 26 per cent agreed; among
the college educated the figure is 11 per cent. Seven per cent of Catholic respondents
said that Catholics have too much power.

personally refuse to sell to a Negro, or would move out of a neighborhood if it threatened to become integrated. However, we know that few middle-class neighborhoods are integrated, that state and local anti-housing-discrimination laws have been defeated or frustrated, and that the educated tend to support or condone discrimination against Jews in what they define as the private sphere. Just as social club discrimination can be defended by an appeal to the right of private association, so residential segregation can be defended by invoking private property rights.

The finding that the uneducated are much higher than the educated on both anti-Negro and anti-Jewish prejudice is incompatible with the competition theory of prejudice. While the uneducated might be said to be in competition with Negroes, they are not in competition with Jews. (Nor can the competition theory explain why the uneducated tend to be less tolerant of atheists, immigrants, people with beards, and practically every other form of diversity examined in this study.) While the middle-class status of Jews and the lower-class status of Negroes enter into the images and stereotypes that have emerged about each, this by no means implies that middle-class people accept anti-Jewish stereotypes while lower-class people accept anti-Negro stereotypes. Whatever the different origins of anti-Negro prejudice and anti-Semitism, their acceptance in the contemporary individual cannot be explained by special factors peculiar to one or another of the groups against whom prejudice is directed.

The social discrimination of the educated is often construed to mean that they are just as prejudiced and secretly hold the same stereotypes of Negroes as do the uneducated. A good deal of evidence indicates that this is not so, including the tendency of the educated to oppose public and political forms of discrimination. As we emphasized in Chapter 3, there are sources of discrimination other than naked prejudice. For many of the educated who are otherwise unprejudiced, admitting Negroes into their neighborhoods still lies outside the limits of their tolerance. The mere fact that pejorative images of Negroes exist and are widespread stigmatizes Negroes as socially undesirable, and social uneasiness—or "polite prejudice"—may persist among whites even after they have rejected traditional stereotypes as false and unjust.

There are inherent value conflicts in any democratic society, especially one that comprises culturally diverse groups. One conflict arises from the difficulty of deciding where the realm of the private ends and the realm of the public begins. The expansion of the democratic conscience in recent years has partly been a process of limiting private rights in light of their public consequences. When the unprejudiced claim a right to discriminate in private spheres, they reflect an unresolved dilemma of our normative order.

10 : Conclusion

Two basic conclusions emerge from this study: anti-Semitism continues at significant levels, and lack of education is the primary factor in its acceptance. Since both conclusions are open to misinterpretation, it may be helpful in this final chapter to make explicit what the findings imply and what they do not imply.

Anti-Semitism is widespread and pervasive, but not in a dangerous form. Evidence for the continued viability of anti-Semitism is of three kinds. First, there is a sizable reservoir of anti-Semitic beliefs and stereotypes in the population. Over a third of Americans are anti-Semitic as measured by an eleven-item Index of Anti-Semitic Belief. Even the nominally unprejudiced—that third of the population free or virtually free of traditional stereotypes—cannot be said to constitute a solid nucleus of opposition to anti-Semitism. Many give evidence of failing to oppose it in principle, either by answering "don't know" to crucial questions about Jews or by acquiescing in some form of discrimination.

Second, social club discrimination is widely accepted, even among the least prejudiced third of the population. Over a quarter of the sample defended the right of social clubs to exclude Jews. Another 29 per cent, while opposed in principle, indicated they would do little or nothing to combat social club discrimination in practice. Firm opposition is confined to a minority of 36 per cent. Moreover, defense of social club discrimination is at its highest among the most educated. This means that anti-Semitism receives substantial support in one form or another from every stratum of American society.

Third, a substantial minority are susceptible to political anti-Semitism. While only a handful said they would be inclined to vote for an anti-Semitic candidate, over a third indicated that his anti-Semitism would make no difference to them. Like social club discrimination, indifference is common among the least prejudiced third of the population. However, it is the uneducated non-anti-Semite who tends to be susceptible to political anti-Semitism, the educated non-anti-Semite who tends to defend social club discrimination.

The viability of anti-Semitism must be measured by opposition as well as support. A third of the population consistently reject anti-Semitic stereotypes; a third firmly oppose social club discrimination; more than half say they would vote against an anti-Semitic candidate. Only 16 per cent of the sample meet all three criteria, and on this strict standard only a small minority of the population can be described as principled and consistent opponents of anti-Semitism. On the other hand support for the more clearly illegitimate forms of discrimination is at unprecedentedly low levels. A mere 5 per cent said they would vote for the anti-Semitic candidate; only 10 per cent failed to support equality in employment; only 11 per cent agreed that Jews have too much power in the United States. Today no more than 5 to 10 per cent can be called rabid anti-Semites.[1]

Nevertheless, a resurgence of anti-Semitism cannot be ruled out. This study has presented a large body of evidence pointing to the conclusion that cultural resources for fascism are widespread in American society. The continued existence of anti-Semitic prejudice would not by itself justify such a conclusion. As our data show, the anti-Semitism of most Americans does not go beyond acceptance of anti-Semitic beliefs and support of mild forms of discrimination. Nor is it a foregone conclusion that political reaction in the United States would be accompanied by anti-Semitism. However, simplistic beliefs and authoritarian attitudes, ignorance and disregard of democratic norms, a low threshold of tolerance for social and political diversity, insensitivity to the suffering of others—these are tendencies that characterize large numbers of Americans. Given a crisis situation and political leadership, they constitute a potential threat to the democratic order.

Lack of education is the most important factor in anti-Semitism, but it is not the only one. From the array of factors examined in Part II, education emerged as the one most powerfully related to anti-Semitism. Its impact is just as great in the South as in the North, among Negroes as among whites, among Protestants as among Catholics. Furthermore, analysis showed that certain other factors predict anti-Semitism only because they are related to education. For example, workers in blue-collar

---

[1] "The great majority of prejudiced persons carry prejudice at a low temperature. . . . They are not paranoid, anti-Semitic fascists, nor obsessive-compulsive fanatics" [Robin M. Williams, Jr., *Strangers Next Door* (Englewood Cliffs, N.J.: Prentice-Hall, 1964), p. 9].

occupations exhibit a comparatively high rate of anti-Semitism, but this has little to do with their occupations or life situation; it is largely a function of their relative lack of education. While persons from lower-class backgrounds, Negroes, immigrants, the elderly, and those living in rural areas are relatively high on anti-Semitism, part of the reason is to be found in their lower levels of education.

Education does not tell the whole story. Other factors such as age and race are related to anti-Semitism apart from education. But no other factor has an impact approaching that of education.

Though the relation between education and anti-Semitism is strong, it is not perfect. In previous chapters we sometimes spoke of "the uneducated" and "the educated" as polar opposites. We did this to simplify the presentation, certainly not to imply that the uneducated are uniformly anti-Semitic, the educated uniformly unprejudiced. Implicitly, all our assertions have been comparative and probabilistic: compared to the less educated, a lower proportion of the more educated hold pejorative images of Jews. Such a statement takes for granted the existence of unprejudiced grade schoolers and anti-Semitic college graduates. Indeed much attention was given to exploring the conditions under which certain individuals deviate from the "norm" for their educational group. It was found that existential factors, such as social isolation and job dissatisfaction, did not increase or decrease anti-Semitism among the uneducated. However, when grade schoolers exhibited cognitive sophistication—when they knew the Constitution and rejected simplistic beliefs—their rate of anti-Semitism was about half that for grade schoolers as a whole. Conversely, when college graduates were not knowledgeable or were simplistic, their rate of anti-Semitism increased sharply. But sophisticated grade schoolers and unsophisticated college graduates are exceptional. As the data show, an enlightened belief system is rarely acquired except through participation in the formal educational system. Theoretically, it can be acquired in other ways. In fact, this seldom happens.

It could be argued that the liberalizing effect of college education is spurious because persons with an intellectually unsophisticated and morally unenlightened belief system are unlikely to go to college in the first place. In other words, because of selective factors the college educated may already be unprejudiced prior to entering institutions of higher learning. No doubt a study of high schoolers would find that those who intend to go on to college are more liberal and tolerant in their attitudes than those who do not. But this is only to say that they already tend to identify with the values of modern education. As our data abundantly show, it is relatively rare to find the unprejudiced rejecting the values of contemporary education, or the prejudiced embracing them. Furthermore, past studies have shown that though entering freshmen may start low on prejudice, they become still less prejudiced by the time they finish college.[2]

Anti-Semitism among the college educated is generally low, but it is far from trivial in its social consequences. The educated are the guardians of the ideal values of our society. They constitute a cultural elite whose responsibility is to form and maintain standards of belief and behavior. Because they typically occupy positions of power and prestige, they also constitute a social and political elite, tending to define for others what is respectable in the realm of belief and permissible in the realm of conduct. For this reason, any prejudice among the college educated cannot be ignored.

The same logic applies to social club discrimination, which finds its strongest support among the college educated. The intentions of some college graduates when they condone social club discrimination may be entirely innocent; abstractly, freedom of personal association is a democratic right. But in a society pervaded by ethnic and racial prejudice this innocent intention has less than innocent consequences. Whatever its source or rationale, social club discrimination helps to create and maintain the image of Jews as socially undesirable and to cast the Jew into the role of the outsider. It reduces the moral authority of the educated to speak out against prejudice, and it implicitly legitimates the virulent expressions of anti-Semitism that the educated disavow for themselves. However unprejudiced they may be, the college educated who support social club discrimination condone one of the historic institutions of prejudice.

The social discrimination of the educated shows that an aura of social undesirability still stigmatizes Jews. This has important consequences for the position of Jews in the social and economic order, and ultimately for the persistence of anti-Semitism. Excluded from the stable center of the economic order, many Jews end up in marginal industries and marginal economic roles often characterized by marginal business practices. A recent study of the legal profession in New York City showed that Jewish lawyers are still largely excluded from coveted positions in the profession: ". . . a Jewish lawyer who . . . [made] law review in an Ivy League law school has no better chance of being in a large firm than a Protestant lawyer who did not 'make law review' and who attended a non-Ivy League law school."[3] As a result, Jewish lawyers tend to be in the smaller, less

[2] At least two studies have administered tests to the same college students at one- or two-year intervals. They found a decline in the proportion holding anti-Semitic stereotypes, as well as other unenlightened beliefs similar to those in the F scale. [Reported in Philip E. Jacob, *Changing Values in College* (New York: Harper & Row, 1957), pp. 41–45.]

[3] Jerome E. Carlin, *Lawyers' Ethics: A Survey of the New York City Bar* (New York: Russell Sage Foundation, 1966), p. 31.

prestigious, and less affluent law firms, characterized by intense competition and low profit margins. Such firms have low status and unstable clienteles, and are typically engaged in areas of the law where unprofessional standards are customary. For Jews and non-Jews alike, these conditions create great pressures to engage in extralegal and unethical practices. This is the familiar vicious circle created by prejudice: Discrimination forces its victims to live out the stereotypes; their behavior is then used to validate the stereotypes and justify continued discrimination. At the same time, similar conduct on the part of others goes unnoticed. Discrimination against Jews by the educated elite, even when unmotivated by hard-core anti-Semitic beliefs, has far-reaching consequences, as the New York study illustrates. Whatever its roots, social discrimination by the educated leaves Jews perennially on the margin of respectability.

Social-class factors, while at present largely irrelevant to acceptance of anti-Semitic beliefs, may be crucial in other respects. This has been a study of routine anti-Semitism. The data were collected during a period of unprecedented economic prosperity. The anti-Semitism we have found is what is "normal" and routine for American society. Except for economic anti-Semitism among Negroes, nothing in the data suggests that present-day anti-Semitism is an expression of social-class resentments. In an economic crisis of sufficient magnitude, however, Jews could well become an object of hostility and blamed for society's ills, as the scapegoat theory of prejudice suggests. Many of those susceptible to political anti-Semitism might vote for an anti-Semitic candidate with a promised economic solution, as happened in Germany. Since the working class are most apt to suffer in an economic crisis, their present acceptance of anti-Semitic beliefs takes on more than incidental significance. In normal times the relative economic deprivation of the working class has little to do with their acceptance of anti-Semitic beliefs. In a period of crisis, however, it could be crucial.

The same logic applies to downward mobility, sometimes identified as a source of anti-Semitism. Our data indicate that generational mobility, whether upward or downward, is unrelated to anti-Semitism when education is taken into account. However, an economic crisis would produce personal downward mobility on a massive scale, as well as heightened anti-Semitic propaganda. Under such circumstances the downwardly mobile might seize upon the Jews as a scapegoat, especially if they were uneducated and already held anti-Semitic beliefs.[4]

Finally, while anti-Semitic beliefs and most discriminatory attitudes are

[4] Bruno Bettelheim and Morris Janowitz, *Social Change and Prejudice* (New York: Free Press of Glencoe, 1964) found that World War II veterans faced with downward occupational mobility were especially prone to express anti-Semitic sentiments.

largely functions of lack of education, support of social club discrimination does tend to be a social-class phenomenon. To the extent that defense of social club discrimination increases with greater income it is plausible that status concerns and social-class snobbery are involved. While education and income are highly related, to some extent they work at cross purposes. Greater education leads to rejection of anti-Semitic prejudice, greater income to support of social club discrimination.[5]

Personality factors do not explain acceptance of anti-Semitic beliefs; nevertheless they are related to prejudice in other ways. The highly systematic relation between prejudice and years of schooling is strong evidence that acceptance of anti-Semitic beliefs is not a matter of "individual psychology." Anti-Semitic beliefs are accepted routinely along with other cultural beliefs so long as individuals lack the cognitive and moral criteria to reject them. This is not to deny that under some conditions and for some individuals anti-Semitic beliefs have psychological consequences. At the very least, to accept anti-Semitic beliefs is to adopt certain attitudes and to have certain predispositions toward Jews. Moreover, because of their distinctive content anti-Semitic beliefs are easily "activated" and put to psychological use in times of personal and social stress. Nor do we wish to deny that in some instances there may be great congruence between an individual's personal psychopathology and the fantasy images projected by anti-Semitic ideology. But any suggestion that acceptance of anti-Semitic beliefs is typically rooted in the personal psychopathology of individuals seems to be ruled out by the facts. Personal psychopathology may explain the rabid anti-Semite and the few who take an active role in creating and promulgating anti-Semitic propaganda. But, on the whole, initial acceptance of anti-Semitic beliefs is no more distinctively rooted in personal psychopathology than is acceptance of other unenlightened beliefs.[6]

We do not claim that the taking on of anti-Semitic beliefs is psychically

---

However, the Bettelheim-Janowitz study differs from the present one in that it examined personal and not generational mobility, and did so in an era characterized by a great deal of anti-Semitic propaganda, including that emanating from Nazi Germany. We do not doubt that for people who already accept anti-Semitic beliefs downward mobility provides an occasion for the *expression* of their anti-Semitism. But there is no evidence in the Bettelheim-Janowitz study that veterans first experienced downward mobility and only then took on anti-Semitic beliefs.

[5] Income is also an *indirect* factor in prejudice since it influences access to education. However, in an era of state-supported education, income is becoming decreasingly relevant.

[6] What Freud said of religion applies as well to anti-Semitism: ". . . civilization gives the individual these ideas, for he finds them there already; they are presented to him ready-made, and he would not be able to discover them for himself. What he is entering into is the heritage of many generations, and he takes it over as he does the multiplication table, geometry, and similar things" [Sigmund Freud, *The Future of an Illusion* (Garden City, N.Y.: Anchor, 1964), p. 30].

neutral. A pathology is present, but it is in the beliefs, not necessarily in the individual who accepts them. Many prejudiced beliefs have been interpreted as examples of projection, displacement, and reaction-formation, of paranoia and sado-masochism.[7] However, to accept the projective or sado-masochistic beliefs of a culture is not necessarily to be engaged in a personal act of projection or to give evidence of being personally sado-masochistic in any clinical sense of the term. No doubt an anti-Semitic belief system can provide the individual with the same kind of perverse psychic satisfactions he receives from his own more personally inspired fantasies. But the important point is that anti-Semites do not have to invent or seek out the anti-Semitic beliefs they hold; rather they accept them in the same way they accept other beliefs in the culture and their immediate environment. Lack of cognitive sophistication in the individual rather than the psychic significance of unenlightened beliefs appears to be the crucial factor in their acceptance.

This does not mean that anti-Semitic beliefs lack psychodynamic origins. To a large extent, the belief systems and symbols that constitute culture are the social precipitates of man's inner and largely unconscious life. In this sense, anti-Semitic ideology may be ultimately rooted in psychodynamic processes and in the deeper layers of human personality. But the relation is indirect; it is mediated by the routine socialization of individuals into the anti-Semitic culture. Sado-masochistic fantasies and primitive defense mechanisms may be the ultimate psychic forces behind the emergence of anti-Semitic ideology as a cultural fact and the creation of the Jew as a cultural symbol for evil; they also suggest the kinds of psychic satisfactions available in anti-Semitic ideology. But whether the individual accepts or rejects anti-Semitic ideology, as well as the psychic satisfactions it affords, is basically determined by his education. Deep psychic forces may help to answer the question: Why prejudice? They may help to explain why people often cling to their prejudices. But they shed little light on why, in our society at the present time, some individuals are prejudiced and others are not.

In accepting anti-Semitic prejudice, and the many other unenlightened beliefs and attitudes that usually accompany it, the individual acquires certain social orientations and a ready-made outlet for whatever inner problems and conflicts he may have. These are legitimately considered part of his personality. But the issue is how much of the individual's personality is formed in early childhood and how much depends on his subsequent education. Largely ignored in the psychoanalytic literature are

---

[7] For example, in Douglass W. Orr, "Anti-Semitism and the Psychopathology of Everyday Life," in Ernst Simmel (ed.), *Anti-Semitism, A Social Disease* (New York: International Universities Press, 1946), pp. 85–95.

the psychic consequences of knowledge and ignorance, and the role that these play in determining, not only the surface personality, but how the individual deals with his inner needs and conflicts. The enlightened culture, insofar as it is organized around scientific and democratic values, is clearly a culture of sublimation; it explicitly proscribes the primitive psychic satisfactions to be gained by direct expressions of id impulses or obedience to the id-inspired dictates of the superego. Psychoanalytic language aside, the acquisition of knowledge about the world permits a realistic problem-solving attitude toward it. For the cognitively naive, the world is often baffling and inexplicable, and this is an open invitation to fantasy and magical explanations. One aspect of a primitive cognitive style is that it assigns blame and searches for scapegoats precisely because it fails to comprehend impersonal and abstract causes. Jews have been the historical scapegoats of Western society. What needs to be added is that scapegoating is a primitive mode of explanation that tends to characterize the cognitively unsophisticated even in modern society.

Education reduces prejudice, but not any kind of education does so. Certainly it is not the argument of this book that "doing time" in school reduces prejudice. The emphasis we have placed on scientific and democratic norms should make it clear that only a certain kind of education is relevant to rejection of prejudice. Not all education is equal in modernity, in quality, or in relevance to prejudice. Even among college graduates, as past studies have shown, commitment to democratic values varies by major concentration in college, with students in the social sciences and humanities scoring as more civil libertarian than those in the physical sciences or business administration.

More is involved in education than learning that prejudice is not respectable. At its best, education involves a total belief system of a fairly general and abstract nature. It develops an intellectual commitment to rules of evidence, not merely to a body of facts; transmits democratic principles, not mere conformity to specific norms and prohibitions.[8] However, education is not always at its best, and everyone is not equally receptive to it. Doubtless, some of the tolerance of the educated represents outward conformity to respectable opinion and, as we know from the data, the commitment of the educated to democratic norms varies depending on the issue involved. This was seen in their willingness to deprive atheists of their civil rights, in their considerable support of social club discrimination against Jews, and in their level of anti-Negro prejudice and

---

[8] For this reason shotgun "educational" campaigns that seek to eliminate prejudice but leave the individual's belief system otherwise unchanged are not apt to be effective. The prejudiced beliefs of the uneducated are firmly embedded in a system of unenlightened beliefs and alienated attitudes; it is unrealistic to think that one element of this system can be easily excised.

lack of sympathy with the civil rights struggle. These facts raise questions concerning the degree to which even college graduates understand and are committed to democratic values. Nevertheless, the educated are almost always more likely than the uneducated to exhibit liberal, humane, and enlightened attitudes, regardless of the issue at hand.

We have emphasized the consequences as well as the content of education. Education determines one's place in the social system. The college educated not only acquire beliefs and values with which anti-Semitism is incompatible, but after leaving college they enter into an environment of belief that gives at least lip service to norms of tolerance. Conversely, after leaving school the less educated are likely to enter an environment of belief where prejudice is routine, to be excluded from full participation in the larger society, and to have little reason or opportunity to identify with the official normative order. Thus, the different life experiences of the uneducated and the educated reinforce and perpetuate whatever inclinations to prejudice or capacity for tolerance they had when they ended their formal education.

As the educational level in the country rises, anti-Semitic prejudice is likely to decrease; however, education is not a cure-all. Prejudice can be combated either by attacking the social institutions that perpetuate prejudice or by strengthening countervailing institutions. The first strategy is attractive because it gets to the root causes of prejudice, but the second is probably the more realistic. That anti-Semitism and other forms of prejudice are deeply embedded in Western culture cannot be taken lightly.

The data show that at the present time the educational system is the primary countervailing influence leading to the reduction of prejudice. The gradual upgrading in the educational composition of the population should therefore result in a steady reduction of prejudice. However, this reduction will be gradual and small. The number of college graduates will more than double by 1985, but they will still constitute only 15 per cent of the adult population. The major shift in the educational structure of the country will be a decrease in the proportion of those with no more than a grade school education from 34 per cent in 1964 to an estimated 16 per cent in 1985.[9] At that time the modal educational group will be high school graduates of whom a third in the present study scored High on the Index of Anti-Semitic Belief. Moreover, even if the countervailing potential of education were maximized, it would still have to contend with the positive forces making for prejudice in the home, the neighborhood, the church, the community. There will always be those who leave school early and those who are prejudiced despite their education. While education can reach many, it cannot reach all.

[9] Projected estimates are from *Statistical Abstract of the United States, 1966*, U.S. Dept. of Commerce, Bureau of the Census, p. 112.

This book has treated education as both a descriptive and a theoretical variable. From a descriptive point of view, education is a social institution and an attribute of individuals. As such, it has limits, as the data have repeatedly shown. From a theoretical point of view, we have necessarily spoken of education in normative and ideal terms. A commitment to scientific and democratic values, an understanding of their social implications, cognitive and moral sophistication—these are the ideals, not always the realities of modern education. But for all their shortcomings, the educational institutions are the primary means whereby the individual is integrated into the ideal norms and values that constitute and sustain a democratic and humane society.

Appendix A: Interview Schedule

SURVEY RESEARCH SERVICE

National Opinion Research Center
University of Chicago

INTRODUCTION AT DWELLING UNIT:

Hello. I'm _____ from the National Opinion
Research Center. We're conducting a national survey and I'm here
to interview a (man)(woman) who is (INSERT QUOTA QUALIFICATION).
Is there someone here who fits that description?

> If Yes (PROCEED WITH INTERVIEW)

> If No (RECORD CALL ON SURS AND
>   GO ON TO NEXT DU)

ENTER TIME INTERVIEW BEGAN: _____ AM
                                     PM

INTRODUCTION TO INTERVIEW:

We're interested in finding out how people all over the country feel
about some important issues of the day, including how they feel about
certain groups. I'd like to ask you, first . . . .

. . . . .about some things that have been in the news.

001

1. In general, are you in favor of the United Nations or opposed?

> In favor 1 8/
>
> Opposed 2
>
> Don't know X

---

2. Do you feel the United States is losing power in the world or is it becoming more powerful?

> Losing power . (ASK A) . . 1 9/
>
> Becoming more powerful . . 2
>
> Staying the same 3
>
> Don't know X

    A. **IF LOSING POWER:** How much does this disturb you--a great deal, somewhat, or very little?

> A great deal 1 10/
>
> Somewhat 2
>
> Very little 3
>
> Don't know X

---

3. (HAND RESPONDENT CARD A) Which of the statements on this card comes closest to expressing how you feel about the state of morals in this country at the present time?

> They are pretty bad, and getting worse . 1 11/
>
> They are pretty bad, but getting better . 2
>
> They are pretty good, but getting worse . 3
>
> They are pretty good, and getting better . 4
>
> Don't know X

---

4. How great a danger do you feel that American Communists are to this country at the present time--a very great danger, a great danger, some danger, hardly any danger, or no danger?

> A very great danger . . . 1 12/
>
> A great danger 2
>
> Some danger 3
>
> Hardly any danger 4
>
> No danger 5
>
> Don't know X

(HAND RESPONDENT CARD B) In this country, do you think any of the people on this card are more likely than other Americans to be Communists?

None	0	13/__
Union leaders	1	14/__
Negroes	2	15/__
Jews	3	16/__
College teachers	4	17/__
Foreign born	5	18/__
People in the government in Washington	6	19/__
Don't know	X	20/__

A. Are there any other types of people in this country (not on the card) that are more likely than other Americans to be Communists? (RECORD VERBATIM)

---

6. Suppose Congress wanted to pass a law saying that groups who disagree with our form of government could not hold public meetings or make speeches. As far as you know, would Congress have the right under the Constitution to pass such a law?

Yes . . . (ASK A) .	1 21/__
No . . . . (ASK B) .	2
Don't know (ASK B) .	X

A. IF YES: Would you be in favor of a law saying that groups who disagree with our form of government could not hold public meetings or make speeches, or opposed to it?

In favor	1 22/__
Opposed	2
Don't know	X

B. IF NO OR DON'T KNOW: Supposing it were constitutional, would you like to see such a law passed or not?

Yes	1 23/__
No	2
Don't know	X

7. How would you feel about a law saying that the President must be a man who believes in God? As far as you know, would Congress have the right under the Constitution to pass such a law?

                                      Yes . . . (ASK A) . . 1 24/
                                      No   . . . (ASK B) . . 2
                                      Don't know (ASK B) . . X

   A. IF YES: Would you be in favor of a law saying that the President must be a man who believes in God, or opposed to it?

                                      In favor 1 25/
                                      Opposed 2
                                      Don't know X

   B. IF NO OR DON'T KNOW: Supposing it were constitutional, would you like to see such a law passed or not?

                                      Yes 1 26/
                                      No 2
                                      Don't know X

8. Do you think that having a death penalty for the worst crimes is a good idea or are you against the death penalty?

                                      A good idea 1 27/
                                      Against 2
                                      Don't know X

9. Have you heard of the John Birch Society?

                                      Yes . . . (ASK A) . . 1 28/
                                      No 2
                                      Don't know X

   A. IF YES: What is your opinion of the John Birch Society--do you strongly approve of what it stands for, approve somewhat, disapprove somewhat, or strongly disapprove?

                                      Strongly approve . . . 1 29/
                                      Approve somewhat . . . 2
                                      Disapprove somewhat . 3
                                      Strongly disapprove . 4
                                      Don't know X

10. As you see it, are Negroes today demanding more than they have a right to?

                                      Yes 1 30/
                                      No 2
                                      Don't know X

FOR <u>NEGRO RESPONDENTS</u>, SKIP TO Q. 12.

11. I'd like to ask you to compare your feelings about Negroes now with your feel-
    ings a year or so ago. Would you say that you are much less sympathetic to
    Negroes now, somewhat less sympathetic, somewhat more sympathetic, or much
    more sympathetic?

                                    Much less sympathetic . . . 1 31/
                                    Somewhat less sympathetic . 2
                                    Somewhat more sympathetic . 3
                                    Much more sympathetic . . . 4
                                    Feel about the same 5
                                    Don't know X

12. Which religious group do you think is most in favor of racial integration--
    Protestants, Catholics, or Jews?

                                    Protestants 1 32/
                                    Catholics 2
                                    Jews 3
                                    No difference 4
                                    Don't know X

13. Now I am going to read a list of statements to you and I would like to know
    whether you <u>agree</u> or <u>disagree</u> with each one.

		Agree	Disagree	Don't Know	
A.	The Federal government should pass a law to provide medical care for old people.	1	2	X	33/
B.	The Federal government is gradually taking away our basic freedoms.	1	2	X	34/
C.	Most people on welfare could take care of themselves if they really wanted to.	1	2	X	35/
D.	Poor people have no one to blame but themselves	1	2	X	36/
E.	The Supreme Court is goind a good job these days	1	2	X	37/
F.	Many church leaders in this country are playing into the hands of the Communists.	1	2	X	38/
G.	In the past 25 years, this country has moved dangerously close to Socialism	1	2	X	39/
H.	These days you hear too much about the rights of minorities and too little about the rights of the majority.	1	2	X	40/
I.	Catholics are getting too much power in the United States.	1	2	X	41/
J.	America owes a great deal to the immigrants who came here.	1	2	X	42/

13. Continued

		Agree	Disagree	Don't Know	
K.	Persons who insist on wearing beards should not be allowed to teach in public schools. .	1	2	X	43/___
L.	Foreigners who come to live in America should give up their foreign ways and learn to be like other Americans.	1	2	X	44/___
M.	Nothing in other countries can beat the American way of life.	1	2	X	45/___
N.	An owner of property should not have to sell to Negroes if he doesn't want to.	1	2	X	46/___
O.	A restaurant owner should not have to serve Negroes if he doesn't want to.	1	2	X	47/___
P.	Generally speaking, Negroes are lazy and don't like to work hard.	1	2	X	48/___
Q.	Before Negroes are given equal rights, they have to show that they deserve them.	1	2	X	49/___
R.	Negroes who want to work hard can get ahead just as easily as anyone else.	1	2	X	50/___

14. In general, do you think that Negroes are as intelligent as white people--
    that is, can they learn things just as well if they are given the same edu-
    cation and training?

                    Yes . . . . 1 51/___

                    No 2

                    Don't know X

15. Do you think white children and Negro children should go to the same schools
    or to separate but equal schools?

                    Same schools . . . . 1 52/___

                    Separate but equal schools . 2

                    Don't know X

16. Do you think there should be laws against marriages between Negroes and whites?

                                    Yes 1   53/___
                                    No 2
                                    Don't know X

17. (HAND RESPONDENT CARD C)   Please look at this card and tell me whether each
    of the people I mention is a writer, someone in sports, a politician, or an
    entertainer.   Very few people would know all of the names, so if you don't
    know someone, just say so.

		Writer	Sports	Politics	Entertainment	Don't Know	
A.	Roger Maris . . .	1	2	3	4	X	54/___
B.	Robert Frost . .	1	2	3	4	X	55/___
C.	William Holden .	1	2	3	4	X	56/___
D.	Vince Edwards . .	1	2	3	4	X	57/___
E.	William E. Miller	1	2	3	4	X	58/___
F.	Herman Melville .	1	2	3	4	X	59/___
G.	Frank Fontaine .	1	2	3	4	X	60/___
H.	Hubert Humphrey .	1	2	3	4	X	61/___
I.	Y. A. Tittle . .	1	2	3	4	X	62/___
J.	William Faulkner.	1	2	3	4	X	63/___
K.	Dean Rusk	1	2	3	4	X	64/___
L.	Mark Twain . . .	1	2	3	4	X	65/___
M.	Clarence Williams	1	2	3	4	X	66/___
N.	Douglas Dillon .	1	2	3	4	X	67/___
O.	Arnold Palmer . .	1	2	3	4	X	68/___
P.	Paul Newman . . .	1	2	3	4	X	69/___

I've already asked you about several groups in the United States. Now I would like to ask you some questions about Jews.

002

18. Protestants and Catholics go to church on Sundays. Do you happen to know on what day of the week Jews have their weekly religious service?

Monday 1	8/
Tuesday 2	
Wednesday 3	
Thursday 4	
Friday 5	
Saturday 6	
Sunday 7	
Don't know X	

19. The Ten Commandments are part of the Christian religion. As far as you know, are the Ten Commandments also part of the Jewish religion?

Yes 1	9/
No 2	
Don't know X	

20. Do you think of Jews as being more ambitious than other people, less ambitious, or about the same?

More ambitious 1	10/
Less ambitious 2	
About the same 3	
Don't know X	

21. Do you think that on the average Jews have more money than most people, less money, or about the same?

More money . (ASK A) . . 1	11/
Less money 2	
About the same 3	
Don't know X	

A. IF MORE MONEY: Some people have told us that it bothers them that Jews have more money than most people. Does it bother you at all? In what way? (WRITE OUT FULL RESPONSE)

Yes 1	12/
No 2	
Don't know X	

22. Do you think that Jewish children do better in school, worse, or about the same as other children?

Do better 1 13/

Do worse 2

About the same 3

Don't know X

---

23. Do you think Jews today are trying to push in where they are not wanted?

Yes 1 14/

No 2

Don't know X

---

24. Do you think the Jews have too much power in the United States?

Yes (ASK Q. 25 AND Q. 26) . . 1 15/

No 2

Don't know X

---

25. How about the business world--do you think the Jews have too much power in the business world?

Yes . . . . . (ASK Q. 26) . . 1 16/

No 2

Don't know X

---

26. IF YES ON EITHER Q. 24 OR Q. 25:

Do you think something should be done to take some power away from the Jews?

Yes . . . . . . (ASK A) . . 1 17/

No 2

Don't know X

A. IF YES: What do you think should be done? (PROBE: Why do you think so?)

27. Now I am going to read a number of statements about Jews. In each case please tell me whether you think the statement is probably _true_ or probably _false_.

		True	False	Don't Know	
A.	Jews are more willing than others to use shady practices to get what they want.	1	2	X	18/__
B.	Jews are more loyal to Israel than to America. . .	1	2	X	19/__
C.	Jews are just as honest as other businessmen. . .	1	2	X	20/__
D.	Jews have a lot of irritating faults.	1	2	X	21/__
E.	International banking is pretty much controlled by Jews.	1	2	X	22/__
F.	Jews are becoming more and more like other Americans.	1	2	X	23/__
G.	Jews don't care what happens to anyone but their own kind.	1	2	X	24/__
H.	Jews always like to be at the head of things. . .	1	2	X	25/__
I.	Jews stick together too much.	1	2	X	26/__
J.	Jews are always stirring up trouble with their ideas.	1	2	X	27/__
K.	Jews are warm and friendly people.	1	2	X	28/__
L.	Jews should stop complaining about what happened to them in Nazi Germany.	1	2	X	29/__
M.	You can usually tell whether or not a person is Jewish just by the way he looks.	1	2	X	30/__
N.	The movie and television industries are pretty much run by Jews.	1	2	X	31/__
O.	Jews have stirred up a lot of the trouble between whites and Negroes.	1	2	X	32/__
P.	The trouble with Jewish businessmen is that they are so shrewd and tricky that other people don't have a fair chance in competition.	1	2	X	33/__
Q.	Jews still think of themselves as God's Chosen People.	1	2	X	34/__
R.	Jewish employers go out of their way to hire other Jews.	1	2	X	35/__

FOR JEWISH RESPONDENTS, SKIP TO Q. 46.

| S. | The more contact a person has with Jewish people, the more he gets to like them . . . . | 1 | 2 | X | 36/__ |

28. Suppose you had a child who wanted to marry a Jew who had a good education and came from a good family. How would you feel about this--would you object strongly, somewhat, a little, or not at all?

> Strongly 1 37/
> Somewhat 2
> A little 3
> Not at all 4
> Don't know X

29. How do you feel about having Jews in your neighborhood? Would you like to have some Jewish neighbors, wouldn't it make any difference to you, or would you prefer not to have any Jewish neighbors?

> Like to have some Jewish neighbors . . . 1 38/
> Wouldn't make any difference 2
> Prefer not to have any Jewish neighbors . 3
> Don't know X

30. If a candidate for Congress should declare himself as being against the Jews, would this influence you to vote for him or to vote against him?

> Vote for him 1 39/
> Vote against him 2
> Make no difference . . . 3
> Don't know X

31. Suppose your political party wanted to nominate a Jew for President of the United States--that is, a religious Jew who would go to synagogue every week the way a Christian goes to church every Sunday. Would this disturb you very much, somewhat, very little, or not at all?

> Very much 1 40/
> Somewhat 2
> Very little 3
> Not at all 4
> Don't know X

32. If the United States government wanted to pass a law to stop more Jews from immigrating to this country, would you be in favor of this or against it?

> Favor 1 41/
> Against 2
> Wouldn't make any difference 3
> Don't know X

33. (HAND RESPONDENT CARD D) Which of the things on this card do you think big companies should do when they are hiring people?

> Hire the best people whether they are Jewish or not 1 42/
>
> Hire Jews in proportion to the number that there are in the community 2
>
> Hire Jews only when they are so good that no one else could do the job as well 3
>
> Hire no Jews at all 4
> Don't know X

34. Mr. Smith is a member of a social club where there are no Jewish members. Although he knows many of the members would prefer not to have Jews in the club, he decides to try to get his Jewish friend, Mr. Cohen, into the club.

First of all, do you think that the other members have a right to be angry at Mr. Smith for trying to get Mr. Cohen in the club?

Yes 1 43/
No 2
Don't know X

35. Do you think that the other members have a right to keep Mr. Cohen out just because he's Jewish?

Yes 1 44/
No 2
Don't know X

36. Now suppose the members did vote to keep Mr. Cohen out of the club. What do you think Mr. Smith should do--quit the club, stay in the club and keep trying to get Mr. Cohen in, or stay in the club and forget the whole thing?

Quit the club 1 45/
Stay in and keep trying 2
Stay in and forget the whole thing 3
Don't know X

37. Do you think that <u>Mr. Cohen</u> should feel angry or do you think that he should realize that Christians have a right to their own clubs?

Should feel angry 1 46/
Should realize that Christians have a right to their own clubs . 2
Don't know X

38. Some people say that Jews have suffered a great deal in the past. Which of these statements comes closest to your own feelings about this? (HAND RESPONDENT CARD E)

The Jews have suffered no more than anybody else 1 47/
The Jews have suffered but they generally brought it on themselves . 2
The Jews have suffered through no fault of their own 3
Don't know X

39. Which of these statements about Hitler comes closest to what you believe? (HAND RESPONDENT CARD F)

Sometimes I think that Hitler was right in getting rid of the Jews. . 1 48/
Hitler was partly right in trying to get rid of the Jews, but he went too far 2
Hitler was wrong in treating the Jews as he did 3
Don't know X

40. Have you heard or read about the relations between the Jews in Israel and the Arab refugees there?

        Yes . . . (ASK A) . . 1 49/

        No 2

    A. IF YES: As far as you know, have the Arab refugees been treated very well, pretty well, pretty badly, or very badly by the Jews in Israel?

        Very well 3

        Pretty well 4

        Pretty badly 5

        Very badly 6

        Don't know X

41. Suppose there were a war between the Arab nations and Israel. Which side do you think you would probably sympathize with?

        Arab nations 1 50/

        Israel 2

        Neither 3

        Don't know X

42. At the present time, do you come into contact with Jews in any of the following ways--

		Yes	No	Don't Know	
A.	In your neighborhood?	1	2	X	51/
B.	At work or in business?	1	2	X	52/
C.	At stores you shop at?	1	2	X	53/
D.	In clubs or organizations you belong to?	1	2	X	54/
E.	Is your doctor or dentist Jewish?	1	2	X	55/
F.	Have you ever had a close friend who was Jewish?	1	2	X	56/
G.	Thinking of the eight or ten people you know best at the present time, are any of them Jewish?	1	2	X	57/
H.	Is someone in your family married to a Jew?	1	2	X	58/

43. Are there any ways that I have not mentioned that you've come into contact with Jews? How?

1. _____ 59/

2. _____ 60/

3. _____ 61/

4. _____ 62/

44. Thinking of Jews as a group, would you say you feel more friendly toward them now than you used to, less friendly, or have you always felt as you do now?

More friendly (ASK A) . . 1   63/
Less friendly (ASK A) . . 2
Same 3
Don't know X

A. IF MORE OR LESS FRIENDLY: What would you say are the reasons that you feel (more)(less) friendly? (PROBE: Any other reasons?)

64/
65/

45. Do you think that <u>Jews</u> have changed in some ways during recent years?

Yes . . . . . (ASK A) . . 1   66/
No 2
Don't know X

A. IF YES: In what ways do you think Jews have changed? (PROBE: Any other ways?)

67/
68/

ASK EVERYONE: 003
46. I'd like to change the subject and ask you how often you read a newspaper-- every day, several days a week, about once a week, or less often than that?

Every day 1   8/
Several days a week . . . 2
About once a week 3
Less often than that . . 4

47. Are there any magazines that you read fairly regularly?

                                          Yes . . (ASK A) . . 1   9/
                                          No 2

    A. IF YES: Which ones are they?   (CIRCLE AS MANY AS APPLY)

                                   Life 1   10/
                                   Look 1   11/
                                   Newsweek 1   12/
                                   New Yorker 1   13/
                                   Reader's Digest 1   14/
                                   Saturday Evening Post 1 15/
                                   Time 1   16/
                                   U S. News and World Report . . 1 17/
                                   1 other 1   18/
                                   2 others 2   18/
                                   3 or more others 3   18/

48. On the average, how many hours a day do you watch television?

                                   _____   19/

49. (HAND RESPONDENT CARD G) Would you use this card and tell me which answer comes closest to how often you do the following things--

	Almost Every Day	Once or Twice a Week	Several Times a Month	About Once a Month	Several Times a Year	About Once a Year	Never	Don't Know	
A. Spend a social evening with relatives? . .	1	2	3	4	5	6	7	X	20/
B. Spend a social evening with someone who lives in your neighborhood?	1	2	3	4	5	6	7	X	21/
C. Spend a social evening with friends who live outside the neighbor-hood?	1	2	3	4	5	6	7	X	22/
D. Go to a bar or tavern? . . .	1	2	3	4	5	6	7	X	23/
E. Listen to the news on radio or television?	1	2	3	4	5	6	7	X	24/

50. Do you belong to any organizations or clubs, such as a union, lodge, church group, political organization, or social club?

Yes . . (ASK A) . . 1 25/___

No 2

A. IF YES: Could you tell me what these are? (PROBE FOR FULL DESCRIPTION OF ANY LOCAL ORGANIZATION OR GROUP WHICH IS NOT GENERALLY KNOWN)

_____

_____

_____

_____

26/___

27/___

_____

---

51. I am going to read you some things that some people believe and some people don't. For each statement, please tell me whether you agree or disagree?

		Agree	Disagree	Don't Know	
A.	No weakness or difficulty can hold us back if we have enough will power.	1	2	X	28/___
B.	Sex crimes, such as rape and attacks on children deserve more than mere imprisonment; such criminals ought to be publicly whipped, or worse.	1	2	X	29/___
C.	Much of our lives are controlled by plots hatched in secret places.	1	2	X	30/___
D.	Reading the stars can tell us a great deal about the future.	1	2	X	31/___
E.	People can be divided into two distinct classes--the weak and the strong.	1	2	X	32/___
F.	The answers to our country's problems are much simpler than the experts would have us believe.	1	2	X	33/___
G.	Teachers should be allowed to paddle children who do not behave in school.	1	2	X	34/___
H.	A little practical experience is worth all the books put together.	1	2	X	35/___
I.	Getting to the top is more a matter of luck than ability.	1	2	X	36/___
J.	Most people in government are not really interested in the problems of the average man.	1	2	X	37/___
K.	You sometimes can't help wondering whether anything is worthwhile anymore.	1	2	X	38/___
L.	Most people will go out of their way to help someone else.	1	2	X	39/___
M.	Nowadays a person has to live pretty much for today and let tomorrow take care of itself.	1	2	X	40/___
N.	If you try hard enough, you can usually get what you want.	1	2	X	41/___
O.	It is safest to assume that all people have a vicious streak and it will come out when they are given a chance.	1	2	X	42/___

004

52. What is your religion?

Protestant . . (ASK A) . . 1   8/
Catholic . . . (ASK B) . . 2
Jewish . . . . (ASK C) . . 3
Other (SPECIFY)

_____ 4

None 5

A. IF PROTESTANT: What denomination is that?

Presbyterian . . . . . . (ASK [1])   9/
Lutheran . . . . (ASK [2])
Baptist . . . . (ASK [3])
United Church of Christ . (ASK [4])
Other Denomination (SPECIFY)

_____ 10/

[1] Is that the . . . . . United Presbyterian Church or 1
Presbyterian Church, USA? 2

[2] Is that the . . . . . Missouri Lutheran Church 3
American Lutheran Church or 4
Lutheran Church in America 5

[3] Is that the . . . . . American Baptist 6

Southern Baptist 7

or some other Baptist Church 8

[4] Was your church originally . . . Congregationalist 9

or was it . . . Evangelical Reform 0

B. IF CATHOLIC: Have you ever attended a parochial school?

Yes: How many years? _____ . . 1 11/

No 2

C. IF JEWISH: Are you a member of a synagogue?

Yes 1 12/

No 2

53. (HAND RESPONDENT CARD H) Please look at this card and tell me which statement comes closest to expressing what you believe about God.

I don't believe in God 1 13/

I don't know whether there is a God and I don't believe there is any way to find out 2

I don't believe in a personal God, but I do believe in a higher power of some kind 3

I find myself believing in God some of the time, but not at other times. 4

While I have doubts, I feel that I do believe in God 5

I know God really exists and I have no doubts about it 6

Don't know X

FOR <u>JEWISH RESPONDENTS</u> SKIP TO Q. 56.

54. Do you think that a person who doesn't accept Jesus can be saved?

Yes 1   14/

No 2

Other (SPECIFY)

_____ 3

Don't know X

---

55. What about the belief that the Devil actually exists? Are you absolutely sure or are you pretty sure that the Devil exists or are you absolutely sure or pretty sure that the Devil does not exist?

Absolutely sure there is a Devil . 1   15/

Pretty sure there is a Devil . . . 2

Absolutely sure there is no Devil . 3

Pretty sure there is no Devil . . . 4

Don't know X

---

56. How sure are you that there is a life beyond death? Are you absolutely sure or pretty sure there is a life beyond death or are you absolutely or pretty sure there is <u>no</u> life beyond death?

Absolutely sure there is a life beyond death . 1   16/

Pretty sure there is a life beyond death . . . 2

Absolutely sure there is no life beyond death. 3

Pretty sure there is no life beyond death . . 4

Don't know X

---

57. All in all, how important would you say that religion is to you--extremely important, quite important, fairly important, not too important, or not important at all?

Extremely important 1   17/

Quite important 2

Fairly important 3

Not too important 4

Not important at all 5

Don't know X

---

58. About how often do you attend worship services? (CIRCLE CODE FOR CATEGORY THAT COMES CLOSEST)

Several times a week 1   18/

Every week 2

Nearly every week 3

2-3 times a month 4

About once a month 5

Several times a year 6

About once or twice a year 7

Less than once a year 8

Never 9

Don't know . . . . **X**

59. The Old Testament tells that God picked a certain group to be his Chosen People. Can you tell me what group this was--the Romans, the Greeks, the Jews, the Christians, or who?

                                    The Romans 1   19/
                                    The Greeks 2
                                    The Jews 3
                                    The Christians 4
                                    Some other group (SPECIFY)

                                    _____ 5
                                    Don't know X

---

60. Who do you think are God's Chosen People today? (DO NOT READ CATEGORIES)

                                    No one 1   20/
                                    Christians 2
                                    Protestants 3
                                    Catholics 4
                                    Jews 5
                                    Other (SPECIFY)

                                    _____ 6
                                    Don't know X

---

61. Who do you think was most responsible for crucifying Christ--the Romans, the Greeks, the Jews, the Christians, or who?

                                    The Romans 1   21/
                                    The Greeks 2
                                    The Jews 3
                                    The Christians 4
                                    Some other group (SPECIFY)

                                    _____ 5
                                    Don't know X

---

62. Some people believe that the reason Jews have so much trouble is because God is punishing them for rejecting Jesus. Do you agree with this?

                                    Yes 1   22/
                                    No 2
                                    Don't know X

---

63. Suppose a man admitted in public that he did not believe in God.
    A. Do you think he should be allowed to teach in a public high school?

                                    Yes 1   23/
                                    No 2
                                    Don't know X

    B. Should he be allowed to hold public office?

                                    Yes 1   24/
                                    No 2
                                    Don't know X

    C. Do you think that a book he wrote should be removed from a public library?

                                    Yes 1   25/
                                    No 2
                                    Don't know X

64. Do you feel that a public school teacher should teach Christmas carols to her
class even if some of the children are Jewish?

Yes (unqualified) . . . 1 26/___
Yes (qualified) 2
If _____
No 3
Don't know X

65. Suppose the parents of some Jewish children go to the principal and ask that the
Christmas carols not be sung in the classroom. How much would you sympathize
with the Jewish parents--very much, somewhat, a little, or not at all?

Very much . . . . 1 27/___
Somewhat 2
A little 3
Not at all 4
Don't know X

66. What do you think should be done--continue singing the Christmas carols, or
stop singing them? (DO NOT READ CATEGORIES)

Continue singing them (unqualified) . . . . 1 28/___
Continue singing them if Jewish children are excused . 2
Continue singing them if Jewish songs are also sung . 3
Stop singing them 4
Other (SPECIFY)_____ 5
Don't know X

67. How do you feel about prayers being said in the public schools--are you strongly
in favor, somewhat in favor, somewhat opposed, or strongly opposed?

Strongly in favor . . . 1 29/___
Somewhat in favor . . . 2
Somewhat opposed . . . 3
Strongly opposed . . . 4
Don't know X

68. Now I'm going to read you another list of statements. For each statement,
please tell me whether it's true for you or not.

	Yes True	No Not True	Not Don't Know	
A. I worry a lot	1	2	X	30/___
B. When problems come up I'm generally able to find out how to solve them.	1	2	X	31/___
C. I don't like to hear a lot of arguments I disagree with	1	2	X	32/___
D. I worry quite a bit about what people think of me. . .	1	2	X	33/___
E. It bothers me to see immigrants succeeding more than Americans who were born here.	1	2	X	34/___
F. To be frank, I would not like my child to go to school with a lot of Negroes.	1	2	X	35/___
G. I like to hear all sides of an argument before I make up my mind.	1	2	X	36/___
H. I am suspicious of people who try to be different from everybody else.	1	2	X	37/___
I. I am the kind of person who likes to get things done rather than to spend a lot of time thinking about it..	1	2	X	38/___
J. I often feel quite lonely.	1	2	X	39/___
K. I tend to go to pieces in a crisis..	1	2	X	40/___

69. Do you think most people can be trusted?

                              Yes 1   41/
                              No 2
                              Don't know X

Now I'd like to ask some questions about your own background.

70. What was the last grade you completed in school?

    No formal schooling . . . . . ⌉ 1   42/
    Grammar school: 1 . . . . . . │ 2
                     2 . . . . . . │ 3
                     3 . . . . . . │ 4
                     4 . . . . . . │ 5
                     5 . . . . . . │ 6
                     6 . . . . . . │ 7
                     7 . . . . . . ├(ASK A) . . 8
    8 (finished grammar school) . . │ 9
    High school: 9 . . . . . . │ 1   43/
                    10 . . . . . . │ 2
                    11 . . . . . . │ 3
    12 (graduated from high school) ⌋ 4
    1 year college . . . . ⌉ 5
    2 years college . . . . │ 6
    3 years college . . . . ├(ASK B) . . 7
    4 years college (graduated) . . │ 8
    Postgraduate . . . . ⌋ 9

   A. IF NO COLLEGE: Have you ever attended a trade school, a business or com-
       mercial school, or some other special school of this kind?

                              Yes 1   44/
                              No 2

   B. IF ANY COLLEGE: How would you rate the college you went to? Would you say
       that scholastically it was among the very top in the
       country, somewhat above average, about average, or some-
       what below average?

                  Among the very top in the country . . 1   45/
                  Somewhat above average 2
                  About average 3
                  Somewhat below average 4
                  Don't know X

71. Compared to other people who have had the same amount of education, would you
    say that you have been more successful, less successful, or would you say that
    you have had about the same amount of success?

                              More successful 1   46/
                              Less successful 2
                              Same amount 3
                              Don't know X

72. Are you working at the present time, are you in your own business, are you unemployed, or something else? (PROBE)

Self-employed . . . . ⎤ 1   47/_
Employed full-time . . ⎥ 2
Employed part-time . . ⎬ (ASK A AND B) 3
Laid off temporarily . ⎥ 4
Out of a job . . . . . ⎥ 5
Retired . . . . ⎦ 6
Housewife . . . (SKIP TO QUESTION 75) . . 7
Student . . . . (SKIP TO QUESTION 75) . . 8
Military . . . (SKIP TO QUESTION 73) . . 9

IF SELF-EMPLOYED, EMPLOYED, UNEMPLOYED, OR RETIRED:

A. What kind of work (do you)(did you normally) do?   (PROBE FOR EXACT DESCRIPTION OF OCCUPATION)

48/_
49/_
50/_
51/_

B. In what kind of business or industry (is)(was) that?

52/_
53/_
54/_
55/_
56/_
57/_
58/_
59/_

FOR PRESENTLY WORKING RESPONDENTS, ASK Q. 73 AND Q. 74.   ALL OTHERS SKIP TO Q. 75.

---

73. All in all, how satisfied are you with your present job--very satisfied, fairly satisfied, or not too satisfied?

Very satisfied 1   60/_
Fairly satisfied 2
Not too satisfied . . . 3
Don't know X

DO NOT ASK Q. 74 FOR SELF-EMPLOYED RESPONDENTS.

74. A. Do you supervise anyone as part of your job?

Yes 1   61/_
No 2
Don't know X

B. How important is it to you to get a promotion on your job--very important, somewhat important, not very important, or not important at all?

Very important 1   62/_
Somewhat important . . . 2
Not very important . . . 3
Not important at all . . 4
Don't know X

C. Would you say your chances of promotion in the next few years are excellent, good, fair, or poor?

Excellent 1   63/_
Good 2
Fair 3
Poor 4
Don't know X

75. Taken altogether, how would you say things are these days--would you say that
you are very happy, pretty happy, or not too happy?

> Very happy 1 64/
> Pretty happy 2
> Not too happy . . . 3

---

76. What year were you born? (CIRCLE LAST TWO DIGITS OF YEAR)

0 1 2 3 4 5 6 7 8 9 X   65/

(IF DON'T KNOW, CIRCLE X AND ASK A)   66/

0 1 2 3 4 5 6 7 8 9 X   67/

A. IF DON'T KNOW: Can you tell me about how old you are? _____   68/

---

77. Would you say your health is usually excellent, good, fair, or poor?

> Excellent 1   69/
> Good 2
> Fair 3
> Poor 4
> Don't know X

                                                                       005
78. Were you born in the United States?   Yes . (ASK A TO G) . . 1   8/
                                                  No . (ASK H AND I) . . 2
                                                  Don't know X
     IF YES:

A. In what state did you spend most of your childhood? _____   9/
                                                                            10/

B. In what country was your father born?

> In U.S. . . . . (ASK C AND D)   11/
> Other _____(SKIP TO E)   12/

C. Do you know in what country his father was born?

> _____   13/
>   14/

D. And in what country was his mother born?

> _____   15/
>   16/

E. And your mother--in what country was she born?

> In U.S. . . . . (ASK F AND G)   17/
> Other _____(SKIP TO Q. 79)   18/

F. Do you know in what country her father was born?

>   19/
> _____   20/

G. And in what country was her mother born?

>   21/
> _____   22/

     IF NO:
H. In what country were you born? _____   23/
                                                                          24/

I. About how old were you when you came to the United States? _____   25/

79. For the most part, were you raised on a farm, in a small town, in a small city, a medium-sized city, a big city, or a suburb of a big city?

```
                    Farm . . . . . . . . . . . . . 1   26/
                    Small town . . . . . . . . . 2
                    Small city . . . . . . . . . 3
                    Medium-sized city  . . . . . 4
                    Big city . . . . . . . . . . 5
                    Suburb to a big city . . . . 6
                    Don't know . . . . . . . . . X
```

80. A. What was the last grade your father completed in school?

B. And your mother--what was the last grade in school she completed?

			A Father 27/	B Mother 28/
Never attended school			1	1
Grammar school:	1 - 4 years		2	2
	5 - 7 years		3	3
	8 years		4	4
High school:	9 - 11 years		5	5
	12 years (finished high school) . .		6	6
College:	1 to 3 years college		7	7
	4 years college (finished college)		8	8
	Postgraduate		9	9
Don't know			X	X

81. A. What kind of work did your father do when you were about 16 years old? (PROBE FOR EXACT DESCRIPTION OF OCCUPATION)

```
                                                              29/
                                                              30/
                                                              31/
                                                              32/
B. In what kind of business or industry (is)(was) that?       33/
                                                              34/
                                                              35/
                                                              36/
C. Was he self-employed at that time?   Yes . . . . . . . . . . . . . 1   37/
                                        No . . . . . . . . . . . . . 2
```

82. Generally speaking, were your parents more religious than you are, less religious, or about the same?

```
                    More religious . . . . . . . 1   38/
                    Less religious . . . . . . . 2
                    About the same . . . . . . . 3
                    Don't know . . . . . . . . . X
```

83. I would like to ask you to compare your parents' feelings toward Jews around the time you were growing up with the way you yourself feel now. Would you say your parents felt more friendly toward Jews than you do now, less friendly, or about the same?

```
                    More friendly . . . . . . . 1   39/
                    Less friendly . . . . . . . 2
                    About the same . . . . . . . 3
                    Don't know . . . . . . . . . X
```

84. Are you single, married, divorced, separated, or widowed?

```
Single . . . . . . . . . . (SKIP TO QUESTION 89) . . 1    40/
Presently married and living with spouse⌐ . . . . . . 2
Separated . . . . . . . . . . . . . .               . . 3
Divorced . . . . . . . . . . . . . . >(ASK A)      . . 4
Widowed . . . . . . . . . . . . . . .⌐ . . . . . . 5
```

A. IF EVER MARRIED: How many children do you have?

```
None . . . . . . . . . . . . 1    41/
One . . .⌐ . . . . . . . . 2
Two . . . . . . . . . . . 3
Three . . . >(ASK B AND C) . 4
Four . . . . . . . . . . . 5
Five . . . . . . . . . . . 6
Six or more⌐ . . . . . . . 7
```

IF ANY CHILDREN:

B. How many of them under twenty-one?   _____   42/

C. How many of them under twelve?   _____   43/

FOR PRESENTLY MARRIED, ASK Q's. 85 TO 87:

FOR WIDOWED, DIVORCED, OR SEPARATED WOMEN, SKIP TO Q. 88.

FOR ALL OTHERS, SKIP TO Q. 89.

---

85. What was the last grade your (husband)(wife) completed in school?

```
Never attended school . . . . . . . . . 1    44/
1 - 4 years . . . . . . . . . . . . . 2
5 - 7 years . . . . . . . . . . . . . 3
8 years . . . . . . . . . . . . . . 4
9 - 11 years . . . . . . . . . . . . 5
12 years (finished high school) . . . . 6
1 - 3 years college . . . . . . . . . 7
4 years college (finished college) . . . 8
Postgraduate . . . . . . . . . . . . 9
Don't know . . . . . . . . . . . . . X
```

86. Is your (husband)(wife) working at the present time, does (he)(she) have (his)
(her) own business, is (he)(she) unemployed, or what?

```
Self-employed . . . .⌐ . . . . . . . . 1    45/
Employed full-time . . .| . . . . . . . 2
Employed part-time . . .| . . . . . . . 3
Laid off temporarily . .>(ASK A AND B)  4
Out of a job . . . . . .| . . . . . . . 5
Retired . . . . . . . .⌐ . . . . . . . 6
Housewife . .⌐ . . . . . . . . . . . . 7
Student . . . .>(SKIP TO QUESTION 89) . 8
Military . . . .⌐ . . . . . . . . . . . 9
```

IF SELF-EMPLOYED, EMPLOYED, UNEMPLOYED, OR RETIRED:

A. What kind of work (does he/she)(did he/she normally) do?   (PROBE FOR
    EXACT DESCRIPTION OF OCCUPATION)

B. In what kind of business or industry (is)(was) that?

```
46/
47/
48/
49/
50/
51/
52/
53/
54/
55/
```

IF SPOUSE IS PRESENTLY WORKING, ASK Q. 87:
87. How satisfied would you say (he)(she) is with (his)(her) present job--very sat-
    isfied, fairly satisfied, or not too satisfied?

Very satisfied 1   56/
Fairly satisfied . . . 2
Not too satisfied . . . 3
Don't know X

FOR WIDOWED, DIVORCED, OR SEPARATED WOMEN, ASK Q. 88:
88. A. What kind of work did your husband do during most of the time that you were
       living together? (PROBE FOR EXACT DESCRIPTION OF OCCUPATION)   57/
                                                                        58/
                                                                        59/
                                                                        60/
                                                                        61/
    B. What kind of business or industry was that?   62/
                                                                        63/
                                                                        64/
                                                                        65/
                                                                        66/

ASK EVERYONE:
89. And how many years have you lived in this house?

Less than 1 year . . . 1   67/
1 up to 2 years 2
2 up to 3 years 3
3 up to 6 years 4
6 up to 10 years . . . 5
10 up to 20 years . . . 6
20 up to 30 years . . . 7
More than 30 years . . 8
Don't know X

---

90. About how many years have you lived in (name city or town)?

Less than 1 year . . . 1   68/
1 up to 2 years 2
2 up to 3 years 3
3 up to 6 years 4
6 up to 10 years . . . 5
10 up to 20 years . . . 6
20 up to 30 years . . . 7
More than 30 years . . 8
Don't know X

---

91. Is this the kind of neighborhood you would like to continue living in?

Yes 1   69/
No 2
Don't know X

---

92. Do you own your own home or do you rent?

Own 1   70/
Rent 2
Other 3

93. (HAND RESPONDENT CARD I) Will you please look at this card and tell me which
     figure comes closest to your total family income for the past year--before
     taxes, that is? Just tell me the letter next to the figure that fits you
     best.

                                        A. Less than $1,000 . . . 1   71/___
                                        B. $ 1,000 to $ 1,999 . . 2
                                        C. $ 2,000 to $ 2,999 . . 3
                                        D. $ 3,000 to $ 3,999 . . 4
                                        E. $ 4,000 to $ 4,999 . . 5
                                        F. $ 5,000 to $ 5,999 . . 6
                                        G. $ 6,000 to $ 6,999 . . 7
                                        H. $ 7,000 to $ 7,999 . . 8
                                        I. $ 8,000 to $ 8,999 . . 9
                                        J. $ 9,000 to $ 9,999 . . 1   72/___
                                        K. $10,000 to $11,999 . . 2
                                        L. $12,000 to $14,999 . . 3
                                        M. $15,000 to $19,999 . . 4
                                        N. $20,000 to $24,999 . . 5
                                        O. $25,000 or more . . . 6
                                        P. Don't know X

---

94. How satisfied would you say that you are with your present income--very satis-
     fied, fairly satisfied, or not too satisfied?

                                        Very satisfied 1   73/___

                                        Fairly satisfied 2

                                        Not too satisfied 3

                                        Don't know X

---

95. By and large, do you think of yourself as being of the upper class, upper middle
     class, middle class, working class, or lower class?

                                        Upper 1   74/___

                                        Upper middle 2

                                        Middle 3

                                        Working 4

                                        Lower 5

                                        Don't know X

---

96. Thinking back to the time you were growing up, would you say that your family
     was of the upper class, upper middle class, middle class, working class, or
     lower class?

                                        Upper 1   75/___

                                        Upper middle 2

                                        Middle 3

                                        Working 4

                                        Lower 5

                                        Don't know X

I have only a few more questions to ask you.

97. Do you usually think of yourself as a Republican, a Democrat, an Independent, or what?

> Republican 1   8/
>
> Democrat 2
>
> Independent . (ASK A) . . 3
>
> Other _____ 4
>
> Don't know X

A. IF INDEPENDENT: Even though you think of yourself as an Independent, do you usually lean more toward the Republicans or more toward the Democrats?

> Republicans 1
>
> Democrats 2
>
> Won't choose . . . . . . y

---

98. As things stand now, which candidate do you prefer in this coming election-- the Democrat, Johnson, or the Republican, Goldwater?

> Johnson 1   9/
>
> Goldwater 2
>
> Don't know . (ASK A) . . X

A. IF DON'T KNOW: The way it looks now, if you had to choose who would you prefer--Johnson or Goldwater?

> Johnson 1
>
> Goldwater 2
>
> Can't choose . . . . . . y

---

99. Do you think you will certainly vote, probably vote, or aren't you sure yet?

> Certainly 1   10/
>
> Probably 2
>
> Not sure 3
>
> Probably not 4
>
> Certainly not 5
>
> Don't know X

---

100. Did you vote in the last presidential election in 1960 when Kennedy ran against Nixon, or did something happen to keep you from voting?

> Did vote . . (ASK A) . . 1   11/
>
> Did not vote 2

A. IF DID VOTE: Who did you vote for--Kennedy or Nixon?

> Kennedy 1   12/
>
> Nixon 2
>
> Don't know X

101. Do you happen to know what President Johnson's religious background is? What? (RECORD VERBATIM)

13/

102. And how about Senator Goldwater's religious background--do you know what that is? What? (RECORD VERBATIM)

14/

103. (HAND RESPONDENT CARD J) Here is a list of issues that have been talked about in the campaign.

A. Please tell me for each one whether it is important to you or not important to you in deciding which candidate you favor?

B. Now look at the card again and tell me for each issue which candidate you agree with most--Senator Goldwater or President Johnson?

	A		B Agree with Most			
	Important	Not Important	Goldwater	Johnson	Don't Know	
The war in Viet Nam	1	2	3	4	X	15/
Medical Care for the Aged .	1	2	3	4	X	16/
Crime in the streets . . .	1	2	3	4	X	17/
Control of nuclear weapons.	1	2	3	4	X	18/
Negro-white relations . . .	1	2	3	4	X	19/
Government spending	1	2	3	4	X	20/
Morality and corruption in government	1	2	3	4	X	21/
Power of the Supreme Court.	1	2	3	4	X	22/
Relations with communist countries	1	2	3	4	X	23/
None of these	1	2	3	4	X	24/

I have just one more, and a rather different, question.

104. Is there anyone in your immediate family who is blind?

Yes . . . (ASK A AND B) . . 1 25/
No 2

IF YES:
A. How is that person related to you?

Self 1 26/
Parent or parent-in-law . . 2
Sibling or sibling-in-law . 3
Spouse 4
Child or grandchild 5
Other relative (SPECIFY)

_____ 6

B. Could we have his name and address? (We may be planning a study of the blind sometime in the future, and it would be helpful to have his/her name and address.)

Name _____

Address _____

City and State _____

105. May I have your name and telephone number in case my office wants to verify this interview?

NAME: _____

TELEPHONE NUMBER _____ AREA CODE _____

Thank you very much for your time and cooperation. (You have been very helpful.)

FILL IN FOLLOWING ITEMS IMMEDIATELY
AFTER LEAVING RESPONDENT.   TIME INTERVIEW ENDED: _____ AM
                                                                     PM

1. Respondent's Sex: Male 1 27/
                                              Female . . . 2

2. Respondent's Race: White . . . 1 28/
                                              Negro . . . 2
                                              Oriental . . 3
                                              Other
                                              _____ 4

3. Respondent's Address:
                                                              29/
_____ _____   30/
   Street or Rural Route   City or Town and State   31/
                                                              32/
4. Date of Interview: _____ 5. S. U. Number _____ 33/
                                                              34/
6. Interviewer's Signature: 35/
                                                              36/
          _____   37/
                                                              38/
                                                              39/
                                                              40/

INTERVIEWER'S OBSERVATIONS

7. Would you say the respondent was unusually tall, somewhere in the normal range, or unusually short?

Unusually tall 1   41/

Normal range 2

Unusually short 3

---

8. Would you say that the respondent was unusually fat, somewhere in the normal range, or unusually thin?

Unusually fat 1   42/

Normal range 2

Unusually thin 3

---

9. Generally speaking, would you say that the respondent was unusually attractive, somewhere in the normal range, or unusually unattractive?

Unusually attractive . . . 1   43/

Normal range 2

Unusually unattractive . . 3

---

10. The respondent seemed:

Truthful 1   44/

Evasive 2

Untruthful 3

Can't be determined X

---

11. Standard of living of neighborhood:

Upper class 1   45/

Middle class 2

Upper middle 3

Lower middle 4

Working class 5

Lower class 6

---

12. Racial composition of neighborhood:

All white 1   46/

All Negro 2

Mixed 3

Can't tell X

13. How did the respondent's home compare to others in the neighborhood?

Much better 1 47/

Slightly better 2

Slightly worse 3

Much worse 4

About the same 5

Appendix B

The following table reports the responses of the 61 Jewish respondents to the eighteen questions about Jews listed in Table 1. Three observations stand out:

1. Acceptance ranges from zero per cent on the belief that "Jews have too much power in the United States" to 39 per cent on the belief that "the movie and television industries are pretty much controlled by Jews." With the exception of this latter belief, every belief in the series was rejected by a majority of Jewish respondents.

2. Of the eleven items in the Index of Anti-Semitic Belief, seven were rejected by over 90 per cent of the Jewish respondents. The three most often accepted by Jews are also the three most often accepted by the least prejudiced third of the population. As indicated earlier, these are weak indicators of anti-Semitism, but were included in the Index to isolate those who would not accept even mildly negative characterizations of Jews.

3. The pattern of responses of the Jewish respondents closely resembles that of the least prejudiced third of the population (Table 5). On none of the eleven beliefs in the Index is acceptance greater among the least anti-Semitic third than among Jewish respondents. This is another indication that as a group those defined as unprejudiced are indeed unprejudiced.

Appendix B.   RESPONSES OF JEWISH RESPONDENTS TO
QUESTIONS ABOUT JEWS[a]
(N = 61)

	True	False	Don't Know
Jews are always stirring up trouble with their ideas.	5%	95%	0%
Jews have too much power in the United States.	0	100	0
Jews have stirred up a lot of the trouble bewteen whites and Negroes.	3	93	4
Jews today are trying to push in where they are not wanted.	12	81	7
Jews don't care what happens to anyone but their own kind.	5	93	2
Jews are just as honest as other businessmen.	92	5	3
Jews have too much power in the business world.	5	95	0
Jews are more loyal to Israel than to America.	3	95	2
International banking is pretty much controlled by Jews.	17	64	19
The trouble with Jewish businessmen is that they are so shrewd and tricky that other people don't have a fair chance in competition.	8	90	2
Jews have a lot of irritating faults.	28	67	5
Jews are more willing than others to use shady practices to get what they want.	10	88	2
You can usually tell whether or not a person is Jewish just by the way he looks.	15	85	0
The movie and television industries are pretty much controlled by Jews.	40	46	14
Jewish employers go out of their way to hire other Jews.	13	80	7
Jews stick together too much.	27	73	0
Jews always like to be at the head of things.	36	60	4
Jews still think of themselves as God's Chosen People.	29	64	7

[a]For the responses of non-Jewish respondents, see Table 1.

Appendix C. CORRELATION MATRIX: INDEX OF ANTI-SEMITIC BELIEF

(whites only)

	1	2	3	4	5	6	7	8	9	10	11
1. Too much power in U.S.	X	.23	−.23	.48	.26	.29	.31	.22	.24	.24	.25
2. Care only about own kind	.32	X	−.38	.34	.39	.26	.47	.30	.40	.36	.35
3. Just as honest as other businessmen	−.23	−.38	X	−.32	−.35	−.20	−.43	−.31	−.53	−.29	−.29
4. Too much power in business world	.48	.34	−.32	X	.26	.32	.40	.26	.33	.34	.29
5. More loyal to Israel than America	.26	.39	−.35	.26	X	.24	.39	.27	.37	.32	.26
6. Control international banking	.29	.26	−.20	.32	.24	X	.29	.26	.25	.21	.27
7. Shrewd and tricky in business	.31	.47	−.43	.40	.39	.29	X	.35	.50	.39	.37
8. Have a lot of irritating faults	.22	.30	−.31	.26	.27	.26	.35	X	.35	.25	.37
9. Use shady practices to get ahead	.24	.40	−.53	.33	.37	.25	.50	.35	X	.35	.34
10. Stick together too much	.24	.36	−.29	.34	.32	.21	.39	.25	.35	X	.34
11. Always like to head things	.25	.35	−.29	.29	.26	.27	.37	.37	.34	.34	X

Appendix D. PRINCIPAL-COMPONENT FACTOR ANALYSIS OF VARIOUS BELIEFS ABOUT JEWS, WITH A VARIMAX ROTATION[a]

(whites only)

I Conventional Anti-Semitism		II Political Anti-Semitism		III Positive Stereotypes		IV Quasi-factual Beliefs	
More loyal to Israel than to America	.619	Too much power in U.S.	.697	The more contact, the more one likes Jews	.697	More ambitious	.711
Hire only their own kind	.602	Too much power in business world	.571	Warm and friendly	.585	Have more money	.604
Shrewd and tricky in business	.566	Push in where not wanted	.557	Just as honest as other businessmen	.565	Control movies and TV	.501
Use shady practices to get ahead	.533	Stir up trouble with ideas	.556	More and more like other Americans	.523		
Think of themselves as God's Chosen People	.526	Stir up trouble between whites and Negroes	.528	Use shady practices to get ahead	-.431		
Stick together too much	.490	Control international banking	.525				
Care only about own kind	.463	Control movies and TV	.459				
Tell a Jew by his looks	.441						
Just as honest as other businessmen	-.434						
Should stop complaining	.419						
Always like to head things	.379						
Have irritating faults	.355						

[a]All twenty-four belief items included in the factor analysis are shown above. Each is listed under the factor on which it had the highest loading. In addition, three items with high loadings (above 4) on more than one factor are listed twice. These are: "The movie and television industries are pretty much run by Jews," "Jews are just as honest as other businessmen," and "Jews are more willing than others to use shady practices to get what they want."

Index

Revised January, 1970

hARPER ⚡ ꞇORCҺBOOKS

† The New American Nation Series, edited by Henry Steele Commager and Richard B. Morris.
‡ American Perspectives series, edited by Bernard Wishy and William E. Leuchtenburg.
α History of Europe series, edited by J. H. Plumb.
§ The Library of Religion and Culture, edited by Benjamin Nelson.
‖ Researches in the Social, Cultural, and Behavioral Sciences, edited by Benjamin Nelson.
א Harper Modern Science Series, edited by James R. Newman.
° Not for sale in Canada.
+ Documentary History of the United States series, edited by Richard B. Morris.
# Documentary History of Western Civilization series, edited by Eugene C. Black and Leonard W. Levy.
Λ The Economic History of the United States series, edited by Henry David et al.
¶ European Perspectives series, edited by Eugene C. Black.
** Contemporary Essays series, edited by Leonard W Levy.
* The Stratum Series, edited by John Hale.

History: Renaissance & Reformation

JACOB BURCKHARDT: The Civilization of the Renaissance in Italy. *Introduction by Benjamin Nelson and Charles Trinkaus. Illus.* Vol. I TB/40; Vol. II TB/41
JOEL HURSTFIELD: The Elizabethan Nation TB/1312
ALFRED VON MARTIN: Sociology of the Renaissance. ° *Introduction by W. K. Ferguson* TB/1099
J. H. PARRY: The Establishment of the European Hegemony: 1415-1715: *Trade and Exploration in the Age of the Renaissance* TB/1045

History: Modern European

MAX BELOFF: The Age of Absolutism, 1660-1815 TB/1062
ALAN BULLOCK: Hitler, A Study in Tyranny. ° *Revised Edition. Illus.* TB/1123
JOHANN GOTTLIEB FICHTE: Addresses to the German Nation. *Ed. with Intro. by George A. Kelly* ¶ TB/1366
H. STUART HUGHES: The Obstructed Path: *French Social Thought in the Years of Desperation* TB/1451
JOHAN HUIZINGA: Dutch Cviilization in the 17th Century and Other Essays TB/1453
JOHN MCMANNERS: European History, 1789-1914: *Men, Machines and Freedom* TB/1419
FRANZ NEUMANN: Behemoth: *The Structure and Practice of National Socialism, 1933-1944* TB/1289
A. J. P. TAYLOR: From Napoleon to Lenin: *Historical Essays* ° TB/1268
H. R. TREVOR-ROPER: Historical Essays TB/1269

Philosophy

HENRI BERGSON: Time and Free Will: *An Essay on the Immediate Data of Consciousness* ° TB/1021
G. W. F. HEGEL: Phenomenology of Mind. ° || *Introduction by George Lichtheim* TB/1303
H. J. PATON: The Categorical Imperative: *A Study in Kant's Moral Philosophy* TB/1325
MICHAEL POLANYI: Personal Knowledge: *Towards a Post-Critical Philosophy* TB/1158
LUDWIG WITTGENSTEIN: The Blue and Brown Books ° TB/1211
LUDWIG WITTGENSTEIN: Notebooks, 1914-1916 TB/1441

Political Science & Government

C. E. BLACK: The Dynamics of Modernization: *A Study in Comparative History* TB/1321
DENIS W. BROGAN: Politics in America. *New Introduction by the Author* TB/1469
KARL R. POPPER: The Open Society and Its Enemies *Vol. I: The Spell of Plato* TB/1101 *Vol: II: The High Tide of Prophecy: Hegel, Marx, and the Aftermath* TB/1102
CHARLES SCHOTTLAND, Ed.: The Welfare State ** TB/1323
JOSEPH A. SCHUMPETER: Capitalism, Socialism and Democracy TB/3008
PETER WOLL, Ed.: Public Administration and Policy: *Selected Essays* TB/1284

Psychology

LUDWIG BINSWANGER: Being-in-the-World: *Selected Papers.* || *Trans. with Intro. by Jacob Needleman* TB/1365

MIRCEA ELIADE: Cosmos and History: *The Myth of the Eternal Return* § TB/2050
SIGMUND FREUD: On Creativity and the Unconscious: *Papers on the Psychology of Art, Literature, Love, Religion.* § *Intro. by Benjamin Nelson* TB/45
J. GLENN GRAY: The Warriors: *Reflections on Men in Battle. Introduction by Hannah Arendt* TB/1294
WILLIAM JAMES: Psychology: *The Briefer Course. Edited with an Intro. by Gordon Allport* TB/1034

Religion

TOR ANDRAE: Mohammed: *The Man and his Faith* TB/62
KARL BARTH: Church Dogmatics: *A Selection. Intro. by H. Hollwitzer. Ed. by G. W. Bromiley* TB/95
NICOLAS BERDYAEV: The Destiny of Man TB/61
MARTIN BUBER: The Prophetic Faith TB/73
MARTIN BUBER: Two Types of Faith: *Interpenetration of Judaism and Christianity* TB/75
RUDOLF BULTMANN: History and Eschatalogy: *The Presence of Eternity* TB/91
EDWARD CONZE: Buddhism: *Its Essence and Development. Foreword by Arthur Waley* TB/58
H. G. CREEL: Confucius and the Chinese Way TB/63
FRANKLIN EDGERTON, Trans. & Ed.: The Bhagavad Gita TB/115
M. S. ENSLIN: Christian Beginnings TB/5
M. S. ENSLIN: The Literature of the Christian Movement TB/6
HENRI FRANKFORT: Ancient Egyptian Religion: *An Interpretation* TB/77
IMMANUEL KANT: Religion Within the Limits of Reason Alone. *Introduction by Theodore M. Greene and John Silber* TB/67
GABRIEL MARCEL: Homo Viator: *Introduction to a Metaphysic of Hope* TB/397
H. RICHARD NIEBUHR: Christ and Culture TB/3
H. RICHARD NIEBUHR: The Kingdom of God in America TB/49
SWAMI NIKHILANANDA, Trans. & Ed.: The Upanishads TB/114
F. SCHLEIERMACHER: The Christian Faith. *Introduction by Richard R. Niebuhr.* Vol. I TB/108 Vol. II TB/109

Sociology and Anthropology

KENNETH B. CLARK: Dark Ghetto: *Dilemmas of Social Power. Foreword by Gunnar Myrdal* TB/1317
KENNETH CLARK & JEANNETTE HOPKINS: A Relevant War Against Poverty: *A Study of Community Action Programs and Observable Social Change* TB/1480
GARY T. MARX: Protest and Prejudice: *A Study of Belief in the Black Community* TB/1435
ROBERT K. MERTON, LEONARD BROOM, LEONARD S. COTTRELL, JR., Editors: Sociology Today: *Problems and Prospects* || Vol. I TB/1173; Vol. II TB/1174
GILBERT OSOFSKY: Harlem: The Making of a Ghetto: *Negro New York, 1890-1930* TB/1381
PHILIP RIEFF: The Triumph of the Therapeutic: *Uses of Faith After Freud* TB/1360
GEORGE ROSEN: Madness in Society: *Chapters in the Historical Sociology of Mental Illness.* || *Preface by Benjamin Nelson* TB/1337